Viktor Mayer-Schönberger is Professor of Internet Governance and Regulation at Oxford University, following a decade on the faculty of Harvard's Kennedy School. He is one of the most respected authorities on what is happening in the big data arena. His book, *Delete: The Virtue of Forgetting in the Digital Age*, is considered a seminal work on the ever-presence of data.

Kenneth Cukier is the Data Editor of *The Economist* and a leading thinker on developments in big data. His writing on technology, business and society has appeared in *Foreign Affairs*, *New York Times*, *Wall Street Journal*, *Financial Times* and elsewhere. He is a member of the Council on Foreign Relations.

Praise for *Big Data*:

'An excellent primer' *Financial Times*

'Fascinating' *Observer*

'An elegant and readable primer' *New Scientist*

'Every decade, there are a handful of books that change the way you look at everything. This is one of those books. Society has begun to reckon the change that big data will bring. This book is an incredibly important start'
Lawrence Lessig, Professor of Law, Harvard Law School, and author of *Remix* and *Free Culture*

'In *Big Data*, Mayer-Schönberger and Cukier break new ground in identifying how today's avalanche of information fundamentally shifts our basic understanding of the world. Argued boldly and written beautifully, the book clearly shows how companies can unlock value, how policymakers need to be on guard, and how everyone's cognitive models need to change'
Joi Ito, Director of the MIT Media Lab

A Revolution That

BIG

Will Transform How We

DATA

Live, Work, and Think

VIKTOR MAYER-SCHÖNBERGER
and KENNETH CUKIER

JOHN MURRAY

First published in Great Britain in 2013 by John Murray (Publishers)
An Hachette UK Company

First published in paperback in 2013

1

A CIP catalogue record for this title is available from the British Library

ISBN 978-1-84854-792-6

Typeset in Mercury Text G2

Printed and bound by Clays Ltd, St Ives plc

John Murray policy is to use papers that are natural, renewable and
recyclable products and made from wood grown in sustainable forests.
The logging and manufacturing processes are expected to conform to the
environmental regulations of the country of origin.

John Murray (Publishers)
338 Euston Road
London NW1 3BH

www.johnmurray.co.uk

To B and v

V.M.S.

To my parents

K.N.C.

CONTENTS

BIG DATA

1

NOW

IN 2009 A NEW FLU virus was discovered. Combining elements of the viruses that cause bird flu and swine flu, this new strain, dubbed H1N1, spread quickly. Within weeks, public health agencies around the world feared a terrible pandemic was under way. Some commentators warned of an outbreak on the scale of the 1918 Spanish flu that had infected half a billion people and killed tens of millions. Worse, no vaccine against the new virus was readily available. The only hope public health authorities had was to slow its spread. But to do that, they needed to know where it already was.

In the United States, the Centers for Disease Control and Prevention (CDC) requested that doctors inform them of new flu cases. Yet the picture of the pandemic that emerged was always a week or two out of date. People might feel sick for days but wait before consulting a doctor. Relaying the information back to the central organizations took time, and the CDC only tabulated the numbers once a week. With a rapidly spreading disease, a two-week lag is an eternity. This delay completely blinded public health agencies at the most crucial moments.

As it happened, a few weeks before the H1N1 virus made headlines, engineers at the Internet giant Google published a remarkable paper in the scientific journal *Nature*. It created a splash among health officials and computer scientists but was otherwise overlooked. The authors explained how Google could "predict" the spread of the winter flu in the United States, not just nationally, but down to specific regions and even states. The company could achieve this by looking at what people were searching for on the Internet. Since Google receives more than three billion search queries every day and saves them all, it had plenty of data to work with.

Google took the 50 million most common search terms that Americans type and compared the list with CDC data on the spread of seasonal flu between 2003 and 2008. The idea was to identify areas infected by the flu virus by what people searched for on the Internet. Others had tried to do this with Internet search terms, but no one else had as much data, processing power, and statistical know-how as Google.

While the Googlers guessed that the searches might be aimed at getting flu information — typing phrases like "medicine for cough and fever" — that wasn't the point: they didn't know, and they designed a system that didn't care. All their system did was look for correlations between the frequency of certain search queries and the spread of the flu over time and space. In total, they processed a staggering 450 million different mathematical models in order to test the search terms, comparing their predictions against actual flu cases from the CDC in 2007 and 2008. And they struck gold: their software found a combination of 45 search terms that, when used together in a mathematical model, had a strong correlation between their prediction and the official figures nationwide. Like the CDC, they could tell where the flu had spread, but unlike the CDC they could tell it in near real time, not a week or two after the fact.

Thus when the H1N1 crisis struck in 2009, Google's system proved to be a more useful and timely indicator than government statistics with their natural reporting lags. Public health officials were armed with valuable information.

Strikingly, Google's method does not involve distributing mouth swabs or contacting physicians' offices. Instead, it is built on "big data" — the ability of society to harness information in novel ways to produce useful insights or goods and services of significant value. In 2012 it identified a sudden surge in flu cases but overstated the amount, perhaps because of a barrage of media attention about the flu. Yet what is clear is that the next time a pandemic comes around, the world will have a better tool at its disposal to predict and thus prevent its spread.

Public health is only one area where big data is making a big difference. Entire business sectors are being reshaped by big data as well. Buying airplane tickets is a good example.

In 2003 Oren Etzioni needed to fly from Seattle to Los Angeles for his younger brother's wedding. Months before the big day, he went online and bought a plane ticket, believing that the earlier you book, the less you pay. On the flight, curiosity got the better of him and he asked the fellow in the next seat how much his ticket had cost and when he had bought it. The man turned out to have paid considerably less than Etzioni, even though he had purchased the ticket much more recently. Infuriated, Etzioni asked another passenger and then another. Most had paid less.

For most of us, the sense of economic betrayal would have dissipated by the time we closed our tray tables and put our seats in the full, upright, and locked position. But Etzioni is one of America's foremost computer scientists. He sees the world as a series of big-data problems — ones that he can solve. And he has been mastering them since he graduated from Harvard in 1986 as its first undergrad to major in computer science.

From his perch at the University of Washington, he started a slew of big-data companies before the term "big data" became known. He helped build one of the Web's first search engines, MetaCrawler, which was launched in 1994 and snapped up by InfoSpace, then a major online property. He co-founded Netbot, the first major comparison-shopping website, which he sold to Excite. His startup for extracting meaning from text documents, called ClearForest, was later acquired by Reuters.

Back on terra firma, Etzioni was determined to figure out a way for people to know if a ticket price they see online is a good deal or not. An airplane seat is a commodity: each one is basically indistinguishable from others on the same flight. Yet the prices vary wildly, based on a myriad of factors that are mostly known only by the airlines themselves.

Etzioni concluded that he didn't need to decrypt the rhyme or reason for the price differences. Instead, he simply had to predict whether the price being shown was likely to increase or decrease in the future. That is possible, if not easy, to do. All it requires is analyzing all the ticket sales for a given route and examining the prices paid relative to the number of days before the departure.

If the average price of a ticket tended to decrease, it would make sense to wait and buy the ticket later. If the average price usually increased, the system would recommend buying the ticket right away at the price shown. In other words, what was needed was a souped-up version of the informal survey Etzioni conducted at 30,000 feet. To be sure, it was yet another massive computer science problem. But again, it was one he could solve. So he set to work.

Using a sample of 12,000 price observations that was obtained by "scraping" information from a travel website over a 41-day period, Etzioni created a predictive model that handed its simulated passengers a tidy savings. The model had no understanding of *why,* only *what.* That is, it didn't know any of the variables that go into airline pricing decisions, such as number of seats that remained unsold, seasonality, or whether some sort of magical Saturday-night-stay might reduce the fare. It based its prediction on what it did know: probabilities gleaned from the data about other flights. "To buy or not to buy, that is the question," Etzioni mused. Fittingly, he named the research project Hamlet.

The little project evolved into a venture capital–backed startup called Farecast. By predicting whether the price of an airline ticket was likely to go up or down, and by how much, Farecast empowered consumers to choose when to click the "buy" button. It armed them with information to which they had never had access before. Upholding the virtue of transparency against itself, Farecast even scored the degree of confidence it had in its own predictions and presented that information to users too.

To work, the system needed lots of data. To improve its performance, Etzioni got his hands on one of the industry's flight reservation databases. With that information, the system could make predictions based on every seat on every flight for most routes in American commercial aviation over the course of a year. Farecast was now crunching nearly 200 billion flight-price records to make its predictions. In so doing, it was saving consumers a bundle.

With his sandy brown hair, toothy grin, and cherubic good looks, Etzioni hardly seemed like the sort of person who would deny the airline industry millions of dollars of potential revenue. In fact, he set his sights on doing even more than that. By 2008 he was planning to apply the method to other goods like hotel rooms, concert tickets, and used cars: anything with little product differentiation, a high degree of price variation, and tons of data. But before he could hatch his plans, Microsoft came knocking on his door, snapped up Farecast for around $110 million, and integrated it into the Bing search engine. By 2012 the system was making the correct call 75 percent of the time and saving travelers, on average, $50 per ticket.

Farecast is the epitome of a big-data company and an example of where the world is headed. Etzioni couldn't have built the company five or ten years earlier. "It would have been impossible," he says. The amount of computing power and storage he needed was too expensive. But although changes in technology have been a critical factor making it possible, something more important changed too, something subtle. There was a shift in mindset about how data could be used.

Data was no longer regarded as static or stale, whose usefulness was finished once the purpose for which it was collected was achieved, such as after the plane landed (or in Google's case, once a search query had been processed). Rather, data became a raw material of business, a vital economic input, used to create a new form of economic value. In fact, with the right mindset, data can be cleverly reused to become a fountain of innovation and new services. The data can reveal secrets to those with the humility, the willingness, and the tools to listen.

Letting the data speak

The fruits of the information society are easy to see, with a cellphone in every pocket, a computer in every backpack, and big information technology systems in back offices everywhere. But less noticeable is the information itself. Half a century after computers entered mainstream society, the data has begun to accumulate to the point where something new and special is taking place. Not only is the world awash with more information than ever before, but that information is growing faster. The change of scale has led to a change of state. The quantitative change has led to a qualitative one. The sciences like astronomy and genomics, which first experienced the explosion in the 2000s, coined the term "big data." The concept is now migrating to all areas of human endeavor.

There is no rigorous definition of big data. Initially the idea was that the volume of information had grown so large that the quantity being examined no longer fit into the memory that computers use for processing, so engineers needed to revamp the tools they used for analyzing it all. That is the origin of new processing technologies like Google's MapReduce and its open-source equivalent, Hadoop, which came out of Yahoo. These let one manage far larger quantities of data than before, and the data — importantly — need not be placed in tidy rows or classic database tables. Other data-crunching technologies that dispense with the rigid hierarchies and homogeneity of yore are also on the horizon. At the same time, because Internet companies could collect vast troves of data and had a burning financial incentive to make sense of them, they became the leading users of the latest processing technologies, superseding offline companies that had, in some cases, decades more experience.

One way to think about the issue today — and the way we do in the book — is this: big data refers to things one can do at a large scale that cannot be done at a smaller one, to extract new insights or create new forms of value, in ways that change markets, organizations, the relationship between citizens and governments, and more.

But this is just the start. The era of big data challenges the way we live and interact with the world. Most strikingly, society will need to shed some of its obsession for causality in exchange for simple correlations: not knowing *why* but only *what*. This overturns centuries of established practices and challenges our most basic understanding of how to make decisions and comprehend reality.

Big data marks the beginning of a major transformation. Like so many new technologies, big data will be a victim of Silicon Valley's notorious hype cycle: after being feted on the cover of magazines and at industry conferences, the trend will be dismissed and many of the data-smitten startups will flounder. But both the infatuation and the damnation profoundly misunderstand the importance of what is taking place. Just as the telescope enabled us to comprehend the universe and the microscope allowed us to understand germs, the new techniques for collecting and analyzing huge bodies of data will help us make sense of our world in ways we are just starting to appreciate. In this book we are not so much big data's evangelists, but merely its messengers. And, again, the real revolution is not in the machines that calculate data but in data itself and how we use it.

To appreciate the degree to which an information revolution is already under way, consider trends from across the spectrum of society. Our digital universe is constantly expanding. Take astronomy. When the Sloan Digital Sky Survey began in 2000, its telescope in New Mexico collected more data in its first few weeks than had been amassed in the entire history of astronomy. By 2010 the survey's archive teemed with a whopping 140 terabytes of information. But a successor, the Large Synoptic Survey Telescope in Chile, due to come on stream in 2016, will acquire that quantity of data every five days.

Such astronomical quantities are found closer to home as well. When scientists first decoded the human genome in 2003, it took them a decade of intensive work to sequence the three billion base pairs. Now, a decade later, a single facility can sequence that much DNA in a day. In finance, about seven billion shares change hands every day on U.S. equity markets, of which around two-thirds is traded by computer algorithms based on mathematical models that crunch mountains of data to predict gains while trying to reduce risk.

Internet companies have been particularly swamped. Google processes more than 24 petabytes of data per day, a volume that is thousands of times the quantity of all printed material in the U.S. Library of Congress. Facebook, a company that didn't exist a decade ago, gets more than 10 million new photos uploaded every hour. Facebook members click a "like" button or leave a comment nearly three billion times per day, creating a digital trail that the company can mine to learn about users' preferences. Meanwhile, the 800 million monthly users of Google's YouTube service upload over an hour of video every second. The number of messages on Twitter grows at around 200 percent a year and by 2012 had exceeded 400 million tweets a day.

From the sciences to healthcare, from banking to the Internet, the sectors may be diverse yet together they tell a similar story: the amount of data in the world is growing fast, outstripping not just our machines but our imaginations.

Many people have tried to put an actual figure on the quantity of information that surrounds us and to calculate how fast it grows. They've had varying degrees of success because they've measured different things. One of the more comprehensive studies was done by Martin Hilbert of the University of Southern California's Annenberg School for Communication and Journalism. He has striven to put a figure on everything that has been produced, stored, and communicated. That would include not only books, paintings, emails, photographs, music, and video (analog and digital), but video games, phone calls, even car navigation systems and letters sent through the mail. He also included broadcast media like television and radio, based on audience reach.

By Hilbert's reckoning, more than 300 exabytes of stored data existed in 2007. To understand what this means in slightly more human terms, think of it like this. A full-length feature film in digital form can be compressed into a one gigabyte file. An exabyte is one billion gigabytes. In short, it's a lot. Interestingly, in 2007 only about 7 percent of the data was analog (paper, books, photographic prints, and so on). The rest was digital. But not long ago the picture looked very different. Though the ideas of the "information revolution" and "digital age" have been around since the 1960s, they have only just become a reality by some measures. As recently as the year 2000, only a quarter of the stored information in the world was digital. The other three-quarters were on paper, film, vinyl LP records, magnetic cassette tapes, and the like.

The mass of digital information then was not much — a humbling thought for those who have been surfing the Web and buying books online for a long time. (In fact, in 1986 around 40 percent of the world's general-purpose computing power took the form of pocket calculators, which represented more processing power than all personal computers at the time.) But because digital data expands so quickly — doubling a little more than every three years, according to Hilbert — the situation quickly inverted itself. Analog information, in contrast, hardly grows at all. So in 2013 the amount of stored information in the world is estimated to be around 1,200 exabytes, of which less than 2 percent is non-digital.

There is no good way to think about what this size of data means. If it were all printed in books, they would cover the entire surface of the United States some 52 layers thick. If it were placed on CD-ROMs and stacked up, they would stretch to the moon in five separate piles. In the third century B.C., as Ptolemy II of Egypt strove to store a copy of every written work, the great Library of Alexandria represented the sum of all knowledge in the world. The digital deluge now sweeping the globe is the equivalent of giving every person living on Earth today 320 times as much information as is estimated to have been stored in the Library of Alexandria.

Things really are speeding up. The amount of stored information grows four times faster than the world economy, while the processing power of computers grows nine times faster. Little wonder that people complain of information overload. Everyone is whiplashed by the changes.

Take the long view, by comparing the current data deluge with an earlier information revolution, that of the Gutenberg printing press, which was invented around 1439. In the fifty years from 1453 to 1503 about eight million books were printed, according to the historian Elizabeth Eisenstein. This is considered to be more than all the scribes of Europe had produced since the founding of Constantinople some 1,200 years earlier. In other words, it took 50 years for the stock of information to roughly double in Europe, compared with around every three years today.

What does this increase mean? Peter Norvig, an artificial intelligence expert at Google, likes to think about it with an analogy to images. First, he asks us to consider the iconic horse from the cave paintings in Lascaux, France, which date to the Paleolithic Era some 17,000 years ago. Then think of a photograph of a horse — or better, the dabs of Pablo Picasso, which do not look much dissimilar to the cave paintings. In fact, when Picasso was shown the Lascaux images he quipped that, since then, "We have invented nothing."

Picasso's words were true on one level but not on another. Recall that photograph of the horse. Where it took a long time to draw a picture of a horse, now a representation of one could be made much faster with photography. That is a change, but it may not be the most essential, since it is still fundamentally the same: an image of a horse. Yet now, Norvig implores, consider capturing the image of a horse and speeding it up to 24 frames per second. Now, the quantitative change has produced a qualitative change. A movie is fundamentally different from a frozen photograph. It's the same with big data: by changing the amount, we change the essence.

Consider an analogy from nanotechnology — where things get smaller, not bigger. The principle behind nanotechnology is that when you get to the molecular level, the physical properties can change. Knowing those new characteristics means you can devise materials to do things that could not be done before. At the nanoscale, for example, more flexible metals and stretchable ceramics are possible. Conversely, when we increase the scale of the data that we work with, we can do new things that weren't possible when we just worked with smaller amounts.

Sometimes the constraints that we live with, and presume are the same for everything, are really only functions of the scale in which we operate. Take a third analogy, again from the sciences. For humans, the single most important physical law is gravity: it reigns over all that we do. But for tiny insects, gravity is mostly immaterial. For some, like water striders, the operative law of the physical universe is surface tension, which allows them to walk across a pond without falling in.

With information, as with physics, size matters. Hence, Google is able to identify the prevalence of the flu just about as well as official data based on actual patient visits to the doctor. It can do this by combing through hundreds of billions of search terms — and it can produce an answer in near real time, far faster than official sources. Likewise, Etzioni's Farecast can predict the price volatility of an airplane ticket and thus shift substantial economic power into the hands of consumers. But both can do so well only by analyzing hundreds of billions of data points.

These two examples show the scientific and societal importance of big data as well as the degree to which big data can become a source of economic value. They mark two ways in which the world of big data is poised to shake up everything from businesses and the sciences to healthcare, government, education, economics, the humanities, and every other aspect of society.

Although we are only at the dawn of big data, we rely on it daily. Spam filters are designed to automatically adapt as the types of junk email change: the software couldn't be programmed to know to block "via6ra" or its infinity of variants. Dating sites pair up couples on the basis of how their numerous attributes correlate with those of successful previous matches. The "autocorrect" feature in smartphones tracks our actions and adds new words to its spelling dictionary based on what we type. Yet these uses are just the start. From cars that can detect when to swerve or brake to IBM's Watson computer beating humans on the game show *Jeopardy!*, the approach will revamp many aspects of the world in which we live.

At its core, big data is about predictions. Though it is described as part of the branch of computer science called artificial intelligence, and more specifically, an area called machine learning, this characterization is misleading. Big data is not about trying to "teach" a computer to "think" like humans. Instead, it's about applying math to huge quantities of data in order to infer probabilities: the likelihood that an email message is spam; that the typed letters "teh" are supposed to be "the"; that the trajectory and velocity of a person jaywalking mean he'll make it across the street in time — the self-driving car need only slow slightly. The key is that these systems perform well because they are fed with lots of data on which to base their predictions. Moreover, the systems are built to improve themselves over time, by keeping a tab on what are the best signals and patterns to look for as more data is fed in.

In the future — and sooner than we may think — many aspects of our world will be augmented or replaced by computer systems that today are the sole purview of human judgment. Not just driving or matchmaking, but even more complex tasks. After all, Amazon can recommend the ideal book, Google can rank the most relevant website, Facebook knows our likes, and LinkedIn divines whom we know. The same technologies will be applied to diagnosing illnesses, recommending treatments, perhaps even identifying "criminals" before one actually commits a crime. Just as the Internet radically changed the world by adding communications to computers, so too will big data change fundamental aspects of life by giving it a quantitative dimension it never had before.

More, messy, good enough

Big data will be a source of new economic value and innovation. But even more is at stake. Big data's ascendancy represents three shifts in the way we analyze information that transform how we understand and organize society.

The first shift is described in Chapter Two. In this new world we can analyze far more data. In some cases we can even process *all* of it relating to a particular phenomenon. Since the nineteenth century, society has depended on using samples when faced with large numbers. Yet the need for sampling is an artifact of a period of information scarcity, a product of the natural constraints on interacting with information in an analog era. Before the prevalence of high-performance digital technologies, we didn't recognize sampling as artificial fetters — we usually just took it for granted. Using all the data lets us see details we never could when we were limited to smaller quantities. Big data gives us an especially clear view of the granular: subcategories and submarkets that samples can't assess.

Looking at vastly more data also permits us to loosen up our desire for exactitude, the second shift, which we identify in Chapter Three. It's a tradeoff: with less error from sampling we can accept more measurement error. When our ability to measure is limited, we count only the most important things. Striving to get the exact number is appropriate. It is no use selling cattle if the buyer isn't sure whether there are 100 or only 80 in the herd. Until recently, all our digital tools were premised on exactitude: we assumed that database engines would retrieve the records that perfectly matched our query, much as spreadsheets tabulate the numbers in a column.

This type of thinking was a function of a "small data" environment: with so few things to measure, we had to treat what we did bother to quantify as precisely as possible. In some ways this is obvious: a small store may count the money in the cash register at the end of the night down to the penny, but we wouldn't — indeed couldn't — do the same for a country's gross domestic product. As scale increases, the number of inaccuracies increases as well.

Exactness requires carefully curated data. It may work for small quantities, and of course certain situations still require it: one either does or does not have enough money in the bank to write a check. But in return for using much more comprehensive datasets we can shed some of the rigid exactitude in a big-data world.

Often, big data is messy, varies in quality, and is distributed among countless servers around the world. With big data, we'll often be satisfied with a sense of general direction rather than knowing a phenomenon down to the inch, the penny, the atom. We don't give up on exactitude entirely; we only give up our devotion to it. What we lose in accuracy at the micro level we gain in insight at the macro level.

These two shifts lead to a third change, which we explain in Chapter Four: a move away from the age-old search for causality. As humans we have been conditioned to look for causes, even though searching for causality is often difficult and may lead us down the wrong paths. In a big-data world, by contrast, we won't have to be fixated on causality; instead we can discover patterns and correlations in the data that offer us novel and invaluable insights. The correlations may not tell us precisely *why* something is happening, but they alert us *that* it is happening.

And in many situations this is good enough. If millions of electronic medical records reveal that cancer sufferers who take a certain combination of aspirin and orange juice see their disease go into remission, then the exact cause for the improvement in health may be less important than the fact that they lived. Likewise, if we can save money by knowing the best time to buy a plane ticket without understanding the method behind airfare madness, that's good enough. Big data is about *what*, not *why*. We don't always need to know the cause of a phenomenon; rather, we can let data speak for itself.

Before big data, our analysis was usually limited to testing a small number of hypotheses that we defined well before we even collected the data. When we let the data speak, we can make connections that we had never thought existed. Hence, some hedge funds parse Twitter to predict the performance of the stock market. Amazon and Netflix base their product recommendations on a myriad of user interactions on their sites. Twitter, LinkedIn, and Facebook all map users' "social graph" of relationships to learn their preferences.

Of course, humans have been analyzing data for millennia. Writing was developed in ancient Mesopotamia because bureaucrats wanted an efficient tool to record and keep track of information. Since biblical times governments have held censuses to gather huge datasets on their citizenry, and for two hundred years actuaries have similarly collected large troves of data concerning the risks they hope to understand — or at least avoid.

Yet in the analog age collecting and analyzing such data was enormously costly and time-consuming. New questions often meant that the data had to be collected again and the analysis started afresh.

The big step toward managing data more efficiently came with the advent of digitization: making analog information readable by computers, which also makes it easier and cheaper to store and process. This advance improved efficiency dramatically. Information collection and analysis that once took years could now be done in days or even less. But little else changed. The people who analyzed the data were too often steeped in the analog paradigm of assuming that datasets had singular purposes to which their value was tied. Our very processes perpetuated this prejudice. As important as digitization was for enabling the shift to big data, the mere existence of computers did not make big data happen.

There's no good term to describe what's taking place now, but one that helps frame the changes is *datafication,* a concept that we introduce in Chapter Five. It refers to taking information about all things under the sun — including ones we never used to think of as information at all, such as a person's location, the vibrations of an engine, or the stress on a bridge — and transforming it into a data format to make it quantified. This allows us to use the information in new ways, such as in predictive analysis: detecting that an engine is prone to a breakdown based on the heat or vibrations that it produces. As a result, we can unlock the implicit, latent value of the information.

There is a treasure hunt under way, driven by the insights to be extracted from data and the dormant value that can be unleashed by a shift from causation to correlation. But it's not just one treasure. Every single dataset is likely to have some intrinsic, hidden, not yet unearthed value, and the race is on to discover and capture all of it.

Big data changes the nature of business, markets, and society, as we describe in Chapters Six and Seven. In the twentieth century, value shifted from physical infrastructure like land and factories to intangibles such as brands and intellectual property. That now is expanding to data, which is becoming a significant corporate asset, a vital economic input, and the foundation of new business models. It is the oil of the information economy. Though data is rarely recorded on corporate balance sheets, this is probably just a question of time.

Although some data-crunching techniques have been around for a while, in the past they were only available to spy agencies, research labs, and the world's biggest companies. After all, Walmart and Capital One pioneered the use of big data in retailing and banking and in so doing changed their industries. Now many of these tools have been democratized (although the data has not).

The effect on individuals may be the biggest shock of all. Specific area expertise matters less in a world where probability and correlation are paramount. In the movie *Moneyball,* baseball scouts were upstaged by statisticians when gut instinct gave way to sophisticated analytics. Similarly, subject-matter specialists will not go away, but they will have to contend with what the big-data analysis says. This will force an adjustment to traditional ideas of management, decision-making, human resources, and education.

Most of our institutions were established under the presumption that human decisions are based on information that is small, exact, and causal in nature. But the situation changes when the data is huge, can be processed quickly, and tolerates inexactitude. Moreover, because of the data's vast size, decisions may often be made not by humans but by machines. We consider the dark side of big data in Chapter Eight.

Society has millennia of experience in understanding and overseeing human behavior. But how do you regulate an algorithm? Early on in computing, policymakers recognized how the technology could be used to undermine privacy. Since then society has built up a body of rules to protect personal information. But in an age of big data, those laws constitute a largely useless Maginot Line. People willingly share information online — a central feature of the services, not a vulnerability to prevent.

Meanwhile the danger to us as individuals shifts from privacy to probability: algorithms will predict the likelihood that one will get a heart attack (and pay more for health insurance), default on a mortgage (and be denied a loan), or commit a crime (and perhaps get arrested in advance). It leads to an ethical consideration of the role of free will versus the dictatorship of data. Should individual volition trump big data, even if statistics argue otherwise? Just as the printing press prepared the ground for laws guaranteeing free speech — which didn't exist earlier because there was so little written expression to protect — the age of big data will require new rules to safeguard the sanctity of the individual.

In many ways, the way we control and handle data will have to change. We're entering a world of constant data-driven predictions where we may not be able to explain the reasons behind our decisions. What does it mean if a doctor cannot justify a medical intervention without asking the patient to defer to a black box, as the physician must do when relying on a big-data-driven diagnosis? Will the judicial system's standard of "probable cause" need to change to "probabilistic cause" — and if so, what are the implications of this for human freedom and dignity?

New principles are needed for the age of big data, which we lay out in Chapter Nine. Although they build upon the values that were developed and enshrined for the world of small data, it's not simply a matter of refreshing old rules for new circumstances, but recognizing the need for new principles altogether.

The benefits to society will be myriad, as big data becomes part of the solution to pressing global problems like addressing climate change, eradicating disease, and fostering good governance and economic development. But the big-data era also challenges us to become better prepared for the ways in which harnessing the technology will change our institutions and ourselves.

Big data marks an important step in humankind's quest to quantify and understand the world. A preponderance of things that could never be measured, stored, analyzed, and shared before is becoming datafied. Harnessing vast quantities of data rather than a small portion, and privileging more data of less exactitude, opens the door to new ways of understanding. It leads society to abandon its time-honored preference for causality, and in many instances tap the benefits of correlation.

The ideal of identifying causal mechanisms is a self-congratulatory illusion; big data overturns this. Yet again we are at a historical impasse where "god is dead." That is to say, the certainties that we believed in are once again changing. But this time they are being replaced, ironically, by better evidence. What role is left for intuition, faith, uncertainty, acting in contradiction of the evidence, and learning by experience? As the world shifts from causation to correlation, how can we pragmatically move forward without undermining the very foundations of society, humanity, and progress based on reason? This book intends to explain where we are, trace how we got here, and offer an urgently needed guide to the benefits and dangers that lie ahead.

2

MORE

BIG DATA IS ALL ABOUT seeing and understanding the relations within and among pieces of information that, until very recently, we struggled to fully grasp. IBM's big-data expert Jeff Jonas says you need to let the data "speak to you." At one level this may sound trivial. Humans have looked to data to learn about the world for a long time, whether in the informal sense of the myriad observations we make every day or, mainly over the last couple of centuries, in the formal sense of quantified units that can be manipulated by powerful algorithms.

The digital age may have made it easier and faster to process data, to calculate millions of numbers in a heartbeat. But when we talk about data that speaks, we mean something more — and different. As noted in Chapter One, big data is about three major shifts of mindset that are interlinked and hence reinforce one another. The first is the ability to analyze vast amounts of data about a topic rather than be forced to settle for smaller sets. The second is a willingness to embrace data's real-world messiness rather than privilege exactitude. The third is a growing respect for correlations rather than a continuing quest for elusive causality. This chapter looks at the first of these shifts: using all the data at hand instead of just a small portion of it.

The challenge of processing large piles of data accurately has been with us for a while. For most of history we worked with only a little data because our tools to collect, organize, store, and analyze it were

poor. We winnowed the information we relied on to the barest minimum so we could examine it more easily. This was a form of uncon-
scious self-censorship: we treated the difficulty of interacting with
data as an unfortunate reality, rather than seeing it for what it was, an
artificial constraint imposed by the technology at the time. Today the
technical environment has changed 179 degrees. There still is, and always will be, a constraint on how much data we can manage, but it is
far less limiting than it used to be and will become even less so as time
goes on.

In some ways, we haven't yet fully appreciated our new freedom
to collect and use larger pools of data. Most of our experience and
the design of our institutions have presumed that the availability of
information is limited. We reckoned we could only collect a little information, and so that's usually what we did. It became self-fulfilling.
We even developed elaborate techniques to use as little data as possible. One aim of statistics, after all, is to confirm the richest finding using the smallest amount of data. In effect, we codified our practice of
stunting the quantity of information we used in our norms, processes,
and incentive structures. To get a sense of what the shift to big data
means, the story starts with a look back in time.

Not until recently have private firms, and nowadays even individuals, been able to collect and sort information on a massive scale. In
the past, that task fell to more powerful institutions like the church
and the state, which in many societies amounted to the same thing.
The oldest record of counting dates is from around 5000 B.C., when
Sumerian merchants used small clay beads to denote goods for trade.
Counting on a larger scale, however, was the purview of the state.
Over millennia, governments have tried to keep track of their people
by collecting information.

Consider the census. The ancient Egyptians are said to have conducted censuses, as did the Chinese. They're mentioned in the Old
Testament, and the New Testament tells us that a census imposed
by Caesar Augustus — "that all the world should be taxed" (Luke 2:1)
— took Joseph and Mary to Bethlehem, where Jesus was born. The
Domesday Book of 1086, one of Britain's most venerated treasures,

was at its time an unprecedented, comprehensive tally of the English people, their land and property. Royal commissioners spread across the countryside compiling information to put in the book — which later got the name "Domesday," or "Doomsday," because the process was like the biblical Final Judgment, when everyone's life is laid bare.

Conducting censuses is both costly and time-consuming; King William I, who commissioned the Domesday Book, didn't live to see its completion. But the only alternative to bearing this burden was to forgo collecting the information. And even after all the time and expense, the information was only approximate, since the census takers couldn't possibly count everyone perfectly. The very word "census" comes from the Latin term "censere," which means "to estimate."

More than three hundred years ago, a British haberdasher named John Graunt had a novel idea. Graunt wanted to know the population of London at the time of the plague. Instead of counting every person, he devised an approach — which today we would call "statistics" — that allowed him to *infer* the population size. His approach was crude, but it established the idea that one could extrapolate from a small sample useful knowledge about the general population. But how one does that is important. Graunt just scaled up from his sample.

His system was celebrated, even though we later learned that his numbers were reasonable only by luck. For generations, sampling remained grossly flawed. Thus for censuses and similar "big data-ish" undertakings, the brute-force approach of trying to count every number ruled the day.

Because censuses were so complex, costly, and time-consuming, they were conducted only rarely. The ancient Romans, who long boasted a population in the hundreds of thousands, ran a census every five years. The U.S. Constitution mandated one every decade, as the growing country measured itself in millions. But by the late nineteenth century even that was proving problematic. The data outstripped the Census Bureau's ability to keep up.

The 1880 census took a staggering eight years to complete. The information was obsolete even before it became available. Worse still, officials estimated that the 1890 census would have required a full 13 years to tabulate — a ridiculous state of affairs, not to mention a violation of the Constitution. Yet because the apportionment of taxes and congressional representation was based on population, getting not only a correct count but a timely one was essential.

The problem the U.S. Census Bureau faced is similar to the struggle of scientists and businessmen at the start of the new millennium, when it became clear that they were drowning in data: the amount of information being collected had utterly swamped the tools used for processing it, and new techniques were needed. In the 1880s the situation was so dire that the Census Bureau contracted with Herman Hollerith, an American inventor, to use his idea of punch cards and tabulation machines for the 1890 census.

With great effort, he succeeded in shrinking the tabulation time from eight years to less than one. It was an amazing feat, which marked the beginning of automated data processing (and provided the foundation for what later became IBM). But as a method of acquiring and analyzing big data it was still very expensive. After all, every person in the United States had to fill in a form and the information had to be transferred to a punch card, which was used for tabulation. With such costly methods, it was hard to imagine running a census in any time span shorter than a decade, even though the lag was unhelpful for a nation growing by leaps and bounds.

Therein lay the tension: Use all the data, or just a little? Getting all the data about whatever is being measured is surely the most sensible course. It just isn't always practical when the scale is vast. But how to choose a sample? Some argued that purposefully constructing a sample that was representative of the whole would be the most suitable way forward. But in 1934 Jerzy Neyman, a Polish statistician, forcefully showed that such an approach leads to huge errors. The key to avoid them is to aim for randomness in choosing whom to sample.

Statisticians have shown that sampling precision improves most dramatically with randomness, not with increased sample size. In fact, though it may sound surprising, a randomly chosen sample of 1,100 individual observations on a binary question (yes or no, with roughly equal odds) is remarkably representative of the whole population. In 19 out of 20 cases it is within a 3 percent margin of error, regardless of whether the total population size is a hundred thousand or a hundred million. Why this should be the case is complicated mathematically, but the short answer is that after a certain point early on, as the numbers get bigger and bigger, the marginal amount of new information we learn from each observation is less and less.

The fact that randomness trumped sample size was a startling insight. It paved the way for a new approach to gathering information. Data using random samples could be collected at low cost and yet extrapolated with high accuracy to the whole. As a result, governments could run small versions of the census using random samples every year, rather than just one every decade. And they did. The U.S. Census Bureau, for instance, conducts more than two hundred economic and demographic surveys every year based on sampling, in addition to the decennial census that tries to count everyone. Sampling was a solution to the problem of information overload in an earlier age, when the collection and analysis of data was very hard to do.

The applications of this new method quickly went beyond the public sector and censuses. In essence, random sampling reduces big-data problems to more manageable data problems. In business, it was used to ensure manufacturing quality — making improvements much easier and less costly. Comprehensive quality control originally required looking at every single product coming off the conveyor belt; now a random sample of tests for a batch of products would suffice. Likewise, the new method ushered in consumer surveys in retailing and snap polls in politics. It transformed a big part of what we used to call the humanities into the social *sciences*.

Random sampling has been a huge success and is the backbone of modern measurement at scale. But it is only a shortcut, a second-best alternative to collecting and analyzing the full dataset. It comes with a number of inherent weaknesses. Its accuracy depends on ensuring randomness when collecting the sample data, but achieving such randomness is tricky. Systematic biases in the way the data is collected can lead to the extrapolated results being very wrong.

There are echoes of such problems in election polling using landline phones. The sample is biased against people who only use cellphones (who are younger and more liberal), as the statistician Nate Silver has pointed out. This has resulted in incorrect election predictions. In the 2008 presidential election between Barack Obama and John McCain, the major polling organizations of Gallup, Pew, and ABC/Washington Post found differences of between one and three percentage points when they polled with and without adjusting for cellphone users — a hefty margin considering the tightness of the race.

Most troublingly, random sampling doesn't scale easily to include subcategories, as breaking the results down into smaller and smaller subgroups increases the possibility of erroneous predictions. It's easy to understand why. Suppose you poll a random sample of a thousand people about their voting intentions in the next election. If your sample is sufficiently random, chances are that the entire population's sentiment will be within a 3 percent range of the views in the sample. But what if plus or minus 3 percent is not precise enough? Or what if you then want to break down the group into smaller subgroups, by gender, geography, or income?

And what if you want to combine these subgroups to target a niche of the population? In an overall sample of a thousand people, a subgroup such as "affluent female voters in the Northeast" will be much smaller than a hundred. Using only a few dozen observations to predict the voting intentions of *all* affluent female voters in the Northeast will be imprecise even with close to perfect randomness. And tiny biases in the overall sample will make the errors more pronounced at the level of subgroups.

Hence, sampling quickly stops being useful when you want to drill deeper, to take a closer look at some intriguing subcategory in the data. What works at the macro level falls apart in the micro. Sampling is like an analog photographic print. It looks good from a distance, but as you stare closer, zooming in on a particular detail, it gets blurry.

Sampling also requires careful planning and execution. One usually cannot "ask" sampled data-fresh questions if they have not been considered at the outset. So though as a shortcut it is useful, the trade-off is that it's, well, a shortcut. Being a sample rather than everything, the dataset lacks a certain extensibility or malleability, whereby the same data can be reanalyzed in an entirely new way than the purpose for which it was originally collected.

Consider the case of DNA analysis. The cost to sequence an individual's genome approached a thousand dollars in 2012, moving it closer to a mass-market technique that can be performed at scale. As a result, a new industry of individual gene sequencing is cropping up. Since 2007 the Silicon Valley startup 23andMe has been analyzing people's DNA for only a couple of hundred dollars. Its technique can reveal traits in people's genetic codes that may make them more susceptible to certain diseases like breast cancer or heart problems. And by aggregating its customers' DNA and health information, 23andMe hopes to learn new things that couldn't be spotted otherwise.

But there's a hitch. The company sequences just a small portion of a person's genetic code: places that are known to be markers indicating particular genetic weaknesses. Meanwhile, billions of base pairs of DNA remain unsequenced. Thus 23andMe can only answer questions about the markers it considers. Whenever a new marker is discovered, a person's DNA (or more precisely, the relevant part of it) has to be sequenced again. Working with a subset, rather than the whole, entails a tradeoff: the company can find what it is looking for faster and more cheaply, but it can't answer questions that it didn't consider in advance.

Apple's legendary chief executive Steve Jobs took a totally different approach in his fight against cancer. He became one of the first people in the world to have his entire DNA sequenced as well as that of his tumor. To do this, he paid a six-figure sum — many hundreds of times more than the price 23andMe charges. In return, he received not a sample, a mere set of markers, but a data file containing the entire genetic codes.

In choosing medication for an average cancer patient, doctors have to hope that the patient's DNA is sufficiently similar to that of patients who participated in the drug's trials to work. However, Steve

Jobs's team of doctors could select therapies by how well they would work given his specific genetic makeup. Whenever one treatment lost its effectiveness because the cancer mutated and worked around it, the doctors could switch to another drug — "jumping from one lily pad to another," Jobs called it. "I'm either going to be one of the first to be able to outrun a cancer like this or I'm going to be one of the last to die from it," he quipped. Though his prediction went sadly unfulfilled, the method — having all the data, not just a bit — gave him years of extra life.

From some to all

Sampling is an outgrowth of an era of information-processing constraints, when people were measuring the world but lacked the tools to analyze what they collected. As a result, it is a vestige of that era too. The shortcomings in counting and tabulating no longer exist to the same extent. Sensors, cellphone GPS, web clicks, and Twitter collect data passively; computers can crunch the numbers with increasing ease.

The concept of sampling no longer makes as much sense when we can harness large amounts of data. The technical tools for handling data have already changed dramatically, but our methods and mindsets have been slower to adapt.

Yet sampling comes with a cost that has long been acknowledged but shunted aside. It loses detail. In some cases there is no other way but to sample. In many areas, however, a shift is taking place from collecting some data to gathering as much as possible, and if feasible, getting everything: $N = all$.

As we've seen, using N = all means we can drill down deep into data; samples can't do that nearly as well. Second, recall that in our example of sampling above, we had only a 3 percent margin of error when extrapolating to the whole population. For some situations, that error margin is fine. But you lose the details, the granularity, the ability to look closer at certain subgroups. A normal distribution is, alas, normal. Often, the really interesting things in life are found in places that samples fail to fully catch.

Hence Google Flu Trends doesn't rely on a small random sample but instead uses billions of Internet search queries in the United States. Using all this data rather than a small sample improves the analysis down to the level of predicting the spread of flu in a particular city rather than a state or the entire nation. Oren Etzioni of Farecast initially used 12,000 data points, a sample, and it performed well. But as Etzioni added more data, the quality of the predictions improved. Eventually, Farecast used the domestic flight records for most routes for an entire year. "This is temporal data — you just keep gathering it over time, and as you do, you get more and more insight into the patterns," Etzioni says.

So we'll frequently be okay to toss aside the shortcut of random sampling and aim for more comprehensive data instead. Doing so requires ample processing and storage power and cutting-edge tools to analyze it all. It also requires easy and affordable ways to collect the data. In the past, each one of these was an expensive conundrum. But now the cost and complexity of all these pieces of the puzzle have declined dramatically. What was previously the purview of just the biggest companies is now possible for most.

Using all the data makes it possible to spot connections and details that are otherwise cloaked in the vastness of the information. For instance, the detection of credit card fraud works by looking for anomalies, and the best way to find them is to crunch all the data rather than a sample. The outliers are the most interesting information, and you can only identify them in comparison to the mass of normal transactions. It is a big-data problem. And because credit card transactions happen instantaneously, the analysis usually has to happen in real time too.

Xoom is a firm that specializes in international money transfers and is backed by big names in big data. It analyzes all the data associated with the transactions it handles. The system raised alarm bells in 2011 when it noticed a slightly higher than average number of Discover Card transactions originating from New Jersey. "It saw a pattern when there shouldn't have been a pattern," explained John Kunze, Xoom's chief executive. On its own, each transaction looked legitimate. But it turned out that they came from a criminal group. The only way to spot the anomaly was to examine all the data — sampling might have missed it.

Using all the data need not be an enormous task. Big data is not necessarily big in absolute terms, although often it is. Google Flu Trends tunes its predictions on hundreds of millions of mathematical modeling exercises using billions of data points. The full sequence of a human genome amounts to three billion base pairs. But the absolute number of data points alone, the size of the dataset, is not what makes these examples of big data. What classifies them as big data is that instead of using the shortcut of a random sample, both Flu Trends and Steve Jobs's doctors used as much of the entire dataset as feasible.

The discovery of match fixing in Japan's national sport, sumo wrestling, is a good illustration of why using N = all need not mean big. Thrown matches have been a constant accusation bedeviling the sport of emperors, and always rigorously denied. Steven Levitt, an economist at the University of Chicago, looked for corruption in the records of more than a decade of past matches — all of them. In a delightful research paper published in the *American Economic Review* and reprised in the book *Freakonomics,* he and a colleague described the usefulness of examining so much data.

They analyzed 11 years' worth of sumo bouts, more than 64,000 wrestler-matches, to hunt for anomalies. And they struck gold. Match fixing did indeed take place, but not where most people suspected. Rather than for championship bouts, which may or may not be rigged, the data showed that something funny was happening during the unnoticed end-of-tournament matches. It seems little is at stake, since the wrestlers have no chance of winning a title.

But one peculiarity of sumo is that wrestlers need a majority of wins at the 15-match tournaments in order to retain their rank and income. This sometimes leads to asymmetries of interests, when a wrestler with a 7–7 record faces an opponent with 8–6 or better. The outcome means a great deal to the first wrestler and next to nothing to the second. In such cases, the number-crunching uncovered, the wrestler who needs the victory is very likely to win.

Might the fellows who need the win be fighting more resolutely? Perhaps. But the data suggested that something else is happening as well. The wrestlers with more at stake win about 25 percent more often than normal. It's hard to attribute that large a discrepancy to adrenaline alone. When the data was parsed further, it showed that the very next time the same two wrestlers met, the loser of the previous bout was much more likely to win than when they sparred in later matches. So the first victory appears to be a "gift" from one competitor to the other, since what goes around comes around in the tight-knit world of sumo.

This information was always apparent. It existed in plain sight. But random sampling of the bouts might have failed to reveal it. Even though it relied on basic statistics, without knowing what to look for, one would have no idea what sample to use. In contrast, Levitt and his colleague uncovered it by using a far larger set of data — striving to examine the entire universe of matches. An investigation using big data is almost like a fishing expedition: it is unclear at the outset not only whether one will catch anything but *what* one may catch.

The dataset need not span terabytes. In the sumo case, the entire dataset contained fewer bits than a typical digital photo these days. But as big-data analysis, it looked at more than a typical random sample. When we talk about big data, we mean "big" less in absolute than in relative terms: relative to the comprehensive set of data.

For a long time, random sampling was a good shortcut. It made analysis of large data problems possible in the pre-digital era. But much as when converting a digital image or song into a smaller file, information is lost when sampling. Having the full (or close to the full) dataset provides a lot more freedom to explore, to look at the data from different angles or to look closer at certain aspects of it.

A fitting analogy may be the Lytro camera, which captures not just a single plane of light, as with conventional cameras, but rays from the entire light field, some 11 million of them. The photographers can decide later which element of an image to focus on in the digital file. There is no need to focus at the outset, since collecting all the information makes it possible to do that afterwards. Because rays from the entire light field are included, it is closer to all the data. As a result, the information is more "reuseable" than ordinary pictures, where the photographer has to decide what to focus on before she presses the shutter.

Similarly, because big data relies on all the information, or at least as much as possible, it allows us to look at details or explore new analyses without the risk of blurriness. We can test new hypotheses at many levels of granularity. This quality is what lets us see match fixing in sumo wrestling, track the spread of the flu virus by region, and fight cancer by targeting a precise portion of the patient's DNA. It allows us to work at an amazing level of clarity.

To be sure, using all the data instead of a sample isn't always necessary. We still live in a resource-constrained world. But in an increasing number of cases using all the data at hand does make sense, and doing so is feasible now where before it was not.

One of the areas that is being most dramatically shaken up by N = all is the social sciences. They have lost their monopoly on making sense of empirical social data, as big-data analysis replaces the highly skilled survey specialists of the past. The social science disciplines largely relied on sampling studies and questionnaires. But when the data is collected passively while people do what they normally do anyway, the old biases associated with sampling and questionnaires disappear. We can now collect information that we couldn't before, be it relationships revealed via mobile phone calls or sentiments unveiled through tweets. More important, the need to sample disappears.

Albert-László Barabási, one of the world's foremost authorities on the science of network theory, wanted to study interactions among people at the scale of the entire population. So he and his colleagues examined anonymous logs of mobile phone calls from a wireless operator that served about one-fifth of an unidentified European country's population — all the logs for a four-month period. It was the first network analysis on a societal level, using a dataset that was in the spirit of N = all. Working on such a large scale, looking at all the calls among millions of people over time, produced novel insights that probably couldn't have been revealed in any other way.

Intriguingly, in contrast to smaller studies, the team discovered that if one removes people from the network who have many links within their community, the remaining social network degrades but doesn't fail. When, on the other hand, people with links outside their immediate community are taken off the network, the social net suddenly disintegrates, as if its structure had buckled. It was an important, but somewhat unexpected result. Who would have thought that the people with lots of close friends are far less important to the stability of the network structure than the ones who have ties to more distant people? It suggests that there is a premium on diversity within a group and in society at large.

We tend to think of statistical sampling as some sort of immutable bedrock, like the principles of geometry or the laws of gravity. But the concept is less than a century old, and it was developed to solve a particular problem at a particular moment in time under specific technological constraints. Those constraints no longer exist to the same extent. Reaching for a random sample in the age of big data is like clutching at a horse whip in the era of the motor car. We can still use sampling in certain contexts, but it need not — and will not — be the predominant way we analyze large datasets. Increasingly, we will aim to go for it all.

3

MESSY

USING ALL AVAILABLE DATA is feasible in an increasing number of contexts. But it comes at a cost. Increasing the volume opens the door to inexactitude. To be sure, erroneous figures and corrupted bits have always crept into datasets. Yet the point has always been to treat them as problems and try to get rid of them, in part because we could. What we never wanted to do was consider them unavoidable and learn to live with them. This is one of the fundamental shifts of going to big data from small.

In a world of small data, reducing errors and ensuring high quality of data was a natural and essential impulse. Since we only collected a little information, we made sure that the figures we bothered to record were as accurate as possible. Generations of scientists optimized their instruments to make their measurements more and more precise, whether for determining the position of celestial bodies or the size of objects under a microscope. In a world of sampling, the obsession with exactitude was even more critical. Analyzing only a limited number of data points means errors may get amplified, potentially reducing the accuracy of the overall results.

For much of history, humankind's highest achievements arose from conquering the world by measuring it. The quest for exactitude began in Europe in the middle of the thirteenth century, when astronomers and scholars took on the ever more precise quantification of time and space — "the measure of reality," in the words of the historian Alfred Crosby.

If one could measure a phenomenon, the implicit belief was, one could understand it. Later, measurement was tied to the scientific method of observation and explanation: the ability to quantify, record, and present reproducible results. "To measure is to know," pronounced Lord Kelvin. It became a basis of authority. "Knowledge is power," instructed Francis Bacon. In parallel, mathematicians, and what later became actuaries and accountants, developed methods that made possible the accurate collection, recording, and management of data.

By the nineteenth century France — then the world's leading scientific nation — had developed a system of precisely defined units of measurement to capture space, time, and more, and had begun to get other nations to adopt the same standards. This went as far as laying down internationally accepted prototype units to measure against in international treaties. It was the apex of the age of measurement. Just half a century later, in the 1920s, the discoveries of quantum mechanics shattered forever the dream of comprehensive and perfect measurement. And yet, outside a relatively small circle of physicists, the mindset of humankind's drive to flawlessly measure continued among engineers and scientists. In the world of business it even expanded, as the rational sciences of mathematics and statistics began to influence all areas of commerce.

However, in many new situations that are cropping up today, allowing for imprecision — for messiness — may be a positive feature, not a shortcoming. It is a tradeoff. In return for relaxing the standards of allowable errors, one can get ahold of much more data. It isn't just that "more trumps some," but that, in fact, sometimes "more trumps better."

There are several kinds of messiness to contend with. The term can refer to the simple fact that the likelihood of errors increases as you add more data points. Hence, increasing the stress readings from a bridge by a factor of a thousand boosts the chance that some may be wrong. But you can also increase messiness by combining different types of information from different sources, which don't always align perfectly. For example, using voice-recognition software to characterize complaints to a call center, and comparing that data with the time it takes operators to handle the calls, may yield an imperfect but useful snapshot of the situation. Messiness can also refer to the inconsistency of formatting, for which the data needs to be "cleaned" before being processed. There are a myriad of ways to refer to IBM, notes the big-data expert DJ Patil, from I.B.M. to T. J. Watson Labs, to International Business Machines. And messiness can arise when we extract or process the data, since in doing so we are transforming it, turning it into something else, such as when we perform sentiment analysis on Twitter messages to predict Hollywood box office receipts. Messiness itself is messy.

Suppose we need to measure the temperature in a vineyard. If we have only one temperature sensor for the whole plot of land, we must make sure it's accurate and working at all times: no messiness allowed. In contrast, if we have a sensor for every one of the hundreds of vines, we can use cheaper, less sophisticated sensors (as long as they do not introduce a systematic bias). Chances are that at some points a few sensors may report incorrect data, creating a less exact, or "messier," dataset than the one from a single precise sensor. Any particular reading may be incorrect, but the aggregate of many readings will provide a more comprehensive picture. Because this dataset consists of more data points, it offers far greater value that likely offsets its messiness.

Now suppose we increase the frequency of the sensor readings. If we take one measurement per minute, we can be fairly sure that the sequence with which the data arrives will be perfectly chronological. But if we change that to ten or a hundred readings per second, the accuracy of the sequence may become less certain. As the information travels across a network, a record may get delayed and arrive out of sequence, or may simply get lost in the flood. The information will be a bit less accurate, but its great volume makes it worthwhile to forgo strict exactitude.

In the first example, we sacrificed the accuracy of each data point for breadth, and in return we received detail that we otherwise could not have seen. In the second case, we gave up exactitude for frequency, and in return we saw change that we otherwise would have missed. Although we may be able to overcome the errors if we throw enough resources at them — after all, 30,000 trades per second take place on the New York Stock Exchange, where the correct sequence matters a lot — in many cases it is more fruitful to tolerate error than it would be to work at preventing it.

For instance, we can accept some messiness in return for scale. As Forrester, a technology consultancy, puts it, "Sometimes two plus two can equal 3.9, and that is good enough." Of course the data can't be completely incorrect, but we're willing to sacrifice a bit of accuracy in return for knowing the general trend. Big data transforms figures into something more probabilistic than precise. This change will take a lot of getting used to, and it comes with problems of its own, which we'll consider later in the book. But for now it is worth simply noting that we often will need to embrace messiness when we increase scale.

One sees a similar shift in terms of the importance of more data relative to other improvements in computing. Everyone knows how much processing power has increased over the years as predicted by Moore's Law, which states that the number of transistors on a chip doubles roughly every two years. This continual improvement has made computers faster and memory more plentiful. Fewer of us know that the performance of the algorithms that drive many of our systems has also increased — in many areas more than the improvement of processors under Moore's Law. Many of the gains to society from big data, however, happen not so much because of faster chips or better algorithms but because there is more data.

For example, chess algorithms have changed only slightly in the past few decades, since the rules of chess are fully known and tightly constrained. The reason computer chess programs play far better today than in the past is in part that they are playing their endgame better. And they're doing that simply because the systems have been fed more data. In fact, endgames when six or fewer pieces are left on the chessboard have been completely analyzed and all possible moves (N = all) have been represented in a massive table that when uncompressed fills more than a terabyte of data. This enables chess computers to play the endgame flawlessly. No human will ever be able to outplay the system.

The degree to which more data trumps better algorithms has been powerfully demonstrated in the area of natural language processing: the way computers learn how to parse words as we use them in everyday speech. Around 2000, Microsoft researchers Michele Banko and Eric Brill were looking for a method to improve the grammar checker that is part of the company's Word program. They weren't sure whether it would be more useful to put their effort into improving existing algorithms, finding new techniques, or adding more sophisticated features. Before going down any of these paths, they decided to see what happened when they fed a lot more data into the existing methods. Most machine-learning algorithms relied on corpuses of text that totaled a million words or less. Banko and Brill took four common algorithms and fed in up to three orders of magnitude more data: 10 million words, then 100 million, and finally a billion words.

The results were astounding. As more data went in, the performance of all four types of algorithms improved dramatically. In fact, a simple algorithm that was the worst performer with half a million words performed better than the others when it crunched a billion words. Its accuracy rate went from 75 percent to above 95 percent. Inversely, the algorithm that worked best with a little data performed the least well with larger amounts, though like the others it improved a lot, going from around 86 percent to about 94 percent accuracy. "These results suggest that we may want to reconsider the tradeoff between spending time and money on algorithm development versus spending it on corpus development," Banko and Brill wrote in one of their research papers on the topic.

So more trumps less. And sometimes more trumps smarter. What then of messy? A few years after Banko and Brill shoveled in all that data, researchers at rival Google were thinking along similar lines — but at an even larger scale. Instead of testing algorithms with a billion words, they used a trillion. Google did this not to develop a grammar checker but to crack an even more complex nut: language translation.

So-called machine translation has been a vision of computer pioneers since the dawn of computing in the 1940s, when the devices were made of vacuum tubes and filled an entire room. The idea took on a special urgency during the Cold War, when the United States captured vast amounts of written and spoken material in Russian but lacked the manpower to translate it quickly.

At first, computer scientists opted for a combination of grammatical rules and a bilingual dictionary. An IBM computer translated sixty Russian phrases into English in 1954, using 250 word pairs in the computer's vocabulary and six rules of grammar. The results were very promising. *"Mi pyeryedayem mislyi posryedstvom ryechyi,"* was entered into the IBM 701 machine via punch cards, and out came "We transmit thoughts by means of speech." The sixty sentences were "smoothly translated," according to an IBM press release celebrating the occasion. The director of the research program, Leon Dostert of Georgetown University, predicted that machine translation would be "an accomplished fact" within "five, perhaps three years hence."

But the initial success turned out to be deeply misleading. By 1966 a committee of machine-translation grandees had to admit failure. The problem was harder than they had realized it would be. Teaching computers to translate is about teaching them not just the rules, but the exceptions too. Translation is not just about memorization and recall; it is about choosing the right words from many alternatives. Is *"bonjour"* really "good morning"? Or is it "good day," or "hello," or "hi"? The answer is, it depends. . . .

In the late 1980s, researchers at IBM had a novel idea. Instead of trying to feed explicit linguistic rules into a computer, together with a dictionary, they decided to let the computer use statistical probability to calculate which word or phrase in one language is the most appropriate one in another. In the 1990s IBM's Candide project used ten years' worth of Canadian parliamentary transcripts published in

French and English — about three million sentence pairs. Because they were official documents, the translations had been done to an extremely high quality. And by the standards of the day, the amount of data was huge. Statistical machine translation, as the technique became known, cleverly turned the challenge of translation into one big mathematics problem. And it seemed to work. Suddenly, computer translation got a lot better. After the success of that conceptual leap, however, IBM only eked out small improvements despite throwing in lots of money. Eventually IBM pulled the plug.

But less than a decade later, in 2006, Google got into translation, as part of its mission to "organize the world's information and make it universally accessible and useful." Instead of nicely translated pages of text in two languages, Google availed itself of a larger but also much messier dataset: the entire global Internet and more. Its system sucked in every translation it could find, in order to train the computer. In went to corporate websites in multiple languages, identical translations of official documents, and reports from intergovernmental bodies like the United Nations and the European Union. Even translations of books from Google's book-scanning project were included. Where Candide had used three million carefully translated sentences, Google's system harnessed billions of pages of translations of widely varying quality, according to the head of Google Translate, Franz Josef Och, one of the foremost authorities in the field. Its trillion-word corpus amounted to 95 billion English sentences, albeit of dubious quality.

Despite the messiness of the input, Google's service works the best. Its translations are more accurate than those of other systems (though still highly imperfect). And it is far, far richer. By mid-2012 its dataset covered more than 60 languages. It could even accept voice input in 14 languages for fluid translations. And because it treats language simply as messy data with which to judge probabilities, it can even translate between languages, such as Hindi and Catalan, in which there are very few direct translations to develop the system. In those cases it uses English as a bridge. And it is far more flexible than other approaches, since it can add and subtract words as they come in and out of usage.

The reason Google's translation system works well is not that it has a smarter algorithm. It works well because its creators, like Banko and Brill at Microsoft, fed in more data — and not just of high quality. Google was able to use a dataset *tens of thousands* of times larger than IBM's Candide because it accepted messiness. The trillion-word corpus Google released in 2006 was compiled from the flotsam and jetsam of Internet content — "data in the wild," so to speak. This was the "training set" by which the system could calculate the probability that, for example, one word in English follows another. It was a far cry from the grandfather in the field, the famous Brown Corpus of the 1960s, which totaled one million English words. Using the larger dataset enabled great strides in natural-language processing, upon which systems for tasks like voice recognition and computer translation are based. "Simple models and a lot of data trump more elaborate models based on less data," wrote Google's artificial-intelligence guru Peter Norvig and colleagues in a paper entitled "The Unreasonable Effectiveness of Data."

As Norvig and his co-authors explained, messiness was the key: "In some ways this corpus is a step backwards from the Brown Corpus: it's taken from unfiltered Web pages and thus contains incomplete sentences, spelling errors, grammatical errors, and all sorts of other errors. It's not annotated with carefully hand-corrected part-of-speech tags. But the fact that it's a million times larger than the Brown Corpus outweighs these drawbacks."

More trumps better

Messiness is difficult to accept for the conventional sampling analysts, who for all their lives have focused on preventing and eradicating messiness. They work hard to reduce error rates when collecting samples, and to test the samples for potential biases before announcing their results. They use multiple error-reducing strategies, including ensuring that samples are collected according to an exact protocol and by specially trained experts. Such strategies are costly to implement even for limited numbers of data points, and they are hardly feasible for big data. Not only would they be far too expensive, but exacting standards of collection are unlikely to be achieved consistently at such scale. Even excluding human interaction would not solve the problem.

Moving into a world of big data will require us to change our thinking about the merits of exactitude. To apply the conventional mindset of measurement to the digital, connected world of the twenty-first century is to miss a crucial point. As mentioned earlier, the obsession with exactness is an artifact of the information-deprived analog era. When data was sparse, every data point was critical, and thus great care was taken to avoid letting any point bias the analysis.

Today we don't live in such an information-starved situation. In dealing with ever more comprehensive datasets, which capture not just a small sliver of the phenomenon at hand but much more or all of it, we no longer need to worry so much about individual data points biasing the overall analysis. Rather than aiming to stamp out every bit of inexactitude at increasingly high cost, we are calculating with messiness in mind.

Take the way sensors are making their way into factories. At BP's Cherry Point Refinery in Blaine, Washington, wireless sensors are installed throughout the plant, forming an invisible mesh that produces vast amounts of data in real time. The environment of intense heat and electrical machinery might distort the readings, resulting in messy data. But the huge quantity of information generated from both wired and wireless sensors makes up for those hiccups. Just increasing the frequency and number of locations of sensor readings can offer a big payoff. By measuring the stress on pipes at all times rather than at certain intervals, BP learned that some types of crude oil are more corrosive than others—a quality it couldn't spot, and thus couldn't counteract, when its dataset was smaller.

When the quantity of data is vastly larger and is of a new type, exactitude in some cases is no longer the goal so long as we can divine the general trend. Moving to a large scale changes not only the expectations of precision but the practical ability to achieve exactitude. Though it may seem counterintuitive at first, treating data as something imperfect and imprecise lets us make superior forecasts, and thus understand our world better.

It bears noting that messiness is not inherent to big data. Instead it is a function of the imperfection of the tools we use to measure, record, and analyze information. If the technology were to somehow become perfect, the problem of inexactitude would disappear. But as long as it is imperfect, messiness is a practical reality we must deal with. And it is likely to be with us for a long time. Painstaking efforts to increase accuracy often won't make economic sense, since the value of having far greater amounts of data is more compelling. Just as statisticians in an earlier era put aside their interest in larger sample sizes in favor of more randomness, we can live with a bit of imprecision in return for more data.

The Billion Prices Project offers an intriguing case in point. Every month the U.S. Bureau of Labor Statistics publishes the consumer price index, or CPI, which is used to calculate the inflation rate. The figure is crucial for investors and businesses. The Federal Reserve considers it when deciding whether to raise or lower interest rates. Companies base salary increases on inflation. The federal government uses it to index payments like Social Security benefits and the interest it pays on certain bonds.

To get the figure, the Bureau of Labor Statistics employs hundreds of staff to call, fax, and visit stores and offices in 90 cities across the nation and report back about 80,000 prices on everything from tomatoes to taxi fares. Producing it costs around $250 million a year. For that sum, the data is neat, clean, and orderly. But by the time the numbers come out, they're already a few weeks old. As the 2008 financial crisis showed, a few weeks can be a terribly long lag. Decision-makers need quicker access to inflation numbers in order to react to them better, but they can't get it with conventional methods focused on sampling and prizing precision.

In response, two economists at the Massachusetts Institute of

Technology, Alberto Cavallo and Roberto Rigobon, came up with a big-data alternative by steering a much messier course. Using software to crawl the Web, they collected half a million prices of products sold in the U.S. every single day. The information is messy, and not all the data points collected are easily comparable. But by combining the big-data collection with clever analysis, the project was able to detect a deflationary swing in prices immediately after Lehman Brothers filed for bankruptcy in September 2008, while those who relied on the official CPI data had to wait until November to see it.

The MIT project has spun off a commercial venture called Price-Stats that banks and others use to make economic decisions. It compiles millions of products sold by hundreds of retailers in more than 70 countries every day. Of course, the figures require careful interpretation, but they are better than the official statistics at indicating trends in inflation. Because there are more prices and the figures are available in real time, they give decision-makers a significant advantage. (The method also serves as a credible outside check on national statistical bodies. For example, *The Economist* distrusts Argentina's method of calculating inflation, so it relies on the PriceStats figures instead.)

Messiness in action

In many areas of technology and society, we are leaning in favor of more and messy over fewer and exact. Consider the case of categorizing content. For centuries humans have developed taxonomies and indexes in order to store and retrieve material. These hierarchical systems have always been imperfect, as everyone familiar with a library card catalogue can painfully recall, but in a small-data universe, they worked well enough. Increase the scale many orders of magnitude, though, and these systems, which presume the perfect placement of everything within them, fall apart. For example, in 2011 the photo-sharing site Flickr held more than six billion photos from more than 75 million users. Trying to label each photo according to preset categories would have been useless. Would there really have been one entitled "Cats that look like Hitler"?

Instead, clean taxonomies are being replaced by mechanisms that are messier but also eminently more flexible and adaptable to a world that evolves and changes. When we upload photos to Flickr, we "tag" them. That is, we assign any number of text labels and use them to organize and search the material. Tags are created and affixed by people in an ad hoc way: there are no standardized, predefined categories, no existing taxonomy to which we must conform. Rather, anyone can add new tags just by typing. Tagging has emerged as the de facto standard for content classification on the Internet, used in social media sites like Twitter, blogs, and so on. It makes the vastness of the Web's content more navigable — especially for things like images, videos, and music that aren't text based so word searches don't work.

Of course, some tags may be misspelled, and such mistakes introduce inaccuracy — not to the data itself but to how it's organized. That pains the traditional mind trained in exactitude. But in return for messiness in the way we organize our photo collections, we gain a much richer universe of labels, and by extension, a deeper, broader access to our pictures. We can combine search tags to filter photos in ways that weren't possible before. The imprecision inherent in tagging is about accepting the natural messiness of the world. It is an antidote to more precise systems that try to impose a false sterility upon the hurly-burly of reality, pretending that everything under the sun fits into neat rows and columns. There are more things in heaven and earth than are dreamt of in that philosophy.

Many of the Web's most popular sites flaunt their admiration for imprecision over the pretense of exactitude. When one sees a Twitter icon or a Facebook "like" button on a web page, it shows the number of other people who clicked on it. When the numbers are small, each click is shown, like "63." But as the figures get larger, the number displayed is an approximation, like "4K." It's not that the system doesn't know the actual total; it's that as the scale increases, showing the exact figure is less important. Besides, the amounts may be changing so quickly that a specific figure would be out of date the moment it appeared. Similarly, Google's Gmail presents the time of recent messages with exactness, such as "11 minutes ago," but treats longer durations with a nonchalant "2 hours ago," as do Facebook and some others.

The industry of business intelligence and analytics software was long built on promising clients "a single version of the truth" — the popular buzz words from the 2000s from the technology vendors in these fields. Executives used the phrase without irony. Some still do. By this, they mean that everyone accessing a company's information-technology systems can tap into the same data; that the marketing team and the sales team don't have to fight over who has the correct customer or sales numbers before the meeting even begins. Their interests might be more aligned if the facts were consistent, the thinking goes.

But the idea of "a single version of the truth" is doing an about-face. We are beginning to realize not only that it may be impossible for a single version of the truth to exist, but also that its pursuit is a distraction. To reap the benefits of harnessing data at scale, we have to accept messiness as par for the course, not as something we should try to eliminate.

We are even seeing the ethos of inexactitude invade one of the areas most intolerant of imprecision: database design. Traditional database engines required data to be highly structured and precise. Data wasn't simply stored; it was broken up into "records" that contained fields. Each field held information of a particular type and length. For example, if a numeric field was seven digits long, an amount of 10 million or more could not be recorded. If one wanted to enter "not available" into a field for phone numbers, it couldn't be done. The structure of the database would have had to be altered to accommodate these entries. We still battle with such restrictions on our computers and smartphones, when the software won't accept the data we want to enter.

Traditional indexes, too, were predefined, and that limited what one could search for. Add a new index, and it had to be created from scratch, taking time. Conventional, so-called relational, databases are designed for a world in which data is sparse, and thus can be and will be curated carefully. It is a world in which the questions one wants to answer using the data have to be clear at the outset, so that the database is designed to answer them — and only them — efficiently.

Yet this view of storage and analysis is increasingly at odds with reality. We now have large amounts of data of varying types and quality. Rarely does it fit into neatly defined categories that are known at the outset. And the questions we want to ask often emerge only when we collect and work with the data we have.

These realities have led to novel database designs that break with the principles of old — principles of records and preset fields that reflect neatly defined hierarchies of information. The most common language for accessing databases has long been SQL, or "structured query language." The very name evokes its rigidity. But the big shift in recent years has been toward something called noSQL, which doesn't require a preset record structure to work. It accepts data of varying type and size and allows it to be searched successfully. In return for permitting structural messiness, these database designs require more processing and storage resources. Yet it is a tradeoff we can afford given the plummeting storage and processing costs.

Pat Helland, one of the world's foremost authorities on database design, describes this fundamental shift in a paper entitled "If You Have Too Much Data, Then 'Good Enough' Is Good Enough." After identifying some of the core principles of traditional design that have become eroded by messy data of varying provenance and accuracy, he lays out the consequences: "We can no longer pretend to live in a clean world." Processing big data entails an inevitable loss of information — Helland calls it "lossy." But it makes up for that by yielding a quick result. "It's OK if we have lossy answers — that's frequently what business needs," concludes Helland.

Traditional database design promises to deliver consistent results across time. If you ask for your bank account balance, for example, you expect to receive the exact amount. And if you query it a few seconds later, you want the system to provide the same result, assuming nothing has changed. Yet as the quantity of data collected grows and the number of users who access the system increases, this consistency becomes harder to maintain.

Large datasets do not exist in any one place; they tend to be split up across multiple hard drives and computers. To ensure reliability and speed, a record may be stored in two or three separate locations. If you update the record at one location, the data in the other locations is no longer correct until you update it too. While traditional systems would have a delay until all updates are made, that is less practical when data is broadly distributed and the server is pounded with tens of thousands of queries per second. Instead, accepting messiness is a kind of solution.

The shift is typified by the popularity of Hadoop, an open-source rival to Google's MapReduce system that is very good at processing large quantities of data. It does this by breaking the data down into smaller chunks and parceling them out to other machines. It expects that hardware will fail, so it builds redundancy in. It presumes that the data is not clean and orderly — in fact, it assumes that the data is too huge to be cleaned before processing. Where typical data analysis requires an operation called "extract, transfer, and load," or ETL, to move the data to where it will be analyzed, Hadoop dispenses with such niceties. Instead, it takes for granted that the quantity of data is so breathtakingly enormous that it can't be moved and must be analyzed where it is.

Hadoop's output isn't as precise as that of relational databases: it can't be trusted to launch a spaceship or to certify bank-account details. But for many less critical tasks, where an ultra-precise answer isn't needed, it does the trick far faster than the alternatives. Think of tasks like segmenting a list of customers to send some of them a special marketing campaign. Using Hadoop, the credit-card company Visa was able to reduce the processing time for two years' worth of test records, some 73 billion transactions, from one month to a mere 13 minutes. That sort of acceleration of processing is transformative to businesses.

The experience of ZestFinance, a company founded by the former chief information officer of Google, Douglas Merrill, underscores the point. Its technology helps lenders decide whether or not to offer relatively small, short-term loans to people who seem to have poor credit. Yet where traditional credit scoring is based on just a handful of strong signals like previous late payments, ZestFinance analyzes a huge number of "weaker" variables. In 2012 it boasted a loan default rate that was a third less than the industry average. But the only way to make the system work is to embrace messiness.

"One of the interesting things," says Merrill, "is that there are no people for whom all fields are filled in — there's always a large amount of missing data." The matrix from the information ZestFinance gathers is incredibly sparse, a database file teeming with missing cells. So the company "imputes" the missing data. For instance, about 10 percent of ZestFinance's customers are listed as dead — but as it turns out, that doesn't affect repayment. "So, obviously, when preparing for the zombie apocalypse, most people assume no debt will get repaid. But from our data, it looks like zombies pay back their loans," adds Merrill with a wink.

In return for living with messiness, we get tremendously valuable services that would be impossible at their scope and scale with traditional methods and tools. According to some estimates only 5 percent of all digital data is "structured" — that is, in a form that fits neatly into a traditional database. Without accepting messiness, the remaining 95 percent of unstructured data, such as web pages and videos, remain dark. By allowing for imprecision, we open a window into an untapped universe of insights.

Society has made two implicit tradeoffs that have become so ingrained in the way we act that we don't even see them as tradeoffs anymore, but as the natural state of things. First, we presume that we can't use far more data, so we don't. But the constraint is increasingly less relevant, and there is much to be gained by using something approaching N = all.

The second tradeoff is over the quality of information. It was rational to privilege exactitude in an era of small data, when because we only collected a little information its accuracy had to be as high as possible. In many cases, that may still matter. But for many other things, rigorous accuracy is less important than getting a quick grasp of their broad outlines or progress over time.

The way we think about using the totality of information compared with smaller slivers of it, and the way we may come to appreciate slackness instead of exactness, will have profound effects on our interaction with the world. As big-data techniques become a regular part of everyday life, we as a society may begin to strive to understand the world from a far larger, more comprehensive perspective than before, a sort of N = all of the mind. And we may tolerate blurriness and ambiguity in areas where we used to demand clarity and certainty, even if it had been a false clarity and an imperfect certainty. We may accept this provided that in return we get a more complete sense of reality — the equivalent of an impressionist painting, wherein each stroke is messy when examined up close, but by stepping back one can see a majestic picture.

Big data, with its emphasis on comprehensive datasets and messiness, helps us get closer to reality than did our dependence on small data and accuracy. The appeal of "some" and "certain" is understandable. Our comprehension of the world may have been incomplete and occasionally wrong when we were limited in what we could analyze, but there was a comfortable certainty about it, a reassuring stability. Besides, because we were stunted in the data that we could collect and examine, we didn't face the same compulsion to get everything, to see everything from every possible angle. And in the narrow confines of small data, we could pride ourselves on our precision — even if by measuring the minutiae to the nth degree, we missed the bigger picture.

Ultimately, big data may require *us* to change, to become more comfortable with disorder and uncertainty. The structures of exactitude that seem to give us bearings in life — that the round peg goes into the round hole; that there is only one answer to a question — are more malleable than we may admit; and yet admitting, even embracing, this plasticity brings us closer to reality.

As radical a transformation as these shifts in mindset are, they lead to a third change that has the potential to upend an even more fundamental convention on which society is based: the idea of understanding the reasons behind all that happens. Instead, as the next chapter will explain, finding associations in data and acting on them may often be good enough.

4

CORRELATION

GREG LINDEN WAS 24 years old in 1997 when he took time off from his PhD research in artificial intelligence at the University of Washington to work at a local Internet startup selling books online. It had only been open for two years but was doing a brisk business. "I loved the idea of selling books and selling knowledge — and helping people find the next piece of knowledge they wanted to enjoy," he reminisces. The store was Amazon.com, and it hired Linden as a software engineer to make sure the site ran smoothly.

Amazon didn't just have techies on its staff. At the time, it also employed a dozen or so book critics and editors to write reviews and suggest new titles. While the story of Amazon is familiar to many people, fewer remember that its content was originally crafted by human hand. The editors and critics evaluated and chose the titles featured on Amazon's web pages. They were responsible for what was called "the Amazon voice" — considered one of the company's crown jewels and a source of its competitive advantage. An article in the *Wall Street Journal* around that time feted them as the nation's most influential book critics, since they drove so many sales.

Then Jeff Bezos, Amazon's founder and CEO, began to experiment with a potent idea: What if the company could recommend specific books to customers based on their individual shopping preferences? From its start, Amazon had captured reams of data on all its customers: what they purchased, what books they only looked at but didn't buy, and how long they looked at them. What books they bought in unison.

The quantity of data was so huge that at first Amazon processed it the conventional way, by taking a sample and analyzing it to find similarities among customers. The resulting recommendations were crude. Buy a book on Poland and you'd be bombarded with Eastern European fare. Purchase one about babies and you'd be inundated with more of the same. "They tended to offer you tiny variations on your previous purchase, ad infinitum," recalled James Marcus, an Amazon book reviewer from 1996 to 2001, in his memoir, *Amazonia*. "It felt as if you had gone shopping with the village idiot."

Greg Linden saw a solution. He realized that the recommendation system didn't actually need to compare people with other people, a task that was technically cumbersome. All it needed to do was find associations among products themselves. In 1998 Linden and his colleagues applied for a patent on "item-to-item" collaborative filtering, as the technique is known. The shift in approach made a big difference.

Because the calculations could be done ahead of time, the recommendations were lightning fast. The method was also versatile, able to work across product categories. So when Amazon branched out to sell items other than books, it could suggest movies or toasters too. And the recommendations were much better than before because the system used all the data. "The joke in the group was if it were working perfectly, Amazon should just show you one book — which is the next book you're going to buy," Linden recalls.

Now the company had to decide what should appear on the site. Machine-generated content like personal recommendations and bestseller lists, or reviews written by Amazon's in-house editorial staff? What the clicks said, or what the critics said? It was a battle of mice and men.

When Amazon ran a test comparing sales produced by human editors with sales produced by computer-generated content, the results were not even close. The data-derived material generated vastly more sales. The computer may not have known why a customer who read

Ernest Hemingway might also like to buy F. Scott Fitzgerald. But that didn't seem to matter. The cash register was ringing. Eventually the editors were presented with the precise percentage of sales Amazon had to forgo when it featured their reviews online and the group was disbanded. "I was very sad about the editorial team getting beaten," recalls Linden. "But the data doesn't lie, and the cost was very high."

Today a third of all of Amazon's sales are said to result from its recommendation and personalization systems. With these systems, Amazon has driven many competitors out of business: not only large bookstores and music stores, but also local booksellers who thought their personal touch would insulate them from the winds of change. In fact, Linden's work revolutionized e-commerce, as the method has been adopted by almost everyone. For Netflix, an online film rental company, three-fourths of new orders come from recommendations. Following Amazon's lead, thousands of websites are able to recommend products, content, friends, and groups without knowing why people are likely to be interested in them.

Knowing why might be pleasant, but it's unimportant for stimulating sales. Knowing what, however, drives clicks. This insight has the power to reshape many industries, not just e-commerce. Salespeople in all sectors have long been told that they need to understand what makes customers tick, to grasp the reasons behind their decisions. Professional skills and years of experience have been highly valued. Big data shows that there is another, in some ways more pragmatic approach. Amazon's innovative recommendation systems teased out valuable correlations without knowing the underlying causes. Knowing *what*, not *why*, is good enough.

Predictions and predilections

Correlations are useful in a small-data world, but in the context of big data they really shine. Through them we can glean insights more easily, faster, and more clearly than before.

At its core, a correlation quantifies the statistical relationship between two data values. A strong correlation means that when one of the data values changes, the other is highly likely to change as well. We have seen such strong correlations with Google Flu Trends: the more people in a particular geographic place search for particular terms through Google, the more people in that location have the flu. Conversely, a weak correlation means that when one data value changes little happens to the other. For instance, we could run correlations on individuals' hair length and happiness and find that hair length is not especially useful in telling us much about happiness.

Correlations let us analyze a phenomenon not by shedding light on its inner workings but by identifying a useful proxy for it. Of course, even strong correlations are never perfect. It is quite possible that two things may behave similarly just by coincidence. We may simply be "fooled by randomness," to borrow a phrase from the empiricist Nassim Nicholas Taleb. With correlations, there is no certainty, only probability. But if a correlation is strong, the likelihood of a link is high. Many Amazon customers can attest to this by pointing to a bookshelf laden with the company's recommendations.

By letting us identify a really good proxy for a phenomenon, correlations help us capture the present and predict the future: if A often takes place together with B, we need to watch out for B to predict that A will happen. Using B as a proxy helps us capture what is probably taking place with A, even if we can't measure or observe A directly. Importantly, it also helps us predict what may happen to A in the future. Of course, correlations cannot foretell the future, they can only predict it with a certain likelihood. But that ability is extremely valuable.

Consider the case of Walmart. It is the largest retailer in the world, with more than two million employees and annual sales of around $450 billion — a sum greater than the GDP of four-fifths of the world's countries. Before the Web brought forth so much data, the company held perhaps the biggest set of data in corporate America. In the 1990s it revolutionized retailing by recording every product as data through a system called Retail Link. This let its merchandise suppliers monitor the rate and volume of sales and inventory. Creating this transparency enabled the company to force suppliers to take care of the stockage themselves. In many cases Walmart does not take "ownership" of a product until the point of sale, thereby shedding its inventory risk and reducing its costs. Walmart used data to become, in effect, the world's largest consignment shop.

What could all that historical data reveal if analyzed in the right way? The retailer worked with expert number-crunchers from Teradata, formerly the venerable National Cash Register Company, to uncover interesting correlations. In 2004 Walmart peered into its mammoth databases of past transactions: what item each customer bought and the total cost, what else was in the shopping basket, the time of day, even the weather. By doing so, the company noticed that prior to a hurricane, not only did sales of flashlights increase, but so did sales of Pop-Tarts, a sugary American breakfast snack. So as storms approached, Walmart stocked boxes of Pop-Tarts at the front of stores next to the hurricane supplies, to make life easier for customers dashing in and out — and boosted its sales.

In the past, someone at headquarters would have needed the hunch beforehand in order to gather the data and test the idea. Now, by having so much data and better tools, the correlations surface more quickly and inexpensively. (That said, one must be cautious: when the number of data points increases by orders of magnitude, we also see more spurious correlations — phenomena that appear to be connected even though they aren't. This requires us to take extra care, as we are just beginning to appreciate.)

Long before big data, correlation analysis proved valuable. The concept was set forth in 1888 by Sir Francis Galton, a cousin of Charles Darwin, after he had noticed a relationship between men's height and the length of their forearms. The mathematics behind it is relatively straightforward and robust — which turns out to be one of its essential features, and which has helped make it one of the most widely used statistical measures. Yet before big data, its usefulness was limited. Because data was scarce and collecting it expensive, statisticians often chose a proxy, then collected the relevant data and ran the correlation analysis to find out how good that proxy was. But how to select the right proxy?

To guide them, experts used hypotheses driven by theories — abstract ideas about how something works. Based on such hypotheses, they collected data and used correlation analysis to verify whether the proxies were suitable. If they weren't, then the researchers often tried again, stubbornly, in case the data had been collected wrongly, before finally conceding that the hypothesis they had started with, or even the theory it was based on, was flawed and required amendment. Knowledge progressed through this hypothesis-driven trial and error. And it did so slowly, as our individual and collective biases clouded what hypotheses we developed, how we applied them, and thus what proxies we picked. It was a cumbersome process, but workable in a small-data world.

In the big-data age, it is no longer efficient to make decisions about what variables to examine by relying on hypotheses alone. The datasets are far too big and the area under consideration is probably far too complex. Fortunately, many of the limitations that forced us into a hypothesis-driven approach no longer exist to the same extent. We now have so much data available and so much computing power that we don't have to laboriously pick one proxy or a small handful of them and examine them one by one. Sophisticated computational analysis can now identify the optimal proxy — as it did for Google Flu Trends, after plowing through almost half a billion mathematical models.

No longer do we necessarily require a valid substantive hypothesis about a phenomenon to begin to understand our world. Thus, we don't have to develop a notion about what terms people search for when and where the flu spreads. We don't need to have an inkling of how airlines price their tickets. We don't need to care about the culinary tastes of Walmart shoppers. Instead we can subject big data to correlation analysis and let it tell us what search queries are the best proxies for the flu, whether an airfare is likely to soar, or what anxious families want to nibble on during a storm. In place of the hypothesis-driven approach, we can use a data-driven one. Our results may be less biased and more accurate, and we will almost certainly get them much faster.

Predictions based on correlations lie at the heart of big data. Correlation analyses are now used so frequently that we sometimes fail to appreciate the inroads they have made. And the uses will only increase.

For instance, financial credit scores are being used to predict personal behavior. The Fair Isaac Corporation, now known as FICO, invented credit scores in the late 1950s. In 2011 FICO established the "Medication Adherence Score." To determine how likely people are to take their medication, FICO analyzes a wealth of variables — including ones that may seem irrelevant, such as how long people have lived at the same address, if they are married, how long they've been in the same job, and whether they own a car. The score is intended to help health providers save money by telling them at which patients they ought to target their reminders. There is nothing causal between car ownership and taking antibiotics as directed; the link between them is pure correlation. But findings such as these were enough to inspire FICO's chief executive to boast in 2011, "We know what you're going to do tomorrow."

Other data brokers are getting into the correlation game, too, as documented by the *Wall Street Journal*'s pioneering "What They Know" series. Experian has a product called Income Insight that estimates people's income level partly on the basis of their credit history. It developed the score by analyzing its huge database of credit histories against anonymous tax data from the U.S. Internal Revenue Service. It would cost a business around $10 apiece to confirm someone's income through tax forms, while Experian sells its estimate for less than $1. So in instances like this, using the proxy is more cost effective than going through the rigmarole to get the real thing. Similarly, yet another credit bureau, Equifax, sells an "Ability to Pay Index" and a "Discretionary Spending Index" that promise to predict the plumpness of a person's purse.

The uses of correlations are being extended even further. Aviva, a large insurance firm, has studied the idea of using credit reports and consumer-marketing data as proxies for the analysis of blood and urine samples for certain applicants. The intent is to identify those who may be at higher risk of illnesses like high blood pressure, diabe-

tes, or depression. The method uses lifestyle data that inclu
dreds of variables such as hobbies, the websites people visit, an
amount of television they watch, as well as estimates of their income.

Aviva's predictive model, developed by Deloitte Consulting, was considered successful at identifying health risks. Other insurance firms such as Prudential and AIG have examined similar initiatives. The benefit is that it may let people applying for insurance avoid having to give blood and urine samples, which no one enjoys, and which the insurance companies have to pay for. The lab tests cost around $125 per person, while the purely data-driven approach is about $5.

To some, the method may sound creepy, because it draws upon seemingly unrelated behaviors. It is as if companies can avail themselves of a cyber-snitch that spies on every mouse click. People might think twice before visiting websites of extreme sports or watching sitcoms glorifying couch potatoes if they felt this might result in higher insurance premiums. Admittedly, chilling people's freedom to interact with information would be terrible. On the other hand, the benefit is that making insurance easier and less expensive to obtain may result in more insured people, which is a good thing for society, not to mention for insurance firms.

Yet the poster child, or perhaps the whipping boy, of big-data correlations is the American discount retailer Target, which has relied on predictions based on big-data correlations for years. In an extraordinary bit of reporting, Charles Duhigg, a business correspondent at the *New York Times*, recounted how Target knows when a woman is pregnant without the mother-to-be explicitly telling it so. Basically, its method is to harness data and let the correlations do their work.

Knowing if a customer may be pregnant is important for retailers, since pregnancy is a watershed moment for couples, when their shopping behaviors are open to change. They may start going to new stores and developing new brand loyalties. Target's marketers turned to its analytics division to see if there was a way to discover customers' pregnancies through their purchasing patterns.

The analytics team reviewed the shopping histories of women who signed up for its baby gift-registry. They noticed that these women bought lots of unscented lotion at around the third month of pregnancy, and that a few weeks later they tended to purchase supplements like magnesium, calcium, and zinc. The team ultimately uncovered around two dozen products that, used as proxies, enabled the company to calculate a "pregnancy prediction" score for every customer who paid with a credit card or used a loyalty card or mailed coupons. The correlations even let the retailer estimate the due date within a narrow range, so it could send relevant coupons for each stage of the pregnancy. "Target," indeed.

In his book *The Power of Habit*, Duhigg recounts what happened next. One day, an angry man stormed into a Target store in Minnesota to see a manager. "My daughter got this in the mail!" he shouted. "She's still in high school, and you're sending her coupons for baby clothes and cribs? Are you trying to encourage her to get pregnant?" When the manager called the man a few days later to apologize, however, the voice on the other end of the line was conciliatory. "I had a talk with my daughter," he said. "It turns out there's been some activities in my house I haven't been completely aware of. She's due in August. I owe you an apology."

Finding proxies in social contexts is only one way that big-data techniques are being employed. Equally powerful are correlations with new types of data to solve everyday needs.

One of these is a method called predictive analytics, which is starting to be widely used in business to foresee events before they happen. The term may refer to an algorithm that can spot a hit song, which is commonly used in the music industry to give recording labels a better idea of where to place their bets. The technique is also being used to prevent big mechanical or structural failures: placing sensors on machinery, motors, or infrastructure like bridges makes it possible to monitor the data patterns they give off, such as heat, vibration, stress, and sound, and to detect changes that may indicate problems ahead.

The underlying concept is that when things break down, they generally don't do so all at once, but gradually over time. Armed with sensor data, correlational analysis and similar methods can identify the specific patterns, the telltale signs, that typically crop up before something breaks — the whirring of a motor, excessive heat from an engine, and the like. From then on, one need only look for that pattern to know when something is amiss. Spotting the abnormality early on enables the system to send out a warning so that a new part can be installed or the problem fixed before the breakdown actually occurs. The aim is to identify and then watch a good proxy, and thereby predict future events.

The shipping company UPS has used predictive analytics since the late 2000s to monitor its fleet of 60,000 vehicles in the United States and know when to perform preventive maintenance. A breakdown on the road can cause havoc, delaying deliveries and pick-ups. So to be cautious, UPS used to replace certain parts after two or three years. But that was inefficient, as some of the parts were fine. Since switching to predictive analytics, the company has saved millions of dollars by measuring and monitoring individual parts and replacing them only when necessary. In one case, the data even revealed that an entire group of new vehicles had a defective part that could have spelled trouble unless it had been spotted before they were deployed.

Similarly, sensors are affixed to bridges and buildings to watch for signs of wear and tear. They are also used in large chemical plants and refineries, where a piece of broken equipment could bring production to a standstill. The cost of collecting and analyzing the data that indicates when to take early action is lower than the cost of an outage. Note that predictive analytics may not explain the cause of a problem; it only indicates that a problem exists. It will alert you that an engine is overheating, but it may not tell you whether the overheating is due to a frayed fan belt or a poorly screwed cap. The correlations show *what*, not *why*, but as we have seen, knowing *what* is often good enough.

The same sort of methodology is being applied in healthcare, to prevent breakdowns of the human machine. When a hospital attaches a ganglion of tubes, wires, and instruments to a patient, a vast stream of data is generated. The electrocardiogram alone records

1,000 readings per second. And yet, remarkably, only a fraction of the data is currently used or kept. Most is just tossed away, even though it may hold important clues about the patient's condition and response to treatments. And if kept and aggregated with other patients' data, it could reveal extraordinary insights into which treatments tend to work and which do not.

Discarding data may have been appropriate when the cost and complexity of collecting, storing, and analyzing it were high, but this is no longer the case. Dr. Carolyn McGregor and a team of researchers at the University of Ontario Institute of Technology and IBM are working with a number of hospitals on software to help doctors make better diagnostic decisions when caring for premature babies (known as "preemies"). The software captures and processes patient data in real time, tracking 16 different data streams, such as heart rate, respiration rate, blood pressure, and blood oxygen level, which together amount to around 1,260 data points per second.

The system is still being developed and not yet deployed, but it can detect subtle changes in the preemies' condition that may signal the onset of infection 24 hours before overt symptoms appear. "You can't see it with the naked eye, but a computer can," explains Dr. McGregor. The method does not rely on causality but on correlations. It tells what, not why. But that serves its purpose. The advance warning lets doctors treat the infection earlier with lighter medical interventions, or alerts them sooner if a treatment seems ineffective. This improves patient outcomes. It is hard to think that this technique won't be implemented for vastly more patients and conditions in the future. The algorithm itself may not be making the decisions, but the machines are doing what machines do best, to help human caregivers do what they do best.

Strikingly, Dr. McGregor's big-data analysis was able to identify correlations that in some ways fly in the face of physicians' conventional wisdom. She found, for instance, that very constant vital signs often are detected prior to a serious infection. This is odd, since we would suspect that deteriorating vitals would precede a full-blown infection. One can imagine generations of doctors ending their workday by glancing at a clipboard beside the crib, seeing the infant's vital signs stabilize, and figuring it was safe to go home — only to get a frantic call from the nursing station at midnight informing them that something had gone tragically wrong and their instincts had been misplaced.

McGregor's data suggests that the preemies' stability, rather than a sign of improvement, is more like the calm before the storm — as if the baby's body is telling its tiny organs to batten down the hatches for a rough ride ahead. We can't know for sure: what the data indicates is a correlation, not causality. But we do know that it required statistical methods applied to a huge quantity of data to reveal this hidden association. Lest there be any doubt: big data saves lives.

Illusions and illuminations

In a small-data world, because so little data tended to be available, both causal investigations and correlation analysis began with a hypothesis, which was then tested to be either falsified or verified. But because both methods required a hypothesis to start with, both were equally susceptible to prejudice and erroneous intuition. And the necessary data often was not available. Today, with so much data around and more to come, such hypotheses are no longer crucial for correlational analysis.

There is another difference, which is just starting to gain importance. Before big data, partly because of inadequate computing power, most correlational analysis using large data sets was limited to looking for linear relationships. In reality, of course, many relationships are far more complex. With more sophisticated analyses, we can identify non-linear relationships among data.

As one example, for many years economists and political scientists believed that happiness and income were directly correlated: increase the income and a person on average will get happier. Looking at the data on a chart, however, reveals that a more complex dynamic is at play. For income levels below a certain threshold every rise in income translates into a substantial rise in happiness, but above that level increases in income barely improved a person's happiness. If we were to plot this on a graph, the line would appear as a curve rather than a straight line as assumed by linear analysis.

The finding was important for policymakers. If it were a linear relationship, it would make sense to raise everyone's income to improve overall happiness. But once the non-linear association was identified, the advice changed to focus on income increases for the poor, since the data showed that this would yield more bang for the buck.

And it gets even more complex, such as when the correlational relationship is more multi-faceted. For instance, researchers at Harvard and MIT examined the disparity of measles immunizations among the population: some groups get vaccinated while others don't. At first this disparity seemed to be correlated with the amount people spend on healthcare. Yet a closer look revealed that the correlation is not a neat line; it is an oddly shaped curve. As people spend more money on healthcare, the immunization disparity goes down (as may be expected), but as they spend even more, it surprisingly goes up again — some of the very affluent seem to shy away from measles shots. For public health officials this is crucial to know, but simple linear correlation analysis would not have caught this.

Experts are just now developing the necessary tools to identify and compare non-linear correlations. At the same time, the techniques of correlational analysis are being aided and enhanced by a fast-growing set of novel approaches and software that can tease out non-causal relationships in data from many different angles — rather like the way cubist painters tried to capture the image of a woman's face from multiple viewpoints at once. One of the most vibrant new methods can be found in the burgeoning field of network analysis. This makes it possible to map, measure, and calculate the nodes and links for everything from one's friends on Facebook, to which court decisions cite which precedents, to who calls whom on their cellphones. Together these tools help answer non-causal, empirical questions.

Ultimately, in the age of big data, these new types of analyses will lead to a wave of novel insights and helpful predictions. We will see links we never saw before. We will grasp complex technical and social dynamics that have long escaped our comprehension despite our best efforts. But most important, these non-causal analyses will aid our understanding of the world by primarily asking *what* rather than *why*.

At first, this may sound counterintuitive. After all, as humans, we desire to make sense of the world through causal links; we want to believe that every effect has a cause, if we only look closely enough. Shouldn't that be our highest aspiration, to know the reasons that underlie the world?

To be sure, there is a philosophical debate going back centuries over whether causality even exists. If everything were caused by something else, then logic dictates that we would not be free to decide anything. Human volition would not exist, as every decision we made and every thought we had would be caused by something else that, in turn, was the effect of another cause, and so forth. The trajectory of all life would simply be determined by causes leading to effects. Hence philosophers have bickered over the role of causality in our world, and at times pitted it against free will. That abstract debate, however, is not what we're after here.

Rather, when we say that humans see the world through causalities, we're referring to two fundamental ways humans explain and understand the world: through quick, illusory causality; and via slow, methodical causal experiments. Big data will transform the roles of both.

First is our intuitive desire to see causal connections. We are biased to assume causes even where none exist. This isn't due to culture or upbringing or level of education. Rather, research suggests, it is a matter of how human cognition works. When we see two events happen one after the other, our minds have a great urge to see them in causal terms.

Take the following three sentences: "Fred's parents arrived late. The caterers were expected soon. Fred was angry." When reading them we instantly intuit why Fred was angry — not because the caterers were to arrive soon, but because of his parents' tardiness. Actually, we have no way of knowing this from the information supplied. Still, our minds cannot help creating what we assume are coherent, causal stories out of facts we are given.

Daniel Kahneman, a professor of psychology at Princeton and the recipient of the 2002 Nobel Prize in economics, uses this example to suggest that we have two modes of thinking. One is fast and takes little effort, letting us jump to conclusions in seconds. The other is slow and hard, requiring us to think through a particular issue.

The fast way of thinking is biased heavily toward "seeing" causal links even when there are none. It is prejudiced to confirm our existing knowledge and beliefs. In ancient history, this fast way of thinking helped us survive a dangerous environment, in which we often needed to decide quickly and with limited information. But frequently it falls short of establishing the true cause of an effect.

Unfortunately, Kahneman argues, very often our brain is too lazy to think slowly and methodically. Instead, we let the fast way of thinking take over. As a consequence, we often "see" imaginary causalities, and thus fundamentally misunderstand the world.

Parents often tell their children that they got the flu because they did not wear hats or gloves in cold weather. Yet there is no direct causal link between bundling up and catching the flu. If we visit a restaurant and later fall sick, we intuitively blame the food we ate there (and perhaps avoid the restaurant in the future), even though the food may have nothing to do with our illness. We could have caught a stomach bug in any number of ways, such as shaking hands with an infected person. The fast-thinking side of our brain is hard-wired to jump quickly to whatever causal conclusions it can come up with. It thus often leads us to wrong decisions.

Contrary to conventional wisdom, such human intuiting of causality does not deepen our understanding of the world. In many instances, it's little more than a cognitive shortcut that gives us the illusion of insight but in reality leaves us in the dark about the world around us. Just as sampling was a shortcut we used because we could not process all the data, the perception of causality is a shortcut our brain uses to avoid thinking hard and slow.

In a small-data world, showing how wrong causal intuitions were took a long time. This is going to change. In the future, big-data correlations will routinely be used to disprove our causal intuitions, showing that often there is little if any statistical connection between the effect and its supposed cause. Our "fast thinking" mode is in for an extensive and lasting reality check.

Perhaps that lesson will make us think harder (and slower) as we aim to understand the world. But even our slow thinking — the second way we suss out causalities — will see its role transformed by big-data correlations.

In our daily lives, we think so often in causal terms that we may believe causality can easily be shown. The truth is much less comfortable. Unlike with correlations, where the math is relatively straightforward, there is no obvious mathematical way to "prove" causality. We can't even express causal relationships easily in standard equations. Hence even if we think slow and hard, conclusively finding causal relationships is difficult. Because our minds are used to an information-poor world, we are tempted to reason with limited data, even though too often, too many factors are at play to simply reduce an effect to a particular cause.

Take the case of the vaccine against rabies. On July 6, 1885, the French chemist Louis Pasteur was introduced to nine-year-old Joseph Meister, who had been mauled by a rabid dog. Pasteur had invented vaccination and had worked on an experimental vaccine against rabies. Meister's parents begged Pasteur to use the vaccine to treat their son. He did, and Joseph Meister survived. In the press, Pasteur was celebrated as having saved the young boy from a certain, painful death.

But had he? As it turns out, on average only one in seven people bitten by rabid dogs ever contract the disease. Even assuming Pasteur's experimental vaccine was effective, there was about an 85 percent likelihood that the boy would have survived anyway.

In this example, administering the vaccine was seen as having cured Joseph Meister. But there are two causal connections in question: one between the vaccine and the rabies virus, and the other between being bitten by a rabid dog and developing the disease. Even if the former is true, the latter is true only in a minority of cases.

Scientists have overcome this challenge of demonstrating causality through experiments, in which the supposed cause can be carefully applied or suppressed. If the effects correspond to whether the cause was applied or not, it suggests a causal connection. The more carefully controlled the circumstances, the higher the likelihood that the causal link you identify is correct.

Hence, much like correlations, causality can rarely if ever be proven, only shown with a high degree of probability. But unlike correlations, experiments to infer causal connections are often not practical or raise challenging ethical questions. How could we run a causal experiment to identify the reason why certain search terms best predict the flu? And for a rabies shot, would we subject dozens, perhaps hundreds of patients to a painful death — as part of the "control group" that didn't get the shot — although we had a vaccine for them? Even where experiments are practical, they remain costly and time-consuming.

In comparison, non-causal analyses, such as correlations, are often fast and cheap. Unlike for causal links, we have the mathematical and statistical methods to analyze relationships and the necessary digital tools to demonstrate the strength of them with confidence.

Moreover, correlations are not only valuable in their own right, they also point the way for causal investigations. By telling us which two things are potentially connected, they allow us to investigate further whether a causal relationship is present, and if so, why. This inexpensive and speedy filtering mechanism lowers the cost of causal analysis through specially controlled experiments. Through correlations we can catch a glimpse of the important variables that we then use in experiments to investigate causality.

But we must be careful. Correlations are powerful not only because they offer insights, but also because the insights they offer are relatively clear. These insights often get obscured when we bring causality back into the picture. For instance, Kaggle, a firm that organizes data-mining competitions for companies that are open to anyone to enter, ran a contest in 2012 on the quality of used cars. A used-car dealer supplied data to participating statisticians to build an algorithm to predict which of the vehicles available for purchase at an auction were likely to have problems. A correlation analysis showed that cars painted orange were far less prone to have defects — at about half the rate of the average of other cars.

Even as we read this, we already think about why it might be so: Are people who own orange cars likely to be car enthusiasts and take better care of their vehicles? Is it because a custom color might mean the car has been made in a more careful, customized way in other respects, too? Or, perhaps orange cars are more noticeable on the road and therefore less likely to be in accidents, so they're in better condition when resold?

Quickly we are caught in a web of competing causal hypotheses. But our attempts to illuminate things this way only make them cloudier. Correlations exist; we can show them mathematically. We can't easily do the same for causal links. So we would do well to hold off from trying to explain the reason behind the correlations: the *why* instead of the *what*. Otherwise, we might advise car owners to paint their clunkers orange in order to make the engines less defective — a ridiculous thought.

Taking these facts into account, it is quite understandable that correlation analysis and similar non-causal methods based on hard data are superior to most intuited causal connections, the result of "fast thinking." But in a growing number of contexts, such analysis is also more useful and more efficient than slow causal thinking that is epitomized by carefully controlled (and thus costly and time-consuming) experiments.

In recent years, scientists have tried to lower the costs of experiments to investigate causes, for instance by cleverly combining appropriate surveys to create "quasi-experiments." That may make some causal investigations easier, but the efficiency advantage of non-causal methods is hard to beat. Moreover, big data itself aids causal inquiries as it guides experts toward likely causes to investigate. In many cases, the deeper search for causality will take place after big data has done its work, when we specifically want to investigate the *why*, not just appreciate the *what*.

Causality won't be discarded, but it is being knocked off its pedestal as the primary fountain of meaning. Big data turbocharges non-causal analyses, often replacing causal investigations. The conundrum of exploding manholes in Manhattan is a case in point.

Man versus manhole

Every year a few hundred manholes in New York City start to smolder as their innards catch fire. Sometimes the cast-iron manhole covers, which weigh as much as 300 pounds, explode into the air several stories high before crashing down to the ground. This is not a good thing.

Con Edison, the public utility that provides the city's electricity, does regular inspections and maintenance of the manholes every year. In the past, it basically relied on chance, hoping that a manhole scheduled for a visit might be one that was poised to blow. It was little better than a random walk down Wall Street. In 2007 Con Edison turned to statisticians uptown at Columbia University in hopes that they could use its historical data about the grid, such as previous problems and what infrastructure is connected to what, to predict which manholes were likely to have trouble, so the company would know where to concentrate its resources.

It's a complex big-data problem. There are 94,000 miles of underground cables in New York City, enough to wrap around the Earth three and a half times. Manhattan alone boasts around 51,000 manholes and service boxes. Some of this infrastructure dates back to the days of Thomas Edison, the company's namesake. One in 20 cables were laid before 1930. Though records had been kept since the 1880s, they were in a hodgepodge of forms — and never meant for data analysis. They came from the accounting department or emergency dispatchers who made hand-written notes of "trouble tickets." To say the data was messy is a gross understatement. As just one example, the statisticians reported, the term "service box," a common piece of infrastructure, had at least 38 variants, including SB, S, S/B, S.B, S?B, S.B., SBX, S/BX, SB/X, S/XB, /SBX, S.BX, S &BX, S?BX, S BX, S/B/X, S BOX, SVBX, SERV BX, SERV-BOX, SERV/BOX, and SER-VICE BOX. A computer algorithm had to figure it all out.

"The data was just so incredibly raw," recalls Cynthia Rudin, the statistician and data-miner, now at MIT, who led the project. "I've got a printout of all the different cable tables. If you roll the thing out, you couldn't even hold it up without it dragging on the floor. And you have to make sense out of all of it — to mine it for gold, whatever it takes to get a really good predictive model."

To work, Rudin and her team had to use all the data available, not just a sample, since any of the tens of thousands of manholes could be a ticking time bomb. So it begged for N = all. And though coming up with causal reasons would have been nice, it might have taken a century and still been wrong or incomplete. The better way to accomplish the task is to find the correlations. Rudin cared less about *why* than about *which* — though she knew that when the team sat across from Con Edison executives, the stats geeks would have to justify the basis for their rankings. The predictions might have been made by a machine, but the consumers were human, and people tend to want reasons, to understand.

The data mining unearthed the golden nuggets Rudin hoped to find. After formatting the messy data so that a machine could process it, the team started with 106 predictors of a major manhole disaster. They then condensed that list to a handful of the strongest signals. In a test of the Bronx's power grid, they analyzed all the data they had, up to mid-2008. Then they used that data to predict problem spots for 2009. It worked brilliantly. The top 10 percent of manholes on their list contained a whopping 44 percent of the manholes that ended up having severe incidents.

In the end, the biggest factors were the age of the cables and whether the manholes had experienced previous troubles. This was useful, as it turns out, since it meant that Con Edison's brass could easily grasp the basis for a ranking. But wait. Age and prior problems?

Doesn't that sound fairly obvious? Well, yes and no. On one hand, as the network theorist Duncan Watts likes to say, "Everything is obvious once you know the answer" (the title of one of his books). On the other hand, it is important to remember that there were 106 predictors in the model at the outset. It was not so evident how to weigh them and then prioritize tens of thousands of manholes, each with myriad variables that added up to millions of data points — and the data itself was not even in a form to be analyzed.

The case of exploding manholes highlights the point that data is being put to new uses to solve difficult real-world problems. To achieve this, however, we needed to change the way we operated. We had to use all the data, as much as we could possibly collect, not just a small portion. We needed to accept messiness rather than treat exactitude as a central priority. And we had to put our trust in correlations without fully knowing the causal basis for the predictions.

The end of theory?

Big data transforms how we understand and explore the world. In the age of small data, we were driven by hypotheses about how the world worked, which we then attempted to validate by collecting and analyzing data. In the future, our understanding will be driven more by the abundance of data rather than by hypotheses.

These hypotheses have often been derived from theories of the natural or the social sciences, which in turn help explain and/or predict the world around us. As we transition from a hypothesis-driven world to a data-driven world, we may be tempted to think that we also no longer need theories.

In 2008 *Wired* magazine's editor-in-chief Chris Anderson trumpeted that "the data deluge makes the scientific method obsolete." In a cover story called "The Petabyte Age," he proclaimed that it amounted to nothing short of "the end of theory." The traditional process of scientific discovery — of a hypothesis that is tested against reality using a model of underlying causalities — is on its way out, Anderson argued, replaced by statistical analysis of pure correlations that is devoid of theory.

To support his argument, Anderson described how quantum physics has become an almost purely theoretical field, because experiments are too expensive, too complex, and too large to be feasible. There is theory, he suggested, that has nothing to do anymore with reality. As examples of the new method, he referred to Google's search engine and to gene sequencing. "This is a world where massive amounts of data and applied mathematics replace every other tool that might be brought to bear," he wrote. "With enough data, the numbers speak for themselves. Petabytes allow us to say: 'Correlation is enough.'"

The article unleashed a furious and important debate, even though Anderson quickly backpedaled away from his bolder claims. But his argument is worth examining. In essence, Anderson contends that until recently, as we aimed to analyze and understand the world around us, we required theories to test. In contrast, in a big-data age, the argument goes, we do not need theories: we can just look at the data. If true, this would suggest that all generalizable rules about how the world works, how humans behave, what consumers buy, when parts break, and so on may become irrelevant as analysis of big data takes over.

The "end of theory" seems to imply that while theories have existed in substantive fields like physics or chemistry, big-data analysis has no need of any conceptual models. That is preposterous.

Big data itself is founded on theory. For instance, it employs statistical theories and mathematical ones, and at times uses computer science theory, too. Yes, these are not theories about the causal dynamics of a particular phenomenon like gravity, but they are theories nonetheless. And, as we have shown, models based on them hold very useful predictive power. In fact, big data may offer a fresh look and new insights precisely because it is unencumbered by the conventional thinking and inherent biases implicit in the theories of a specific field.

Moreover, because big-data analysis is based on theories, we can't escape them. They shape both our methods and our results. It begins with how we select the data. Our decisions may be driven by convenience: Is the data readily available? Or by economics: Can the data be captured cheaply? Our choices are influenced by theories. What we choose influences what we find, as the digital-technology researchers danah boyd and Kate Crawford have argued. After all, Google used search terms as a proxy for the flu, not the length of people's hair. Similarly, when we analyze the data, we choose tools that rest on theories. And as we interpret the results we again apply theories. The age of big data clearly is not without theories — they are present throughout, with all that this entails.

Anderson deserves credit for raising the right questions — and doing so, characteristically, before others. Big data may not spell the "end of theory," but it does fundamentally transform the way we make sense of the world. This change will take a lot of getting used to. It challenges many institutions. Yet the tremendous value that it unleashes will make it not only a worthwhile tradeoff, but an inevitable one.

Before we get there, however, it bears noting how we got here. Many people in the tech industry like to credit the transformation to the new digital tools, from fast chips to efficient software, because they are the toolmakers. The technical wizardry does matter, but not as much as one might think. The deeper reason for these trends is that we have far more data. And the reason we have more data is that we are rendering more aspects of reality in a data format, the topic of the next chapter.

5
DATAFICATION

MATTHEW FONTAINE MAURY was a promising U.S. Navy officer headed to a new assignment on the brig *Consort* in 1839, when his stagecoach suddenly slid off its path, toppled over, and hurled him into the air. He landed hard, fracturing his thighbone and dislocating his knee. The joint was snapped back into place by a local doctor but the thigh was badly set and needed to be rebroken a few days later. The injuries left Maury, at 33 years old, partially crippled and unfit for the sea. After nearly three years of recuperation, the Navy placed him behind a desk, as the head of the uninspiringly named Depot of Charts and Instruments.

It turned out to be the perfect place for him. As a young navigator, Maury had been bewildered by the way ships would zigzag across the water rather than take more direct routes. When he quizzed captains about it, they replied it was far better to steer a familiar course than to risk a less known one that might entail hidden dangers. They viewed the ocean as an unpredictable realm, where sailors faced the unexpected with every wind and wave.

Yet from his voyages Maury knew that this wasn't entirely true. He saw patterns everywhere. On an extended stop in Valparaiso, Chile, he witnessed the winds operating like clockwork. A late afternoon gale would abruptly end at sundown and become a gentle breeze, as if someone had turned off a tap. On another voyage he crossed the warm aqua-blue waters of the Gulf Stream as it flowed between the dark walls of Atlantic seawater, as distinguishable and fixed in place as if it were the Mississippi River. Indeed, the Portuguese had navigated the Atlantic for centuries by relying on uniform easterly and westerly winds called the "trades" (which in old English meant "path" or "track," and only later became associated with commerce).

Whenever Midshipman Maury arrived at a new port, he would seek out old sea captains to gain their knowledge, based on the experiences passed down for generations. He learned about tides, winds, and sea currents that acted in regularity — but were nowhere to be found in the books and maps that the Navy issued to its sailors. Instead, they relied on charts that were sometimes a hundred years old, many with vast omissions or outright inaccuracies. In his new position as the Superintendent of the Depot of Charts and Instruments, he aimed to fix that.

Taking up the post, he inventoried the barometers, compasses, sextants, and chronometers in the depot's collection. He also noted the myriad nautical books, maps, and charts that it housed. He found musty crates full of old logbooks from all the past voyages of Navy captains. His predecessors in the job had regarded them as rubbish. With the odd limerick or sketch in the margins, they sometimes seemed more of an escape from the boredom of the passage than a record of ships' whereabouts.

But as Maury dusted off the saltwater-stained books and peered inside, he became very excited. Here was the information he needed: records about the wind, water, and weather at specific locations on specific dates. Though some of the logs offered little of value, many teemed with useful information. Put it all together, Maury realized, and an entirely new form of navigational chart would be possible. Maury and his dozen "computers" — the job title of those who calculated data — began the laborious process of extracting and tabulating the information trapped inside the deteriorating logs.

Maury aggregated the data and divvied up the entire Atlantic into blocks of five degrees of longitude and latitude. For each segment he noted the temperature, the speed and direction of the winds and waves, and also the month, since those conditions differ depending on the time of year. When combined, the data revealed patterns and pointed toward more efficient routes.

Generations of seafarers' advice occasionally had sent ships directly into calms or pitted them against opposing winds and currents. On one common route, from New York to Rio de Janeiro, sailors had long tended to fight nature rather than rely on her. American skippers were taught to avoid the hazards of a straight cruise south to Rio. So their ships flitted about in a southeasterly course before swinging southwesterly after crossing the equator. The distance sailed often amounted to three complete crossings of the Atlantic. The convoluted route turned out to be nonsensical. A roughly direct shot south was fine.

To improve accuracy, Maury needed more information. He created a standard form for logging ships' data and got all U.S. Navy vessels to use and submit it upon landing. Merchant ships desperately wanted to get hold of his charts; Maury insisted that in return they too hand over their logs (an early version of a viral social network). "Every ship that navigates the high seas," he proclaimed, "may henceforth be regarded as a floating observatory, a temple of science." To fine-tune the charts, he sought other data points (just as Google built upon the PageRank algorithm to include more signals). He got captains to throw bottles with notes indicating the day, position, wind, and prevailing current into the sea at regular intervals, and to retrieve any such bottles that they spotted. Many ships flew a special flag to show they were cooperating with the information exchange (presaging the link-sharing icons that appear on some web pages).

From the data, natural sea-lanes presented themselves, where the winds and currents were particularly favorable. Maury's charts cut long voyages, usually by about a third, saving merchants a bundle. "Until I took up your work I had been traversing the ocean blindfold," wrote one appreciative shipmaster. And even old sea dogs who rejected the newfangled charts and relied on the traditional ways or their intuition served a useful function: if their journeys took longer or met with disaster, they proved the utility of Maury's system. By 1855, when he published his magisterial work *The Physical Geogra-*

phy of the Sea, Maury had plotted 1.2 million data points. "Thus the young mariner instead of groping his way along until the lights of experience should come to him . . . would here find, at once, that he had already the experience of a thousand navigators to guide him," he wrote.

His work was essential for laying the first transatlantic telegraph cable. And, after a tragic collision on the high seas, he quickly devised the system of shipping lanes that is commonplace today. He even applied his method to astronomy: when the planet Neptune was discovered in 1846, Maury had the bright idea of combing the archives for mistaken references to it as a star, which enabled its orbit to be plotted.

Maury has been largely ignored in American history books, perhaps because the Virginia native resigned from the (Union) Navy during the Civil War and served as a spy in England for the Confederacy. But years earlier, when he arrived in Europe to drum up international support for his charts, four countries knighted him and he received gold medals from another eight, including the Holy See. At the dawn of the twenty-first century, pilot charts issued by the U.S. Navy still bore his name.

Commander Maury, the "Pathfinder of the Seas," was among the first to realize that there is a special value in a huge corpus of data that is lacking in smaller amounts — a core tenet of big data. More fundamentally, he understood that the Navy's musty logbooks actually constituted "data" that could be extracted and tabulated. In so doing, he was one of the pioneers of datafication, of unearthing data from material that no one thought held any value. Like Oren Etzioni at Farecast, who used the airline industry's old price information to create a lucrative business, or the engineers at Google, who applied old search queries to understand flu outbreaks, Maury took information generated for one purpose and converted it into something else.

His method, broadly similar to big-data techniques today, was astounding considering that it was done with pencil and paper. His story highlights the degree to which the use of data predates digitization. Today we tend to conflate the two, but it is important to keep them separate. To get a fuller sense of how data is being extracted from the unlikeliest of places, consider a more modern example.

Appreciating people's posteriors is the art and science of Shigeomi Koshimizu, a professor at Japan's Advanced Institute of Industrial Technology in Tokyo. Few would think that the way a person sits constitutes information, but it can. When a person is seated, the contours of the body, posture, and distribution of weight can all be quantified and tabulated. Koshimizu and his team of engineers convert backsides into data by measuring the pressure at 360 different points from sensors in a car seat and indexing each point on a scale from zero to 256. The result is a digital code that is unique for each individual. In a trial, the system was able to distinguish among a handful of people with 98 percent accuracy.

The research is not asinine. The technology is being developed as an anti-theft system in cars. A vehicle equipped with it would recognize when someone other than an approved driver was at the wheel and demand a password to continue driving or perhaps cut the engine. Transforming sitting positions into data creates a viable service and a potentially lucrative business. And its usefulness may go far beyond deterring auto theft. For instance, the aggregated data might reveal clues about a relationship between drivers' posture and road safety, such as telltale shifts in position prior to accidents. The system might also be able to sense when a driver slumps slightly from fatigue and send an alert or automatically apply the brakes. And it might not only prevent a car from being stolen but identify the thief from behind (so to speak).

Professor Koshimizu took something that had never been treated as data — or even imagined to have an informational quality — and transformed it into a numerically quantified format. Likewise, Commodore Maury took material that seemed to have little use and extracted the information, turning it into eminently useful data. Doing so allowed the information to be used in a novel way and to create unique value.

The word "data" means "given" in Latin, in the sense of a "fact." It became the title of a classic work by Euclid, in which he explains geometry from what is known or can be shown to be known. Today data refers to a description of something that allows it to be recorded, analyzed, and reorganized. There is no good term yet for the sorts of transformations produced by Commodore Maury and Professor Koshimizu. So let's call them *datafication*. To datafy a phenomenon is to put it in a quantified format so it can be tabulated and analyzed.

Again, this is very different from digitization, the process of converting analog information into the zeros and ones of binary code so computers can handle it. Digitization wasn't the first thing we did with computers. The initial era of the computer revolution was computational, as the etymology of the word suggests. We used machines to do calculations that had taken a long time to do by previous methods: such as missile trajectory tables, censuses, and the weather. Only later came taking analog content and digitizing it. Hence when Nicholas Negroponte of the MIT Media Lab published his landmark book in 1995 called *Being Digital,* one of his big themes was the shift from atoms to bits. We largely digitized text in the 1990s. More recently, as storage capacity, processing power, and bandwidth have increased, we've done it with other forms of content too, like images, video, and music.

Today there is an implicit belief among technologists that big data traces its lineage to the silicon revolution. That simply is not so. Modern IT systems certainly make big data possible, but at its core the move to big data is a continuation of humankind's ancient quest to measure, record, and analyze the world. The IT revolution is evident all around us, but the emphasis has mostly been on the *T*, the technology. It is time to recast our gaze to focus on the *I*, the information.

In order to capture quantifiable information, to datafy, we need to know how to measure and how to record what we measure. This requires the right set of tools. It also necessitates a desire to quantify and to record. Both are prerequisites of datafication, and we developed the building blocks necessary for datafication many centuries before the dawn of the digital age.

Quantifying the world

The ability to record information is one of the lines of demarcation between primitive and advanced societies. Basic counting and measurement of length and weight were among the oldest conceptual tools of early civilizations. By the third millennium B.C. the idea of recorded information had advanced significantly in the Indus Valley, Egypt, and Mesopotamia. Accuracy increased, as did the use of measurement in everyday life. The evolution of script in Mesopotamia provided a precise method of keeping track of production and business transactions. Written language enabled early civilizations to measure reality, record it, and retrieve it later. Together, measuring and recording facilitated the creation of data. They are the earliest foundations of datafication.

This made it possible to replicate human activity. Buildings, for example, could be reproduced from records of their dimensions and materials. It also permitted experimentation: an architect or a builder could alter certain dimensions while keeping others unchanged, creating a new design — which could then be recorded in turn. Commercial transactions could be captured, so one knew how much crop was produced from a harvest or a field (and how much would be taken away by the state in taxes). Quantification enabled prediction and thus planning, even if it was as crude as simply guessing that next year's harvest would be as bountiful as the previous years'. It let partners in a transaction keep tabs on what they owed each other. Without measuring and recording, there could be no money, because there wouldn't have been data to support it.

Over the centuries, measuring extended from length and weight to area, volume, and time. By the beginning of the first millennium A.D., the main features of measuring were in place in the West. But there was a significant shortcoming to the way early civilizations measured. It wasn't optimized for calculations, even relatively simple ones. The counting system of Roman numerals was a poor fit for numerical analysis. Without a base-ten "positional" numbering system or decimals, multiplication and division of large numbers were hard even for experts, and simple addition and subtraction lacked transparency for most of the rest.

An alternative system of numerals was developed in India around the first century A.D. It traveled to Persia, where it was improved, and then was passed on to the Arabs, who greatly refined it. It is the basis of the Arabic numerals we use today. The Crusades may have brought destruction on the lands the Europeans invaded, but knowledge migrated from East to West, and perhaps the most significant transplant was Arabic numerals. Pope Sylvester II, who had studied them, advocated their use at the end of the first millennium. By the twelfth century Arabic texts describing the system were translated into Latin and spread throughout Europe. As a result, mathematics took off.

Even before Arabic numerals arrived in Europe, calculating had been improved through the use of counting boards. These were smooth trays on which tokens were placed to denote amounts. By sliding the tokens in certain areas, one could add or subtract. Yet the method had severe limitations. It was hard to calculate very large and very small numbers at the same time. Most important, the numbers on the boards were fleeting. A wrong move or a careless bump might change a digit, leading to incorrect results. Counting boards may have been tolerable for calculating, but they were bad for recording. And the only way to record and store the numbers shown on the boards was to translate them back into inefficient Roman numerals. (The Europeans were never exposed to the abacuses of the Orient—in hindsight a good thing, since the devices might have prolonged the use of Roman numerals in the West.)

Mathematics gave new meaning to data—it could now be *analyzed,* not just recorded and retrieved. Widespread adoption of Arabic numerals in Europe took hundreds of years, from their introduction in the twelfth century to the late sixteenth century. By that time, mathematicians boasted that they could calculate six times faster with Arabic numerals than with counting boards. What finally helped make Arabic numerals a success was the evolution of another tool of datafication: double-entry bookkeeping.

Accountants invented script in the third millennium B.C. While bookkeeping evolved over the centuries that followed, by and large it remained a system of recording a particular transaction in one place. What it failed to do was to show easily at any given time what book-keepers and their merchant employers care about most: whether a particular account or an entire venture was profitable or not. That began to change in the fourteenth century, when accountants in Italy started recording transactions using two entries, one for credits and one for debits, so that overall the accounts are in balance. The beauty of this system was that it made it easy to see profits and losses. And suddenly dull data began to speak.

Today double-entry bookkeeping is usually considered only for its consequences for accounting and finance. But it also represents a landmark in the evolution of the use of data. It enabled informa-tion to be recorded in the form of "categories" that linked accounts. It worked by means of a set of rules about how to record data — one of the earliest examples of standardized recording of information. One accountant could look at another's books and understand them. It was organized to make a particular type of data query — calculating profits or losses for each account — quick and straightforward. And it provided an audit trail of transactions so that the data was more easily retraceable. Technology geeks can appreciate it today: it had "error correction" built in as a design feature. If one side of the ledger looked amiss, one could check the corresponding entry.

Still, like Arabic numerals, double-entry bookkeeping was not an instant success. Two hundred years after this method had first been devised, it would take a mathematician and a merchant family to alter the history of datafication.

The mathematician was a Franciscan monk named Luca Pacioli. In 1494 he published a textbook, written for the layperson, on math-ematics and its commercial application. The book was a great success and became the de facto mathematics textbook of its time. It was also the first book to use Arabic numerals throughout, and thus its popu-larity facilitated their adoption in Europe. Its most lasting contribu-tion, however, was the section devoted to bookkeeping, where Paci-oli neatly explained the double-entry system of accounting. Over the following decades the material on bookkeeping was separately published in six languages, and it remained the standard reference on the subject for centuries.

As for the merchant family, it was the famous Florentine traders and patrons of the arts, the Medici. In the sixteenth century they became the most influential bankers in Europe, in no small part because they used a superior method of data recording, the double-entry system. Together, Pacioli's textbook and the Medici's success in applying it sealed the victory of double-entry bookkeeping — and by extension established the use of Arabic numerals in the West.

Parallel to advances in the recording of data, ways of measuring the world — denoting time, distance, area, volume, and weight — continued to gain ever increasing precision. The zeal to understand nature through quantification defined science in the nineteenth century, as scholars invented new tools and units to measure and record electric currents, air pressure, temperature, sound frequency, and the like. It was an era when absolutely everything had to be defined, demarcated, and denoted. The fascination went so far as measuring people's skulls as a proxy for their mental ability. Fortunately the pseudo-science of phrenology has mostly withered away, but the desire to quantify has only intensified.

Measuring reality and recording data thrived because of a combination of the tools and a receptive mindset. That combination is the rich soil from which modern datafication has grown. The ingredients for datafying were in place, though in an analog world it was still costly and time-consuming. In many instances it required seemingly infinite patience, or at least a life-long dedication, like Tycho Brahe's fastidious nightly observations of stars and planets in the 1500s. In the limited cases where datafication succeeded in the analog era, such as Commodore Maury's navigational charts, it often did so because of a fortunate confluence of coincidences: Maury, for example, was confined to a desk job but with access to a treasure trove of logbooks. Yet whenever datafication did succeed, enormous value was created from the underlying information and tremendous insights were uncovered.

The arrival of computers brought digital measuring and storage devices that made datafying vastly more efficient. It also greatly enabled mathematical analysis of data to uncover its hidden value. In short, digitization turbocharges datafication. But it is not a substitute. The act of digitization — turning analog information into computer-readable format — by itself does not datafy.

When words become data

The difference between digitization and datafication becomes obvious when we look at a domain where both have happened and compare their consequences. Consider books. In 2004 Google announced an incredibly bold plan. It would take every page of every book it could get hold of and (to the extent possible under copyright laws) permit everyone around the world to search and access the books through the Internet for free. To achieve this feat the company teamed up with some of the world's biggest and most prestigious academic libraries and developed scanning machines that could automatically turn pages, so that scanning millions of books was both feasible and financially viable.

First Google *digitized* text: every page was scanned and captured in a high-resolution digital image file that was stored on Google servers. The page had been transformed into a digital copy that could have easily been retrieved by people everywhere through the Web. Retrieving it, however, would have required either knowing which book had the information one wanted, or doing much reading to find the right bit. One could not have searched the text for particular words, or analyzed it, because the text hadn't been datafied. All that Google had were images that only humans could transform into useful information — by reading.

While this would still have been a great tool — a modern, digital Library of Alexandria, more comprehensive than any library in history — Google wanted more. The company understood that information has stored value that can only be released once it is datafied. And so Google used optical character-recognition software that could take a digital image and recognize the letters, words, sentences, and paragraphs on it. The result was datafied text rather than a digitized picture of a page.

Now the information on the page was usable not just for human readers, but also for computers to process and algorithms to analyze. Datafication made text indexable and thus searchable. And it permitted an endless stream of textual analysis. We now can discover when certain words or phrases were used for the first time, or became popular, knowledge that sheds new light on the spread of ideas and the evolution of human thought across centuries and in many languages.

You can try it yourself. Google's Ngram Viewer (http://books .google.com/ngrams) will generate a graph of the use of words or phrases over time, using the entire Google Books index as a data source. Within seconds we discover that until 1900 the term "causality" was more frequently used than "correlation," but then the ratio reversed. We can compare writing styles and gain insights into authorship disputes. Datafication also makes plagiarism in academic works much easier to discover; as a result, a number of European politicians, including a German defense minister, have been forced to resign.

An estimated 130 million unique books have been published since the invention of the printing press in the mid-fifteenth century. By 2012, seven years after Google began its book project, it had scanned over 20 million titles, more than 15 percent of the world's written heritage — a substantial chunk. This has sparked a new academic discipline called "Culturomics": computational lexicology that tries to understand human behavior and cultural trends through the quantitative analysis of texts.

In one study, researchers at Harvard poured through millions of books (which equated to more than 500 billion words) to reveal that fewer than half the number of English words that appear in books are included in dictionaries. Rather, they wrote, the cornucopia of words "consists of lexical 'dark matter' undocumented in standard references." Moreover, by algorithmically analyzing references to the artist Marc Chagall, whose works were banned in Nazi Germany because he was Jewish, the researchers showed that the suppression or censorship of an idea or person leaves "quantifiable fingerprints." Words are like fossils encased within pages instead of sedimentary rock. The practitioners of culturomics can mine them like archeologists. Of course the dataset entails a zillion implicit biases — are library books a true reflection of the real world or simply one that authors and librarians hold dear? Nevertheless culturomics has given us an entirely new lens with which to understand ourselves.

Transforming words into data unleashes numerous uses. Yes, the data can be used by humans for reading and by machines for analysis. But as the paragon of a big-data company, Google knows that information has multiple potential purposes that can justify its collection and datafication. So Google cleverly used the datafied text from its book-scanning project to improve its machine-translation service. As explained in Chapter Three, the system would take books that are translations and analyze what words and phrases the translators used as alternatives from one language to another. Knowing this, it could then treat translation as a giant math problem, with the computer figuring out probabilities to determine what word best substitutes for another between languages.

Of course Google was not the only organization that dreamed of bringing the richness of the world's written heritage into the computer age, and it was hardly the first to try. Project Gutenberg, a volunteer initiative to place public domain works online as early as 1971, was all about making the texts available for people to read, but it didn't consider ancillary uses of treating the words as data. It was about reading, not reusing. Likewise, publishers for years have experimented with electronic versions of books. They too saw the core value of books as content, not as data — their business model is based on this. Thus they never used or permitted others to use the data inherent in a book's text. They never saw the need, or appreciated the potential.

Many companies are now vying to crack the e-book market. Amazon, with its Kindle e-book readers, seems to have a big early lead. But this is an area where Amazon's and Google's strategies differ greatly.

Amazon, too, has datafied books — but unlike Google, it has failed to exploit possible new uses of the text as data. Jeff Bezos, the company's founder and chief executive, convinced hundreds of publishers to release their books on the Kindle format. Kindle books are not made up of page images. If they were, one wouldn't be able to change the font size or display a page on color as well as black-and-white screens. The text is datafied, not just digital. Indeed, Amazon has done for millions of new books what Google is painstakingly trying to achieve for many older ones.

However, other than Amazon's brilliant service of "statistically significant words" — which uses algorithms to find links among the topics of books that might not otherwise be apparent — the online retailer has not used its wealth of words for big-data analysis. It sees its book business as based on the content that humans read, rather than on analysis of datafied text. And in fairness, it probably faces restrictions from conservative publishers over how it may use the information contained in their books. Google, as the big-data bad boy willing to push the limits, feels no such constraints: its bread is buttered by users' clicks, not by access to publishers' titles. Perhaps it is not unjust to say that, at least for now, Amazon understands the value of digitizing content, while Google understands the value of datafying it.

When location becomes data

One of the most basic pieces of information in the world is, well, the world. But for most of history spatial area was never quantified or used in data form. The geo-location of nature, objects, and people of course constitutes information. The mountain is there; the person is here. But to be most useful, that information needs to be turned into data. To datafy location requires a few prerequisites. We need a method to measure every square inch of area on Earth. We need a standardized way to note the measurements. We need an instrument to monitor and record the data. Quantification, standardization, collection. Only then can we store and analyze location not as place per se, but as data.

In the West, quantification of location began with the Greeks. Around 200 B.C. Eratosthenes invented a system of grid lines to demarcate location, akin to latitude and longitude. But like so many good ideas from antiquity, the practice faded away over time. A millennium and a half later, around 1400 A.D., a copy of Ptolemy's *Geographia* arrived in Florence from Constantinople just as the Renaissance and the shipping trade were igniting interest in science and in know-how from the ancients. Ptolemy's treatise was a sensation, and his old lessons were applied to solve modern navigation challenges. From then on, maps appeared with longitude, latitude, and scale. The system was later improved upon by the Flemish cartographer Gerardus Mercator in 1570, enabling sailors to plot a straight course in a spherical world.

Although by this time there was a means to record location, there was no generally accepted format for sharing that information. A common identification system was needed, just as the Internet benefited from domain names to make things like email work universally. The standardization of longitude and latitude took a long time. It was finally enshrined in 1884 at the International Meridian Conference in Washington, D.C., where 25 nations chose Greenwich, England, as the prime meridian and zero-point of longitude (with the French, who considered themselves the leaders in international standards, abstaining). In the 1940s the Universal Transverse Mercator (UTM) coordinate system was created, which broke the world into 60 zones to increase accuracy.

Geospatial location could now be identified, recorded, tallied, analyzed, and communicated in a standardized, numerical format. Position could be datafied. But because of the high cost of measuring and recording the information in an analog setting, it rarely was. For datafication to happen, tools to measure location cheaply had to be invented. Until the 1970s the only way to determine physical location was by using landmarks, astronomical constellations, dead reckoning, or limited radio-position technology.

A great change occurred in 1978, when the first of the 24 satellites that make up the Global Positioning System (GPS) was launched. Receivers on the ground can triangulate their position by noting the differences in time it takes to receive a signal from the satellites 12,600 miles overhead. Developed by the U.S. defense department, the system was first opened to non-military uses in the 1980s and became fully operational by the 1990s. Its precision was enhanced for commercial applications a decade later. Accurate to one meter, GPS marked the moment when a method to measure location, the dream of navigators, mapmakers, and mathematicians since antiquity, was finally fused with the technical means to achieve it quickly, (relatively) cheaply, and without requiring any specialized knowledge.

Yet the information must actually be generated. There was nothing to prevent Eratosthenes and Mercator from estimating their whereabouts every minute of the day, had they cared to. While feasible, that was impractical. Likewise, early GPS receivers were complex and costly, suitable for a submarine but not for everyone at all times. But this would change, thanks to the ubiquity of inexpensive chips embedded in digital gadgets. The cost of a GPS module tumbled from hundreds of dollars in the 1990s to about a dollar today at high volume. It usually takes only a few seconds for GPS to fix a location, and the coordinates are standardized. So 37° 14′ 06″ N, 115° 48′ 40″ W can only mean that one is at the super-secretive U.S. military base in a remote part of Nevada known as "Area 51," where space aliens are (perhaps!) being kept.

Nowadays GPS is just one system among many to capture location. Rival satellite systems are under way in China and Europe. And even better accuracy can be established by triangulating among cell towers or wifi routers to determine position based on signal strength, since GPS doesn't work indoors or amid tall buildings. That helps explain why firms like Google, Apple, and Microsoft have established their own geo-location systems to complement GPS. Google's Street View cars collected wifi router information as they snapped photos, and the iPhone was a "spyPhone" gathering location and wifi data and sending it back to Apple, without users realizing it. (Google's Android phones and Microsoft's mobile operating system also collected this sort of data.)

It is not just people but objects that can be tracked now. With wireless modules placed inside vehicles, the datafication of location will transform the idea of insurance. The data offers a granular look at the times, locations, and distances of actual driving to better price risk. In the U.S. and Britain, drivers can buy car insurance priced according to where and when they actually drive, not just pay an annual rate based on their age, sex, and past record. This approach to insurance pricing creates incentives for good behavior. It shifts the very nature of insurance from one based on pooled risk to something based on individual action. Tracking individuals by vehicles also changes the nature of fixed costs, like roads and other infrastructure, by tying the use of those resources to drivers and others who "consume" them. This was impossible to do prior to rendering geo-location in data form on a continual basis for everyone and everything — but it is the world we are headed into.

UPS, for example, uses "geo-loco" data in multiple ways. Its vehicles are fitted with sensors, wireless modules, and GPS so that headquarters can predict engine trouble, as we saw in the last chapter. Moreover, it lets the company know the vans' whereabouts in case of delays, to monitor employees, and to scrutinize their itineraries to optimize routes. The most efficient path is determined in part from data on previous deliveries, much as Maury's charts were based on earlier sea voyages.

The analytics program has had extraordinary effects. In 2011 UPS shaved a massive 30 million miles off its drivers' routes, saving three million gallons of fuel and 30,000 metric tons of carbon-dioxide emissions, according to Jack Levis, UPS's director of process management. It also improved safety and efficiency: the algorithm compiles routes with fewer turns that must cross traffic at intersections, which tend to lead to accidents, waste time, and consume more fuel since vans often must idle before turning.

"Prediction gave us knowledge," says Levis at UPS. "But after knowledge is something more: wisdom and clairvoyance. At some point in time, the system will be so smart that it will predict problems and correct them before the user realizes that there was something wrong."

Datafied location across time is most notably being applied to people. For years wireless operators have collected and analyzed information to improve the service level of their networks. But the data is increasingly being used for other purposes and collected by third parties for new services. Some smartphone applications, for example, gather location information regardless of whether the app itself has a location-based feature. In other cases, the whole point of an app is to build a business around knowing the users' locations. An example is Foursquare, which lets people "check in" at their favorite locations. It earns income from loyalty programs, restaurant recommendations, and other location-related services.

The ability to collect users' geo-loco data is becoming extremely valuable. On an individual level, it allows targeted advertising based on where the person is situated or is predicted to go. Moreover, the information can be aggregated to reveal trends. For instance, amassing location data lets firms detect traffic jams without needing to see the cars: the number and speed of phones traveling on a highway reveal this information. The company AirSage crunches 15 billion geo-loco records daily from the travels of millions of cellphone subscribers to create real-time traffic reports in over 100 cities across America. Two other geo-loco companies, Sense Networks and Skyhook, can use location data to tell which areas of a city have the most bustling nightlife, or to estimate how many protesters turned up at a demonstration.

Yet the non-commercial uses of geo-location may turn out to be the most important of all. Sandy Pentland, the director of MIT's Human Dynamics Laboratory, and Nathan Eagle together pioneered what they call "reality mining." This refers to processing huge amounts of data from mobile phones to make inferences and predictions about human behavior. In one study, analyzing movements and call patterns allowed them to successfully identify people who had contracted the flu before they themselves knew they were ill. In the case of a deadly flu outbreak, this ability could save millions of lives by letting public health officials know the most afflicted areas at any moment. But if placed in irresponsible hands, the power of reality mining could have terrible consequences, as we will see later.

Eagle, the founder of the wireless-data startup Jana, has used aggregated cellphone data from more than 200 mobile operators in more than 100 countries — some 3.5 billion people in Latin America, Africa, and Europe — to answer questions dear to marketing execs' hearts, like how many times per week a household does laundry. But he's also used big data to examine questions such as how cities prosper. He and a colleague combined location data on prepaid cellphone subscribers in Africa with the amount of money they spent when they topped off their accounts. The value correlates strongly with income: richer people buy more minutes at a time. But one of Eagle's counterintuitive findings is that slums, rather than being only centers of poverty, also act as economic springboards. The point is that these indirect uses of location data have nothing to do with the routing of mobile communications, the purpose for which the information was initially generated. Rather, once location is datafied, new uses crop up and new value can be created.

When interactions become data

The next frontiers of datafication are more personal: our relationships, experiences, and moods. The idea of datafication is the backbone of many of the Web's social media companies. Social networking platforms don't simply offer us a way to find and stay in touch with friends and colleagues, they take intangible elements of our everyday life and transform them into data that can be used to do new things. Facebook datafied relationships; they always existed and constituted information, but they were never formally defined as data until Facebook's "social graph." Twitter enabled the datafication of sentiment by creating an easy way for people to record and share their stray thoughts, which had previously been lost to the winds of time. LinkedIn datafied our long-past professional experiences, just as Maury transformed old logbooks, turning that information into predictions about our present and future: whom we may know, or a job we may want.

Such uses of the data are still embryonic. In the case of Facebook, it has been shrewdly patient, knowing that unveiling too many new purposes for its users' data too soon could freak them out. Besides, the company is still adjusting its business model (and privacy policy) for the amount and type of data collection it wants to do. Hence much more of the criticism it has faced centers on what information it is capable of collecting than on what it has actually done with that data. Facebook had around one billion users in 2012, who were interconnected through over 100 billion friendships. The resulting social graph represents more than 10 percent of the total world population, datafied and available to a single company.

The potential uses are extraordinary. A number of startups have looked into adapting the social graph to use as signals for establishing credit scores. The idea is that birds of a feather flock together: prudent people befriend like-minded types, while the profligate hang out among themselves. If it pans out, Facebook could be the next FICO, the credit-scoring agency. The rich datasets from social media firms may well form the basis of new businesses that go far beyond the superficial sharing of photos, status updates, and "likes."

Twitter, too, has seen its data used in interesting ways. To some, the 400 million terse tweets sent every day in 2012 by over 140 million monthly users seem like little more than random blather. And, in fact, they're often just that. Yet the company enables the datafication of people's thoughts, moods, and interactions, which could never be captured previously. Twitter has struck deals with two firms, Data-Sift and Gnip, to sell access to the data. (Although all tweets are public, access to the "firehose" comes at a cost.) Many businesses parse tweets, sometimes using a technique called sentiment analysis, to garner aggregate customer feedback or judge the impact of marketing campaigns.

Two hedge funds, Derwent Capital in London and MarketPsych in California, started analyzing the datafied text of tweets as signals for investments in the stock market. (Their actual trading strategies were kept secret: rather than investing in firms that were ballyhooed, they may have bet against them.) Both firms now sell the information to traders. In MarketPsych's case, it teamed up with Thomson Reuters to offer no fewer than 18,864 separate indices across 119 countries, updated each minute, on emotional states like optimism, gloom, joy, fear, anger, and even themes like innovation, litigation, and conflict. The data is used not so much by humans as by computers: Wall Street math whizzes, known as "quants," plug the data into their algorithmic models in order to look for unseen correlations that can be parlayed into profits. The very frequency of tweets on a topic can predict various things, such as Hollywood box-office revenue, according to one of the fathers of social networking analysis, Bernardo Huberman. He and a colleague at HP developed a model that looked at the rate at which new tweets were posted. With this, they were able to forecast a film's success better than other commonly used predictors.

But even more is possible. Twitter messages are limited to a sparse 140 characters, but the metadata — that is, the "information about information" — associated with each tweet is rich. It includes 33 discrete items. Some do not seem very useful, like the "wallpaper" on a user's Twitter page or the software the user employs to access the service. But other metadata is extremely interesting, such as users' language, their geo-location, and the number and names of people they follow and those who follow them. In one study, reported in *Science* in 2011, an analysis of 509 million tweets over two years from 2.4 million people in 84 countries showed that people's moods followed similar daily and weekly patterns across cultures around the world — something that had not been possible to spot before. Moods have been datafied.

Datafication is not just about rendering attitudes and sentiments into an analyzable form, but human behavior as well. This is otherwise hard to track, especially in the context of the broader community and subgroups within it. The biologist Marcel Salathé of Penn State University and the software engineer Shashank Khandelwal analyzed tweets to find that people's attitudes about vaccinations matched their likelihood of actually getting flu shots. Importantly, their study used the metadata of who was connected to whom among Twitter followers to go a step further still. They noticed that subgroups of unvaccinated people may exist. What marks this research as particularly special is that where other studies, such as Google Flu Trends, used aggregated data to consider the state of individuals' health, the sentiment analysis performed by Salathé actually predicted health *behaviors*.

These early findings indicate where datafication will surely go next. Like Google, a gaggle of social media networks such as Facebook, Twitter, LinkedIn, Foursquare, and others sit on an enormous treasure chest of datafied information that, once analyzed, will shed light on social dynamics at all levels, from the individual to society at large.

The datafication of everything

With a little imagination, a cornucopia of things can be rendered into data form — and surprise us along the way. In the same spirit as Professor Koshimizu's work on backsides in Tokyo, IBM was granted a U.S. patent in 2012 on "Securing premises using surface-based computing technology." That's intellectual-property-lawyer-speak for a touch-sensitive floor covering, somewhat like a giant smartphone screen. The potential uses are plentiful. It would be able to identify the objects on it. In basic form, it could know to turn on lights in a room or open doors when a person enters. More important, however, it might identify individuals by their weight or the way they stand and walk. It could tell if someone fell and did not get back up, an important feature for the elderly. Retailers could learn the flow of traffic through their stores. When the floor is datafied, there is no ceiling to its possible uses.

Datafying as much as possible is not as far out as it sounds. Consider the "quantified self" movement. It refers to a disparate group of fitness aficionados, medical maniacs, and tech junkies who measure every element of their bodies and lives in order to live better — or at least, to learn new things they couldn't have known in an enumerated way before. The number of "self-trackers" is small for the moment but growing.

Because of smartphones and inexpensive computing technology, datafication of the most essential acts of living has never been easier. A slew of startups let people track their sleep patterns by measuring brainwaves throughout the night. One firm, Zeo, has already created the world's largest database of sleep activity and uncovered differences in the amounts of REM sleep experienced by men and women. Asthmapolis has attached a sensor to an asthma inhaler that tracks location via GPS; aggregating the information lets the company discern environmental triggers for asthma attacks, such as proximity to certain crops.

The firms Fitbit and Jawbone let people measure their physical activity and sleep. Another company, Basis, lets wearers of its wristband monitor their vital signs, including heart rate and skin conductance, which are measures of stress. Getting the data is becoming easier and less intrusive than ever. In 2009 Apple was granted a patent for collecting data on blood oxygenation, heart rate, and body temperature through its audio earbuds.

There is a lot to learn from datafying how one's body works. Researchers at Gjøvik University College in Norway and Derawi Biometrics have developed an app for smartphones that analyzes an individual's gait while walking and uses the information as a security system to unlock the phone. Meanwhile two professors at Georgia Tech Research Institute, Robert Delano and Brian Parise, are developing a smartphone application called iTrem that uses the phone's built-in accelerometer to monitor a person's body tremors for Parkinson's and other neurological disorders. The app is a boon for both doctors and patients. It allows patients to bypass costly tests done at a physician's office; it also lets medical professionals remotely monitor people's disability and their responses to treatments. According to researchers in Kyoto, a smartphone is only a tiny bit less effective at measuring the tremors than the tri-axial accelerometer used in specialized medical equipment, so it can be reliably used. Once again, a bit of messiness trumps exactitude.

In most of these cases, we're capturing information and putting it into data form that allows it to be reused. This can happen almost everywhere and to nearly everything. GreenGoose, a startup in San Francisco, sells tiny sensors that detect motion, which can be placed on objects to track how much they are used. Putting it on a pack of dental floss, a watering can, or a box of cat litter makes it possible to datafy dental hygiene and the care of plants and pets. The enthusiasm over the "internet of things" — embedding chips, sensors, and communications modules into everyday objects — is partly about networking but just as much about datafying all that surrounds us.

Once the world has been datafied, the potential uses of the information are basically limited only by one's ingenuity. Maury datafied seafarers' previous journeys through painstaking manual tabulation, and thereby unlocked extraordinary insights and value. Today we have the tools (statistics and algorithms) and the necessary equipment (digital processors and storage) to perform similar tasks much faster, at scale, and in many different contexts. In the age of big data, even backsides have upsides.

We are in the midst of a great infrastructure project that in some ways rivals those of the past, from Roman aqueducts to the Enlightenment's *Encyclopédie*. We fail to appreciate this because today's project is so new, because we are in the middle of it, and because unlike the water that flows on the aqueducts the product of our labors is intangible. The project is datafication. Like those other infrastructural advances, it will bring about fundamental changes to society.

Aqueducts made possible the growth of cities; the printing press facilitated the Enlightenment, and newspapers enabled the rise of the nation state. But these infrastructures were focused on flows — of water, of knowledge. So were the telephone and the Internet. In contrast, datafication represents an essential enrichment in human comprehension. With the help of big data, we will no longer regard our world as a string of happenings that we explain as natural or social phenomena, but as a universe comprised essentially of information.

For well over a century, physicists have suggested that this is the case — that not atoms but information is the basis of all that is. This, admittedly, may sound esoteric. Through datafication, however, in many instances we can now capture and calculate at a much more comprehensive scale the physical and intangible aspects of existence and act on them.

Seeing the world as information, as oceans of data that can be explored at ever greater breadth and depth, offers us a perspective on reality that we did not have before. It is a mental outlook that may penetrate all areas of life. Today, we are a numerate society because we presume that the world is understandable with numbers and math. And we take for granted that knowledge can be transmitted across time and space because the idea of the written word is so ingrained. Tomorrow, subsequent generations may have a "big-data consciousness" — the presumption that there is a quantitative component to all that we do, and that data is indispensable for society to learn from. The notion of transforming the myriad dimensions of reality into data probably seems novel to most people at present. But in the future, we will surely treat it as a given (which, pleasingly, harks back to the very origin of the term "data").

In time, the impact of datafication may dwarf that of aqueducts and newspapers, rivaling perhaps the printing press and the Internet by giving us the means to map the world in a quantifiable, analyzable way. For the moment, however, the most advanced users of datafication are in business, where big data is being used to create new forms of value — the subject of the next chapter.

6

VALUE

IN THE LATE 1990s the Web was quickly turning into an unruly, unwelcoming, unfriendly place. "Spambots" were inundating email inboxes and swamping online forums. In 2000 Luis von Ahn, a 22-year-old who had just graduated from college, had an idea for solving the problem: force registrants to prove they are human. So he looked for something that is easy for people to do but hard for machines.

He came up with the idea of presenting squiggly, hard-to-read letters during the sign-up process. People would be able to decipher them and type in the correct text in a few seconds, but computers would be stumped. Yahoo implemented his method and reduced its scourge of spambots overnight. Von Ahn called his creation Captcha (for Completely Automated Public Turing Test to Tell Computers and Humans Apart). Five years later, millions of Captchas were being typed each day.

Captcha brought von Ahn considerable fame and a job teaching computer science at Carnegie Mellon University after he earned his PhD. It was also a factor in his receiving, at 27, one of the MacArthur Foundation's prestigious "genius" awards of half a million dollars. But when he realized that he was responsible for millions of people wasting lots of time each day typing in annoying, squiggly letters — vast amounts of information that was simply discarded afterwards — he didn't feel so smart.

Looking for ways to put all that human computational power to more productive use, he came up with a successor, fittingly named ReCaptcha. Instead of typing in random letters, people type two words from text-scanning projects that a computer's optical character-recognition program couldn't understand. One word is meant to confirm what other users have typed and thus is a signal that the person is a human; the other is a new word in need of disambiguation. To ensure accuracy, the system presents the same fuzzy word to an average of five different people to type in correctly before it trusts it's right. The data had a primary use — to prove the user was human — but it also had a secondary purpose: to decipher unclear words in digitized texts.

The value this unleashes is immense, when one considers what it would cost to hire people instead. At roughly 10 seconds per use, 100-ADD million ReCaptchas a day — the current rate — add up to a quarter of a million hours a day. The minimum wage in the United States was $7.25 an hour in 2012. If one were to turn to the market for disambiguating words that a computer couldn't make sense of, it would cost around $2-ADD million a day, or around $750 million a year. Instead, von Ahn designed a system to do it, in effect, for free. This was so valuable that Google acquired the technology from von Ahn in 2009. Google makes it freely available for any website to use; today it's incorporated into some 200,000 sites, including Facebook, Twitter, and Craigslist.

The story of ReCaptcha underscores the importance of the reuse of data. With big data, the value of data is changing. In the digital age, data shed its role of supporting transactions and often became the good itself that was traded. In a big-data world, things change again. Data's value shifts from its primary use to its potential future uses. This has profound consequences. It affects how businesses value the data they hold and who they let access it. It enables, and may force, companies to change their business models. It alters how organizations think about data and how they use it.

Information has always been essential for market transactions. Data enables price discovery, for instance, which is a signal for how much to produce. This dimension of data is well understood. Certain types of information have long been traded on markets. Content found in books, articles, music, and movies is an example, as is financial information like stock prices. These have been joined in the past few decades by personal data. Specialized data brokers in the United States such as Acxiom, Experian, and Equifax charge handsomely for comprehensive dossiers of personal information on hundreds of millions of consumers. With Facebook, Twitter, LinkedIn, and other social media platforms, our personal connections, opinions, preferences, and patterns of everyday living have joined the pool of personal information already available about us.

In short, although data has long been valuable, it was either seen as ancillary to the core operations of running a business, or limited to relatively narrow categories such as intellectual property or personal information. In contrast, in the age of big data, *all* data will be regarded as valuable, in and of itself.

When we say "all data," we mean even the rawest, most seemingly mundane bits of information. Think of readings from a heat sensor on a factory machine. Or the real-time stream of GPS coordinates, accelerometer readings, and fuel levels from a delivery vehicle — or a fleet of 60,000 of them. Or think of billions of old search queries, or the price of nearly every seat on every commercial airline flight in the United States going back years.

Until recently there were no easy ways to collect, store, and analyze such data, which severely limited the opportunities to extract its potential value. In Adam Smith's celebrated example of the pin maker, with which he discussed the division of labor in the eighteenth century, it would have required observers watching all the workers not just for one particular study, but at all times everyday, taking detailed measurements, and counting the output on thick paper with feathery quill pens. When classical economists considered the factors of production (land, labor, and capital), the idea of harnessing data was largely absent. Though the cost of gathering and using data has declined over the past two centuries, until fairly recently it remained relatively expensive.

What makes our era different is that many of the inherent limitations on the collection of data no longer exist. Technology has reached a point where vast amounts of information often can be captured and recorded cheaply. Data can frequently be collected passively, without much effort or even awareness on the part of those being recorded. And because the cost of storage has fallen so much, it is easier to justify keeping data than discarding it. All this makes much more data available at lower cost than ever before. Over the past half-century, the cost of digital storage has been roughly cut in half every two years, while storage density has increased 50 million-fold. In light of informational firms like Farecast or Google — where raw facts go in at one end of a digital assembly line and processed information comes out at the other — data is starting to look like a new resource or factor of production.

The immediate value of most data is evident to those who collect it. In fact, they probably gather it with a specific purpose in mind. Stores collect sales data for proper financial accounting. Factories monitor their output to ensure it conforms to quality standards. Websites log every click users make — sometimes even where the mouse-cursor moves — for analyzing and optimizing the content the sites present to visitors. These primary uses of the data justify its collection and processing. When Amazon records not only the books that customers buy but the web pages they merely look at, it knows it will use the data to offer personalized recommendations. Similarly, Facebook tracks users' "status updates" and "likes" to determine the most suitable ads to display on its website to earn revenue.

Unlike material things — the food we eat, a candle that burns — data's value does not diminish when it is used; it can be processed again and again. Information is what economists call a "non-rivalrous" good: one person's use of it does not impede another's. And information doesn't wear out with use the way material goods do. Hence Amazon can use data from past transactions when making recommendations to its customers — and use it repeatedly, not only for the customer who generated the data but for many others as well.

Just as data can be used many times for the same purpose, more importantly, it can be harnessed for multiple purposes as well. This point is important as we try to understand how much information will be worth to us in the era of big data. We've seen some of this potential realized already, as when Walmart searched its database of old sales receipts and spotted the lucrative correlation between hurricanes and Pop-Tarts sales.

All this suggests that data's full value is much greater than the value extracted from its first use. It also means that companies can exploit data effectively even if the first or each subsequent use only brings a tiny amount of value, so long as they utilize the data many times over.

The "option value" of data

To get a sense of what the reuse of data means for its ultimate value, consider electric cars. Whether they succeed as a mode of transportation depends on a dizzying array of logistics, which all have something to do with battery life. Drivers need to be able to recharge their car batteries quickly and conveniently, and power companies need to ensure that the energy drawn by these vehicles doesn't destabilize the grid. We have largely effective distribution of gas stations today, but we don't yet know what the recharging needs and placement of stations for electric vehicles will be.

Strikingly, this is not so much an infrastructural problem as an informational one. And big data is an important part of the solution. In a trial in 2012, IBM worked with Pacific Gas and Electric Company in California and the carmaker Honda to collect vast amounts of information to answer fundamental questions about when and where electric cars will draw power and what this will mean for the power supply. IBM developed an elaborate predictive model based on numerous inputs: the car's battery level, the location of the car, the time of day, and the available slots at nearby charging stations. It coupled that data with the current consumption of power from the grid as well as historical power usage patterns. Analyzing the huge streams of real-time and historical data from multiple sources let IBM determine the optimal times and places for drivers to top up their car batteries. It also revealed where to best build recharging stations. Eventually, the system will need to take into account price differences at nearby recharging stations. Even weather forecasts will have to be factored in: for example, if it is sunny and a nearby solar-powered station is teeming with electricity, but the forecast calls for a week of rain in which the solar panels will be idle.

The system takes information generated for one purpose and reuses it for another — in other words, the data moves from primary to secondary uses. This makes it much more valuable over time. The car's battery-level indicator tells drivers when to fill 'er up. The power grid's usage data is collected by the utility so it can manage the stability of the grid. Those are the primary uses. Both sets of data find secondary uses — and new value — when they're applied to a completely different purpose: determining when and where to recharge, and where to build electric-vehicle service stations. On top of this, ancillary information is incorporated, such as the location of the car and historical grid consumption. And IBM processes the data not once but over and over, as it continuously updates its profile of e-car energy intake and its stress on the power grid.

Data's true value is like an iceberg floating in the ocean. Only a tiny part of it is visible at first sight, while much of it is hidden beneath the surface. Innovative companies that understand this can extract that hidden value and reap potentially huge benefits. In short, data's value needs to be considered in terms of all the possible ways it can be employed in the future, not simply how it is used in the present. We have seen this in many of the examples we have highlighted already. Farecast harnessed data from previously sold plane tickets to predict the future price of airfares. Google reused search terms to uncover the prevalence of the flu. Maury repurposed old captains' logs to reveal ocean currents.

Still, the importance of data's reuse is not fully appreciated in business and society. Few executives at Con Edison in New York could have imagined that century-old cable information and maintenance records might be used to prevent future accidents. It took a new generation of statisticians, and a new wave of methods and tools, to unlock the data's value. Even many Internet and technology companies have been unaware until recently how valuable data's reuse can be.

It may be helpful to envision data the way physicists see energy. They refer to "stored" or "potential" energy that exists within an object but lies dormant. Think of a compressed spring or a ball resting at the top of a hill. The energy in these objects remains latent — potential — until it's unleashed, say, when the spring is released or the ball is nudged so that it rolls downhill. Now these objects' energy has become "kinetic" because they're moving and exerting force on other objects in the world. After its primary use, data's value still exists, but lies dormant, storing its potential like the spring or the ball, until the data is applied to a secondary use and its power is released anew. In a big-data age, we finally have the mindset, ingenuity, and tools to tap data's hidden value.

Ultimately, the value of data is what one can gain from all the possible ways it can be employed. These seemingly infinite potential uses are like options — not in the sense of financial instruments, but in the practical sense of choices. The data's worth is the sum of these choices: the "option value" of data, so to speak. In the past, once data's main use was achieved we often thought the data had fulfilled its purpose, and we were ready to erase it, to let it slip away. After all, it seemed the key worth had been extracted. In the big-data age, data is like a magical diamond mine that keeps on giving long after its principal value has been tapped. There are three potent ways to unleash data's option value: basic reuse; merging datasets; and finding "twofers."

THE REUSE OF DATA

A classic example of data's innovative reuse is search terms. At first glance, the information seems worthless after its primary purpose has been fulfilled. The momentary interaction between consumer and search engine produced a list of websites and ads that served a particular function unique to that moment. But old queries can be extraordinarily valuable. Companies like Hitwise, a web-traffic-measurement company owned by the data broker Experian, lets clients mine search traffic to learn about consumer preferences. Marketers can use Hitwise to get a sense of whether pink will be in this spring or black is back. Google makes a version of its search-term analytics openly available for people to examine. It has launched a business-forecasting service with Spain's second-largest bank, BBVA, to look at the tourism sector as well as sell real-time economic indicators based on search data. The Bank of England uses search queries related to property to get a better sense of whether housing prices are rising or falling.

Companies that have failed to appreciate the importance of data's reuse have learned their lesson the hard way. For example, in Amazon's early days it signed a deal with AOL to run the technology behind AOL's e-commerce site. To most people, it looked like an ordinary outsourcing deal. But what really interested Amazon, explains Andreas Weigend, Amazon's former chief scientist, was getting hold of data on what AOL users were looking at and buying, which would improve the performance of its recommendation engine. Poor AOL never realized this. It only saw the data's value in terms of its primary purpose — sales. Clever Amazon knew it could reap benefits by putting the data to a secondary use.

Or take the case of Google's entry into speech recognition with GOOG-411 for local search listings, which ran from 2007 to 2010. The search giant didn't have its own speech-recognition technology so needed to license it. It reached an agreement with Nuance, the leader in the field, which was thrilled to have landed such a prized client. But Nuance was then a big-data dunderhead: the contract didn't specify who got to retain the voice-translation records, and Google kept them for itself. Analyzing the data lets one score the probability that a given digitized snippet of voice corresponds to a specific word. This is essential for improving speech-recognition technology or creating a new service altogether. At the time Nuance perceived itself as in the business of software licensing, not data crunching. As soon as it recognized its error, it began striking deals with mobile operators and handset manufacturers to use its speech-recognition service — so that it could gather up the data.

The value in data's reuse is good news for organizations that collect or control large datasets but currently make little use of them, such as conventional businesses that mostly operate offline. They may sit on untapped informational geysers. Some companies may have collected data, used it once (if at all), and just kept it around because of low storage cost — in "data tombs," as data scientists call the places where such old info resides.

Internet and technology companies are on the front lines of harnessing the data deluge, since they collect so much information just by being online and are ahead of the rest of industry in analyzing it. But all firms stand to gain. The consultants at McKinsey & Company point to a logistics company, whose name they keep anonymous, which noticed that in the process of delivering goods, it was amassing reams of information on product shipments around the globe. Smelling opportunity, it established a special division to sell the aggregated data in the form of business and economic forecasts. In other words, it created an offline version of Google's past-search-query business. Or consider SWIFT, the global interbank system for wire transfers. It found that payments correlate with global economic activity. So SWIFT offers GDP forecasts based on fund transfer data passing over its network.

Some firms, thanks to their position in the information value chain, may be able to collect huge amounts of data, even though they have little immediate need for it or aren't adept at reusing it. For instance, mobile phone operators collect information on their subscribers' locations so they can route calls. For these companies, this data has only narrow technical uses. But it becomes more valuable when it is reused by companies that distribute personalized, location-based advertising and promotions. Sometimes the value comes not from individual data points but from what they reveal in the aggregate. Hence the geo-loco businesses like AirSage and Sense Networks that we saw in the last chapter can sell information on where people are gathering on a Friday night or how slowly cars are crawling in traffic. This massed information can be used to determine real estate values or billboard advertising prices.

Even the most banal information may have special value, if applied in the right way. Look again at mobile phone operators: they have records of where and when the phones connect to base stations, including at what signal strength. Operators have long used that data to fine-tune the performance of their networks, deciding where to add or upgrade infrastructure. But the data has many other potential uses. Handset manufacturers could use it to learn what influences signal strength, for example, to improve the reception quality of their gadgets. Mobile operators have long been loath to monetize that information for fear of running afoul of privacy regulations. But they are starting to soften their stance as their financial fortunes flounder and they regard their data as a potential source of income. In 2012 the large Spanish and international operator Telefonica went so far as to create a separate company, called Telefonica Digital Insights, to sell anonymous and aggregated subscriber-location data to retailers and others.

RECOMBINANT DATA

Sometimes the dormant value can only be unleashed by combining one dataset with another, perhaps a very different one. We can do innovative things by commingling data in new ways. An example of how this can work is a clever study published in 2011 on whether cellphones increase the likelihood of cancer. With around six billion cellphones in the world, almost one for every human on Earth, the question is crucial. Many studies have looked for a link, but they have been hobbled by shortcomings. Their sample sizes were too small, or the time periods they covered were too short, or they were based on self-reported data that was fraught with error. However, a team of researchers at the Danish Cancer Society devised an interesting approach based on previously collected data.

Data on all cellphone subscribers since mobiles were introduced in Denmark was obtained from mobile operators. The study looked at those who had cellphones from 1987 to 1995, with the exception of corporate subscribers and others whose socioeconomic data was not available. It came to 358,403 people. The country also maintained a nationwide registry of all cancer patients, which contained 10,729 people who had tumors of the central nervous system during 1990 to 2007, the follow-up period. Finally, the study used a nationwide registry with information on highest attained education and disposable income for each Danish inhabitant. After combining the three datasets, the researchers looked into whether mobile users showed higher rates of cancer than non-subscribers. And among subscribers, were those who had owned a cellphone for a longer period more likely to get cancer?

Despite the study's scale, the data wasn't messy or imprecise at all: the datasets required fastidious quality standards for medical or commercial or demographic purposes. The information wasn't collected in ways that could introduce biases related to the theme of the study. In fact, the data had been generated years earlier, and for reasons that had nothing to do with this research. Most important, the study was not based on a sample but on something close to N = all: almost every incident of cancer, and nearly every mobile user, which amounted to 3.8 million person-years of cellphone ownership. The fact that it contained almost all cases meant that the researchers could control for subpopulations, such as those with high levels of income.

In the end, the group didn't detect any increase in the risk of cancer associated with use of mobile phones. For that reason, its findings hardly made a splash in the media when they were published in October 2011 in the British medical journal *BMJ*. But if a link had been uncovered, the study would have been front-page news around the world, and the methodology of "recombinant data" would have been celebrated.

With big data, the sum is more valuable than its parts, and when we recombine the sums of multiple datasets together, that sum too is worth more than its individual ingredients. Today Internet users are familiar with basic "mashups," which combine two or more data sources in a novel way. For instance, the property website Zillow superimposes real estate information and prices on a map of neighborhoods in the United States. It also crunches reams of data, such as recent transactions in the neighborhood and the specifications of properties, to predict the value of specific homes in an area. The visual presentation makes the data more accessible. But with big data we can go far beyond this. The Danish cancer study gives us a hint of what is possible.

EXTENSIBLE DATA

One way to enable the reuse of data is to design extensibility into it from the outset so that it is suitable for multiple uses. Though this is not always possible — since one may only realize possible uses long after the data has been collected — there are ways to encourage multiple uses of the same dataset. For instance, some retailers are positioning store surveillance cameras so that they not only spot shoplifters but can also track the flow of customers through the store and where they stop to look. Retailers can use the latter information to design the best layout for the store as well as to judge the effectiveness of marketing campaigns. Prior to this, such video cameras were only for security. Now they are seen as an investment that may increase revenue.

One of the best at collecting data with extensibility in mind is, unsurprisingly, Google. Its controversial Street View cars cruised around snapping pictures of houses and roads, but also gobbling up GPS data, checking mapping information, and even sucking in wifi network names (and, perhaps illegally, the content that flowed over open wireless networks). A single Google Street View drive amassed a myriad of discrete data streams at every moment. The extensibility comes in because Google applied the data not just for a primary use but for lots of secondary uses. For example, the GPS data it garnered improved the company's mapping service and was indispensable for the functioning of its self-driving car.

The extra cost of collecting multiple streams or many more data points in each stream is often low. So it makes sense to gather as much data as possible, as well as to make it extensible by considering potential secondary uses at the outset. That increases the data's option value. The point is to look for "twofers" — where a single dataset can be used in multiple instances if it can be collected in a certain way. Thus the data can do double duty.

DEPRECIATING VALUE OF DATA

As the cost of storing digital data has plummeted, businesses have strong economic motivation to keep data to reuse for the same or similar purposes. But there is a limit to its usefulness.

For instance, as firms like Netflix and Amazon parlay customer purchases, browsing, and reviews into recommendations of new products, they can be tempted to use the records many times over for many years. With that in mind, one might argue that as long as a firm isn't constrained by legal and regulatory limits like privacy laws, it ought to use digital records forever, or at least as long as economically possible. However, the reality is not so simple.

Most data loses some of its utility over time. In such circumstances, continuing to rely on old data doesn't just fail to add value; it actually destroys the value of fresher data. Take a book you bought ten years ago from Amazon, which may no longer reflect your interests. If Amazon uses the decade-old purchase record to recommend other books, you're less likely to buy those titles — or even care about subsequent recommendations the site might offer. As Amazon's recommendations are based on both outdated information and more recent, still valuable data, the presence of the old data diminishes the value of the newer data.

So the company has a huge incentive to use data only so long as it remains productive. It needs to continuously groom its troves and cull the information that has lost value. The challenge is knowing what data is no longer useful. Just basing that decision on time is rarely adequate. Hence, Amazon and others have built sophisticated models to help them separate useful from irrelevant data. For instance, if a customer looks at or buys a book that was recommended based on a previous purchase, e-commerce companies can infer that the older purchase still represents the customer's current preferences. That way they are able to score the usefulness of older data, and thus model more accurate "depreciation rates" for the information.

Not all data depreciates in value at the same pace or in the same way. This explains why some firms believe they need to keep data as long as possible, even if regulators or the public want it erased or anonymized after a period. For instance, Google has long resisted calls to delete users' full Internet Protocol addresses from old search queries. (Instead it erases only the final digits after nine months to quasi-anonymize the query. Thus, the company can still compare year-on-year data, such as for holiday shopping searches — but only on a regional basis, not down to the individual.) Also, knowing the location of searchers can help improve the relevance of results. For instance, if lots of people in New York search for Turkey — and click on sites related to the country, not the bird — the algorithm will rank those pages higher for others in New York. Even if the value of the data diminishes for some of its purposes, its option value may remain strong.

The value of data exhaust

The reuse of data can sometimes take a clever, hidden form. Web firms can capture data on all the things that users do, and then treat each discrete interaction as a signal to use as feedback for personalizing the site, improving a service, or creating an entirely new digital product. We see a piquant illustration of this in a tale of two spell checks.

Over the course of twenty years, Microsoft developed a robust spell checker for its Word software. It worked by comparing a frequently updated dictionary of correctly spelled terms against the stream of characters the users typed. The dictionary established what were known words; the system would treat close variants that weren't in the dictionary as misspellings that it would then correct. Because of the effort needed to compile and update the dictionary,

Microsoft Word's spell check was available only for the most common languages. It cost the company millions of dollars to create and maintain.

Now consider Google. It arguably has the world's most complete spell checker, in basically every living language. The system is constantly improving and adding new words — the incidental outcome of people using the search engine every day. Mistype "iPad"? It's in there. "Obamacare"? Got it.

Moreover, Google seemingly obtained its spell checker for free, reusing the misspellings that are typed into the company's search engine among the three billion queries it handles every day. A clever feedback loop instructs the system what word users actually meant to type. Users sometimes explicitly "tell" Google the answer when it poses the question at the top of the results page — "Did you mean *epidemiology?*" — by clicking on that to start a new search with the correct term. Or the web page where users go implicitly signals the correct spelling, since it's probably more highly correlated with the correctly spelled word than with the incorrect one. (This is more important than it may seem: As Google's spell check continually improved, people stopped bothering to type their searches correctly, since Google could process them well regardless.)

Google's spell-checking system shows that "bad," "incorrect," or "defective" data can still be very useful. Interestingly, Google wasn't the first to have this idea. Around 2000 Yahoo saw the possibility of creating a spell checker from users' mistyped queries. But the idea never went anywhere. Old search-query data was treated largely as rubbish. Likewise, Infoseek and Alta Vista, earlier popular search engines, each had the world's most comprehensive database of misspelled words in its day, but they didn't appreciate the value. Their systems, in a process that was invisible to users, treated typos as "related terms" and performed a search. But it was based on dictionaries that explicitly told the system what was correct, not on the living, breathing sum of user interactions.

Only Google recognized that the detritus of user interactions was actually gold dust that could be gathered up and forged into a shiny ingot. One of Google's top engineers estimated that its spell checker performs better than Microsoft's by at least an order of magnitude (though when pressed, he conceded he had not reliably measured this). And he scoffed at the idea that it was "free" to develop. The raw material — misspellings — might have come without a direct cost, but Google had probably spent a lot more than Microsoft to develop the system, he confessed with a broad smile.

The two companies' different approaches are extremely telling. Microsoft only saw the value of spell check for one purpose, word processing. Google, on the other hand, understood its deeper utility. The firm not only used the typos to develop the world's best and most up-to-date spell checker to improve search, but it applied the system to many other services, such as the "autocomplete" feature in search, Gmail, Google Docs, and even its translation system.

A term of art has emerged to describe the digital trail that people leave in their wake: "data exhaust." It refers to data that is shed as a byproduct of people's actions and movements in the world. For the Internet, it describes users' online interactions: where they click, how long they look at a page, where the mouse-cursor hovers, what they type, and more. Many companies design their systems so that they can harvest data exhaust and recycle it, to improve an existing service or to develop new ones. Google is the undisputed leader. It applies the principle of recursively "learning from the data" to many of its services. Every action a user performs is considered a signal to be analyzed and fed back into the system.

For example, Google is acutely aware of how many times people searched for a term as well as related ones, and of how often they clicked on a link but then returned to the search page unimpressed with what they found, only to search again. It knows whether they clicked on the eighth link on the first page or the first link on the eighth page — or if they abandoned the search altogether. The company may not have been the first to have this insight, but it implemented it with extraordinary effectiveness.

This information is highly valuable. If many users tend to click on a search result at the bottom of the results page, this suggests it is more relevant than those above it, and Google's ranking algorithm knows to automatically place it higher up on the page in subsequent searches. (And it does this for advertisements too.) "We like learning from large, 'noisy' datasets," chirps one Googler.

Data exhaust is the mechanism behind many services like voice recognition, spam filters, language translation, and much more. When users indicate to a voice-recognition program that it has misunderstood what they said, they in effect "train" the system to get better.

Many businesses are starting to engineer their systems to collect and use information in this way. In Facebook's early days, its first "data scientist," Jeff Hammerbacher (and among the people credited with coining the term), examined its rich trove of data exhaust. He and the team found that a big predictor that people would take an action (post content, click an icon, and so on) was whether they had seen their friends do the same thing. So Facebook redesigned its system to put greater emphasis on making friends' activities more visible, which sparked a virtuous circle of new contributions to the site.

The idea is spreading far beyond the Internet sector to any company that has a way to gather up user feedback. E-book readers, for example, capture massive amounts of data on the literary preferences and habits of the people who use them: how long they take to read a page or section, where they read, if they turn the page with barely a skim or close the book forever. The devices record each time users underline a passage or take notes in the margins. The ability to gather this kind of information transforms reading, long a solitary act, into a sort of communal experience.

Once aggregated, the data exhaust can tell publishers and authors things they could never know before in a quantifiable way: the likes, dislikes, and reading patterns of people. This information is commercially valuable. One can imagine e-book firms selling it to publishers to improve the content and structure of books. For instance, Barnes & Noble's analysis of data from its Nook e-book reader revealed that people tended to quit long nonfiction books midway through.

That discovery inspired the company to create a series called "Nook Snaps": short works on topical themes such as health and current affairs.

Or consider online education programs like Udacity, Coursera, and edX. They track the web interactions of students to see what works best pedagogically. Class sizes have been at the level of tens of thousands of students, producing extraordinary amounts of data. Professors can now see if a large percentage of students have rewatched a segment of a lecture, which might suggest they weren't clear on a certain point. In teaching a Coursera class on machine learning, the Stanford professor Andrew Ng noted that around 2,000 students got a particular homework question wrong—but produced the exact same incorrect answer. Clearly, they were all making the same error. But what was it?

With a little bit of investigation, he figured out that they were inverting two algebraic equations in an algorithm. So now, when other students make the same error, the system doesn't simply say they're wrong; it gives them a hint to check their math. The system applies big data, too, by analyzing every forum post that students have read and whether they complete their homework correctly to predict the probability that a student who has read a given post will produce correct results, as a way to determine which forum posts are most useful for students to read. These are things that were utterly impossible to know before, and which could change teaching and learning forever.

Data exhaust can be a huge competitive advantage for companies. It may also become a powerful barrier to entry against rivals. Consider: if a newly launched company devised an e-commerce site, social network, or search engine that was much better than today's leaders like Amazon, Google, or Facebook, it would have trouble competing not simply because of economies of scale and network effects or brand, but because so much of those leading firms' performance is due to the data exhaust they collect from customer interactions and incorporate back into the service. Could a new online education site have the know-how to compete with one that already has a gargantuan amount of data with which it can learn what works best?

The value of open data

Today we're likely to think of sites like Google and Amazon as the pioneers of big data, but of course governments were the original gatherers of information on a mass scale, and they still rival any private enterprise for the sheer volume of data they control. One difference from data holders in the private sector is that governments can often compel people to provide them with information, rather than having to persuade them to do so or offer them something in return. As a consequence, governments will continue to amass vast troves of data.

The lessons of big data apply as much to the public sector as to commercial entities: government data's value is latent and requires innovative analysis to unleash. But despite their special position in capturing information, governments have often been ineffective at using it. Recently the idea has gained prominence that the best way to extract the value of government data is to give the private sector and society in general access to try. There is a principle behind this as well. When the state gathers data, it does so on behalf of its citizens, and thus it ought to provide access to society (except in a limited number of cases, such as when doing so might harm national security or the privacy rights of others).

This idea has led to countless "open government data" initiatives around the globe. Arguing that governments are only custodians of the information they collect, and that the private sector and society will be more innovative, advocates of open data call on official bodies to publicly release data for purposes both civic and commercial. To work, of course, the data must be in a standardized, machine-readable form so it can be easily processed. Otherwise, the information might be considered public only in name.

The idea of open government data got a big boost when President Barack Obama, on his first full day in office on January 21, 2009, issued a presidential memorandum ordering the heads of federal agencies to release as much data as possible. "In the face of doubt, openness prevails," he instructed. It was a remarkable declaration, particularly when compared with the attitude of his predecessor, who had instructed agencies to do precisely the opposite. Obama's order prompted the creation of a website called data.gov, a repository of openly accessible information from the federal government. The site mushroomed from 47 datasets in 2009 to nearly 450,000 across 172 agencies by its third anniversary in July 2012.

Even in reticent Britain, where a lot of government information has been locked up by Crown Copyright and has been difficult and costly to license to use (such as postal codes for e-commerce companies), there has been substantial progress. The UK government has issued rules to encourage open information and supported the creation of an Open Data Institute co-directed by Tim Berners-Lee, the inventor of the World Wide Web, to promote novel uses of open data and ways to free it from the state's grip.

The European Union has also announced open-data initiatives that could soon become continent-wide. Countries elsewhere, such as Australia, Brazil, Chile, and Kenya, have issued and implemented open-data strategies. Below the national level, a growing number of cities and municipalities around the world, too, have embraced open data, as have international organizations such as the World Bank, which has made available hundreds of previously restricted datasets of economic and social indicators.

In parallel, communities of web developers and visionary thinkers have formed around the data to figure out ways to get the most from it, such as Code for America and the Sunlight Foundation in the United States and the Open Knowledge Foundation in Britain.

An early example of the possibilities of open data comes from a website called FlyOnTime.us. Visitors to the site can interactively find out (among many other correlations) how likely it is that inclement weather will delay flights at a particular airport. The website combines flight and weather information from official data sources that are freely available and accessible through the Internet. It was developed by open-data advocates to show the usefulness of information amassed by the federal government. Even the site's software code is open-source, so others can learn from it and reuse it.

FlyOnTime.us lets the data do the talking, and it often says surprising things. One can see that for flights from Boston to New York's
LaGuardia Airport, travelers need to be prepared for delays twice
as long for fog than for snow. This probably isn't what most people
would have guessed as they milled about the departure lounge; snow
would have seemed like a bigger reason for a delay. But it is the sort
of insight that big data makes possible, when one crunches historical
flight-delay data from the Bureau of Transportation with current airport information from the Federal Aviation Administration, alongside
past weather reports from the National Oceanic and Atmospheric
Administration and real-time conditions from the National Weather
Service. FlyOnTime.us highlights how an entity that does not collect
or control information flows, like a search engine or big retailer, can
still obtain and use data to create value.

Valuing the priceless

Whether open to the public or locked away in corporate vaults, data's
value is hard to measure. Consider the events of Friday, May 18, 2012.
On that day, Facebook's 28-year-old founder Mark Zuckerberg sym-
bolically rang NASDAQ's opening bell from the company's headquarters in Menlo Park, California. The world's biggest social network —
which boasted around one out of every ten people on the planet as a
member — began its new life as a public company. The stock immediately jumped 11 percent, as many new technology stocks do on their
first day of trading. However, then something odd happened. Facebook shares began to fall. It didn't help that there was a technical
glitch with NASDAQ's computers that temporarily halted trading. A
bigger problem was afoot. Sensing trouble, the stock's underwriters,
led by Morgan Stanley, actually propped up the listing so that it would
stay above its issue price.

The evening before, Facebook's banks had priced the company at
$38 per share, which translated into a $104 billion valuation. (That,
by way of comparison, was roughly the market capitalizations of Boeing, General Motors, and Dell Computers combined.) What was Face-

book actually worth? In its audited financial accounts for 2011, with which investors sized up the company, Facebook reported assets of $6.3 billion. That represented the value of its computer hardware, office equipment, and other physical stuff. As for the book value placed on the vast stores of information that Facebook held in its corporate vault? Basically zero. It wasn't included, even though the company is almost nothing *but* data.

The situation gets odder. Doug Laney, vice president of research at Gartner, a market research firm, crunched the numbers during the period before the initial public offering (IPO) and reckoned that Facebook had collected 2.1 trillion pieces of "monetizable content" between 2009 and 2011, such as "likes," posted material, and comments. Compared against its IPO valuation, this means that each item, considered as a discrete data point, had a value of about five cents. Another way of looking at it is that every Facebook user was worth around $100, since users are the source of the information that Facebook collects.

How to explain the vast divergence between Facebook's worth under accounting standards ($6.3 billion) and what the market initially valued it at ($104 billion)? There is no good way to do so. Rather, there is widespread agreement that the current method of determining corporate worth, by looking at a company's "book value" (that is, mostly, the worth of its cash and physical assets), no longer adequately reflects the true value. In fact, the gap between book value and "market value" — what the company would fetch on the stock market or if it were bought outright — has been growing for decades. The U.S. Senate even held hearings in the year 2000 about modernizing the financial reporting rules, which emerged in the 1930s when information-based businesses scarcely existed. The issue affects more than just a company's balance sheet: the inability to properly value corporate worth arguably produces business risk and market volatility.

The difference between a company's book value and its market value is accounted for as "intangible assets." It has grown from around 40 percent of the value of publicly traded companies in the United States in the mid-1980s to three-fourths of their value at the dawn of the new millennium. This is a hefty divergence. These intangible assets are considered to include brand, talent, and strategy — anything that's not physical and part of the formal financial-accounting system. But increasingly, intangible assets are coming to mean the data that companies hold and use, too.

Ultimately, what this shows is that there is currently no obvious way to value data. The day Facebook's shares opened, the gap between its formal assets and its unrecorded intangible value was nearly $100 billion. This is ludicrous. Yet gaps like this must and will close as companies find ways to record the value of their data assets on their balance sheets.

Baby steps in this direction are under way. A senior executive at one of America's largest wireless operators confided that the carrier recognized the immense value of its data and studied whether to treat it as a corporate asset in formal accounting terms. But as soon as the company's lawyers heard about the initiative, they stopped it in its tracks. Putting the data on the books may make the firm legally liable for it, the legal eagles argued, which they thought was not such a good idea.

Meanwhile, investors will also start to take notice of the option value of data. Share prices may swell for companies that have data or can collect it easily, while others in less fortunate positions may see their market valuations shrink. The data does not have to formally show up on the balance sheets for this to happen. Markets and investors will price these intangible assets into their valuations — albeit with difficulty, as the seesawing of Facebook's share price in its first few months attests. But as accounting quandaries and liability concerns are alleviated, it is almost certain that the value of data will show up on corporate balance sheets and emerge as a new asset class.

How will data be valued? Calculating its worth will no longer mean simply adding up what's gained from its primary use. Yet if most of data's value is latent and derived from unknown future secondary uses, it is not immediately clear how one might go about estimating it. This resembles the difficulties of pricing financial derivatives prior to the development of the Black-Scholes equation in the 1970s, or the difficulty in valuing patents, where auctions, exchanges, private sales, licensing, and lots of litigation are slowly creating a market for knowledge. If nothing else, putting a price tag on data's option value certainly represents a rich opportunity for the financial sector.

One way to start is to look at the different strategies data holders apply to extract value. The most obvious possibility is for the firm's own use. It is unlikely, however, that a company is capable of uncovering all of the data's latent value. More ambitiously, therefore, one could license the data to third parties. In the big-data age, many data holders may want to opt for an arrangement that pays them a percentage of the value extracted from the data rather than a fixed fee. It is similar to how publishers pay a percentage of book, music, or movie sales as royalties to authors and performers. It also resembles intellectual property deals in biotechnology, where licensors may demand royalties on any subsequent inventions that spring from their technology. This way all parties have an incentive to maximize the value gained from data's reuse.

However, because the licensee may fail to extract the full option value, data holders may not want to grant access to their troves exclusively. Rather, "data promiscuity" may become the norm. That way data holders can hedge their bets.

A number of marketplaces have sprung up to experiment with ways to price data. DataMarket, founded in Iceland in 2008, provides access to free datasets from other sources, such as the United Nations, the World Bank, and Eurostat, and earns revenue by reselling data from commercial providers like market research firms. Other startups have tried to be information middlemen, platforms for third parties to share their data either for free or for a fee. The idea is to let anyone sell the data they happen to have in their databases, just as eBay provided a platform for people to sell the stuff in their attic. Import.io encourages firms to license their data that might otherwise get "scraped" from the Net and used for free. And Factual, founded by a former Googler, Gil Elbaz, is making available datasets it takes the time to compile itself.

Microsoft has entered the arena with the Windows Azure Marketplace. It aims to focus on high-quality data and oversee what is on offer, similar to the way Apple supervises the offerings in its app store. In Microsoft's vision, a marketing executive working on an Excel spreadsheet may want to cross-tabulate her internal company data against GDP growth forecasts from an economic consultancy. So she clicks to buy the data then and there, and it instantly flows into her columns on the screen.

So far there's no telling how the valuation models will play out. But what's certain is that economies are starting to form around data — and that many new players stand to benefit, while a number of old ones will probably find a surprising new lease on life. "Data is a platform," in the words of Tim O'Reilly, a technology publisher and savant of Silicon Valley, since it is a building block for new goods and business models.

The crux of data's worth is its seemingly unlimited potential for reuse: its option value. Collecting the information is crucial but not enough, since most of data's value lies in its use, not its mere possession. In the next chapter, we examine how the data is actually being used and the big-data businesses that are emerging.

7

IMPLICATIONS

In 2011 a clever startup in Seattle called Decide.com opened its online doors with fantastically bold ambitions. It wanted to be a price-prediction engine for zillions of consumer products. But it planned to start relatively modestly: with every possible tech gadget, from mobile phones and flat-screen televisions to digital cameras. Its computers sucked down data feeds from e-commerce sites and scoured the Web for any other price and product information they could find.

Prices on the Web constantly change throughout the day, dynamically updating based on countless, intricate factors. So the company needed to collect pricing data at all times. It isn't just big data but "big text" too, since the system had to analyze words to recognize when a product was being discontinued or a newer model was about to launch, information that consumers ought to know and that affects prices.

A year later, Decide.com was analyzing four million products using over 25 billion price observations. It identified oddities about retailing that people had never been able to "see" before, like the fact that prices might temporarily increase for older models once new ones are introduced. Most people would purchase the older one figuring it would be cheaper, but depending on when they clicked "buy," they might pay more. As online stores increasingly use automated pricing systems, Decide.com can spot unnatural, algorithmic price spikes and warn consumers to wait. The company's predictions, according to its internal measurements, are accurate 77 percent of the time and provide buyers with average potential savings of around $100 per product. So confident is the company, that in cases where its predictions prove incorrect, Decide.com will reimburse the price difference to paying members of the service.

On the surface, Decide.com sounds like many promising startups that aim to harness information in new ways and earn an honest dollar for their effort. What makes Decide.com special isn't the data: the company relies on information it licenses from e-commerce sites and scrapes off the Web, where it is free for the taking. It also isn't technical expertise: the company doesn't do anything so complex that the only engineers in the world capable of pulling it off are the ones at its own office. Rather, although collecting the data and technical skills are important, the essence of what makes Decide.com special is the idea: the company has a "big-data mindset." It spied an opportunity and recognized that certain data could be mined to reveal valuable secrets. And if there seem to be echoes between Decide.com and the airfare prediction site Farecast, there is good reason: each is the brainchild of Oren Etzioni.

In the previous chapter we noted that data is becoming a new source of value in large part because of what we termed its option value, as it's put to novel purposes. The emphasis was on firms that collect data. Now our regard shifts to the companies that use data, and how they fit into the information value chain. We'll consider what this means for organizations and for individuals, both in their careers and in their everyday lives.

Three types of big-data companies have cropped up, which can be differentiated by the value they offer. Think of it as the data, the skills, and the ideas.

First is the data. These are the companies that have the data or at the least have access to it. But perhaps that is not what they are in the business for. Or, they don't necessarily have the right skills to extract its value or to generate creative ideas about what is worth unleashing. The best example is Twitter, which obviously enjoys a massive stream of data flowing through its servers but turned to two independent firms to license it to others to use.

Second are skills. They are often the consultancies, technology vendors, and analytics providers who have special expertise and do the work, but probably do not have the data themselves nor the ingenuity to come up with the most innovative uses for it. In the case of Walmart and Pop-Tarts, for example, the retailer turned to the specialists at Teradata, a data-analytics firm, to help tease out the insights.

Third is the big-data mindset. For certain firms, the data and the know-how are not the main reasons for their success. What sets them apart is that their founders and employees have unique ideas about ways to tap data to unlock new forms of value. An example is Pete Warden, the geeky co-founder of Jetpac, which makes travel recommendations based on the photos users upload to the site.

So far, the first two of these elements get the most attention: the skills, which today are scarce, and the data, which seems abundant. A new profession has emerged in recent years, the "data scientist," which combines the skills of the statistician, software programmer, infographics designer, and storyteller. Instead of squinting into a microscope to unlock a mystery of the universe, the data scientist peers into databases to make a discovery. The McKinsey Global Institute proffers dire predictions about the dearth of data scientists now and in the future (which today's data scientists like to cite to feel special and to pump up their salaries).

Hal Varian, Google's chief economist, famously calls statistician the "sexiest" job around. "If you want to be successful, you want to be complementary and scarce to something that is ubiquitous and cheap," he says. "Data is so widely available and so strategically important that the scarce thing is the knowledge to extract wisdom from it. That is why statisticians, and database managers and machine learning people, are really going to be in a fantastic position."

However, all the focus on the skills and the downplaying of the importance of the data may prove to be short-lived. As the industry evolves, the paucity of personnel will be overcome as the skills that Varian vaunts become commonplace. What's more, there is a mistaken belief that just because there is so much data around, it is free for the taking or its value is meager. In fact, the data is the critical ingredient. To appreciate why, consider the different parts of the big-data value chain, and how they are likely to change over time. To start, let's examine each category — data holder, data specialist, and big-data mindset — in turn.

The big-data value chain

The primary substance of big data is the information itself. So it makes sense to look first at the data holders. They may not have done the original collection, but they control access to information and use it themselves or license it to others who extract its value. For instance, ITA Software, a large airline reservation network (after Amadeus, Travelport, and Sabre), provided data to Farecast for its airfare predictions, but did not do the analysis itself. Why not? ITA perceived its business as using the data for the purpose for which it was designed — selling airline tickets — not for ancillary uses. As such, its core competencies were different. Moreover, it would have had to work around Etzioni's patent.

The company also chose not to exploit the data because of where it sat on the information value chain. "ITA shied away from projects that involved making commercial use of data too closely related to airline revenue," recalls Carl de Marcken, a co-founder of ITA Software and its former chief technology officer. "ITA had special access to such data, required to provide ITA's service, and couldn't afford to jeopardize that." Instead, it delicately stayed an arm's length away by licensing the data but not using it. The majority of the data's secondary value went to Farecast: to its customers in the form of cheaper tickets, and to its employees and owners from the income Farecast earned off ads, commissions, and eventually the sale of the firm.

Some firms have shrewdly positioned themselves in the center of information flows so they can achieve scale and capture value from data. That's been the case in the credit card industry in the United

States. For years, the high cost of fighting fraud led many small and midsized banks to avoid issuing their own credit cards and to turn their card operations over to larger financial institutions, which had the size and scale to invest in the technology. Firms like Capital One and Bank of America's MBNA lapped up the business. But the smaller banks now regret that decision, because having shed the card operations deprives them of data on spending patterns that would let them know more about their customers so they could sell them tailored services.

Instead, the larger banks and the card issuers like Visa and MasterCard seem to be in the sweet spot of the information value chain. By serving many banks and merchants, they can see more transactions over their networks and use them to make inferences about consumer behavior. Their business model shifts from simply processing payments to collecting data. The question then is what they do with it.

MasterCard could license the data to third parties who would extract the value, as ITA did, but the company prefers to do the analysis itself. A division called MasterCard Advisors aggregates and analyzes 65 billion transactions from 1.5 billion cardholders in 210 countries in order to divine business and consumer trends. Then it sells that information to others. It discovered, among other things, that if people fill up their gas tanks at around four o'clock in the afternoon, they're quite likely to spend between $35 and $50 in the next hour at a grocery store or restaurant. A marketer might use that insight to print out coupons for a nearby supermarket on the back of gas-station receipts around that time of day.

As a middleman to information flows, MasterCard is in a prime position to collect data and capture its value. One can imagine a future when card companies forgo their commissions on transactions, processing them for free in return for access to more data, and earn income from selling highly sophisticated analytics based on it.

The second category consists of data specialists: companies with the expertise or technologies to carry out complex analysis. MasterCard chose to do this in house, and some firms migrate between categories. But lots of others turn to specialists. For example, the consultancy Accenture works with firms in many industries to deploy advanced wireless-sensor technologies and to analyze the data the sensors collect. In a pilot project with the city of St. Louis, Missouri, Accenture installed wireless sensors in a score of public buses to monitor their engines to predict breakdowns or determine the optimal time to do regular maintenance. It lowered the cost of ownership by as much as 10 percent. Just one finding — that the city could delay a scheduled part change from every 200,000–250,000 miles to 280,000 miles — saved more than a thousand dollars per vehicle. The client, not the consultancy, reaped the value of the data.

In the realm of medical data, we see another striking example of how outside technology firms can provide useful services. The Med-Star Washington Hospital Center in Washington, D.C., working with Microsoft Research and using Microsoft's Amalga software, analyzed several years of its anonymized medical records — patient demographics, tests, diagnoses, treatments, and more — for ways to reduce readmission rates and infections. These are some of the costliest parts of healthcare, so anything that can lower the rates means huge savings.

The technique uncovered some surprising correlations. One result was a list of all conditions that increased the chances that a discharged patient would return within a month. Some are well known and have no easy solution. A patient with congestive heart failure is likely to be back: it's a hard condition to treat. But the system also spotted another unexpected top predictor: the patient's mental state. The probability that a person would be readmitted within a month of discharge increased markedly if the initial complaint contained words that suggested mental distress, such as "depression."

Although this correlation says nothing to establish causality, it nevertheless suggests that a post-discharge intervention that addresses patients' mental health might improve their physical health too, reducing readmissions and lowering medical costs. This finding, which a machine sifted out of a vast trove of data, is something a person studying the data might never have spotted. Microsoft didn't control the data, which belonged to the hospital. And it didn't have an astonishing idea; that wasn't what was required here. Instead, it offered the software tool, the Amalga software, to spot the insight.

The firms that are big-data holders rely on specialists to extract value from the data. But despite the high praise and chic job titles like "data ninja," the life of technical experts is not always as glamorous as it may seem. They toil in the diamond mines of big data, taking home a pleasant paycheck, but they hand over the gems they unearth to those who have the data.

The third group is made up of companies and individuals with a big-data mindset. Their strength is that they see opportunities before others do — even if they lack the data or the skills to act upon those opportunities. Indeed, perhaps it is precisely because, as outsiders, they lack these things that their minds are free of imaginary prison bars: they see what is possible rather than being limited by a sense of what is feasible.

Bradford Cross personifies what it means to have a big-data mindset. In August 2009, when he was in his mid-twenties, he and some friends created FlightCaster.com. Like FlyOnTime.us, FlightCaster predicted if a flight in the United States was likely to be delayed. To make the predictions, it analyzed every flight over the previous ten years, matched against historic and current weather data.

Interestingly, the data holders themselves couldn't do that. None had the incentive — or the regulatory mandate — to use the data in this way. In fact, if the data sources — the U.S. Bureau of Transportation Statistics, the Federal Aviation Administration, and the National Weather Service — had dared to predict commercial flight delays, Congress would have probably held hearings and bureaucrats' heads would have rolled. And the airlines couldn't do it — or wouldn't. They benefit from keeping their middling performance as obscure as possible. Instead, achieving it took a bunch of engineers in hoodies. In fact, FlightCaster's predictions were so uncannily accurate that even airline employees started using them: airlines don't want to announce delays until the very last minute, so although they're the ultimate source of the information, they aren't the most timely source.

Because of its big-data mindset — its inspired realization that publicly available data could be processed in a way that offered answers that millions of people would crave — Cross's FlightCaster was a first mover, but just barely. In the same month that FlightCaster was launched, the geeks behind FlyOnTime.us began cobbling together open data to build their site. The advantage that FlightCaster enjoyed would soon ebb. In January 2011 Cross and his partners sold the firm to Next Jump, a company that manages corporate-discount programs using big-data techniques.

Then Cross turned his sights on another aging industry where he spotted a niche that an outside innovator could enter: the news media. His startup company Prismatic aggregates and ranks content from across the Web on the basis of text analysis, user preferences, social-network-related popularity, and big-data analytics. Importantly, the system does not make a big distinction between a teenager's blog post, a corporate website, and an article in the *Washington Post:* if the content is deemed relevant and popular (by how widely it is viewed and how much it is shared), it appears at the top of the screen.

As a service, Prismatic is a recognition of the ways a younger generation is interacting with the media. For them the source of information has lost its primal importance. This is a humbling reminder to the high priests of mainstream media that the public is in aggregate more knowledgeable than they are, and that cufflinked journalists must compete against bloggers in their bathrobes. Yet the key point is that it is hard to imagine that Prismatic would have emerged from within the media industry itself, even though it collects lots of information. The regulars around the bar of the National Press Club never thought to reuse online data about media consumption. Nor might the analytics specialists in Armonk, New York, or Bangalore, India, have harnessed the information in this way. It took Cross, a louche outsider with disheveled hair and a slacker's drawl, to presume that by using data he could tell the world what it ought pay attention to better than the editors of the *New York Times.*

The notion of the big-data mindset, and the role of a creative out-sider with a brilliant idea, are not unlike what happened at the dawn of e-commerce in the mid-1990s, when the pioneers were unencum-bered by the entrenched thinking or institutional restraints of older industries. Thus a hedge-fund quant, not Barnes & Noble, founded an online bookstore (Amazon's Jeff Bezos). A software developer, not Sotheby's, built an auction site (eBay's Pierre Omidyar). Today the entrepreneurs with the big-data mindset often don't have the data when they start. But because of this, they also don't have the vested interests or financial disincentives that might prevent them from un-leashing their ideas.

As we've seen, there are cases where one firm combines many of these big-data characteristics. Etzioni and Cross may have had their killer ideas before others did, but they had the skills as well. The fac-tory hands at Teradata and Accenture don't just punch a clock; they too are known to have a great notion from time to time. Still, the ar-chetypes are helpful as a way to appreciate the roles that different firms play. Today's pioneers of big data often come from disparate backgrounds and cross-apply their data skills in a wide variety of ar-eas. A new generation of angel investors and entrepreneurs is emerg-ing, notably from among ex-Googlers and the so-called PayPal Mafia (the firm's former leaders like Peter Thiel, Reid Hoffman, and Max Levchin). They, along with a handful of academic computer scien-tists, are some of the biggest backers of today's data-infused startups.

The creative vision of individuals and firms in the big data food-chain helps us reassess the worth of companies. For instance, Sales-force.com may not simply be a useful platform for firms to host their corporate applications: it is also well placed to unleash value from the data that flows atop its infrastructure. Mobile phone companies, as we saw in the previous chapter, collect a gargantuan amount of data but are often culturally blinded to its worth. They could, however, li-cense it to others who are able to extract novel value from it — just as Twitter decided to grant the rights to license its data to two outside companies.

Some fortunate enterprises straddle the different domains as a matter of conscious strategy. Google collects data like search-query typos, has the bright idea to use it to create a spell checker, and enjoys the in-house skills to execute the idea brilliantly. With many of its other activities, too, Google benefits from vertical integration in the big-data value chain, where it occupies all three positions at once. At the same time, Google also makes some of its data available to others via application programming interfaces (APIs) so it can be reused and further value can be added. One example is Google's maps, which are used throughout the Web by everyone from real estate agencies to government websites for free (though heavily visited websites have to pay).

Amazon, too, has the mindset, the expertise, and the data. In fact, the company approached its business model in that order, which is the inverse of the norm. It initially only had the idea for its celebrated recommendation system. Its stock market prospectus in 1997 described "collaborative filtering" before Amazon knew how it would work in practice or had enough data to make it useful.

Both Google and Amazon span the categories, but their strategies differ. When Google first sets out to collect any sort of data, it has secondary uses in mind. Its Street View cars, as we have seen, collected GPS information not just for its map service but also to train self-driving cars. By contrast, Amazon is more focused on the primary use of data and only taps the secondary uses as a marginal bonus. Its recommendation system, for example, relies on clickstream data as a signal, but the company hasn't used the information to do extraordinary things like predict the state of the economy or flu outbreaks.

Despite Amazon's Kindle e-book readers' being capable of showing whether a certain page has been heavily annotated and underlined by users, the firm does not sell that information to authors and publishers. Marketers would love to learn which passages are most popular and use that knowledge to sell books better. Authors might like to know where in their lofty tomes most readers give up, and could use that information to improve their work. Publishers might spot themes that herald the next big book. But Amazon seems to leave the field of data to lie fallow.

Harnessed shrewdly, big data can transform companies' business models and the ways that long-standing partners interact. In one stunning case, a large European carmaker reshaped its commercial relationship with a parts supplier by harnessing usage data that the component manufacturer lacked. (Because we learned this example on a background basis from one of the principal firms that crunched the data, we regrettably cannot disclose the company names.)

Cars today are stuffed with chips, sensors, and software that upload performance data to the carmakers' computers when the vehicle is serviced. Typical mid-tier vehicles now have some 40 microprocessors; all of a car's electronics account for one-third of its costs. This makes the cars fitting successors to the ships Maury called "floating observatories." The ability to gather data about how car parts are actually used on the road — and to reincorporate this data to improve them — is turning out to be a big competitive advantage for the firms that can get hold of the information.

Working with an outside analytics firm, the carmaker was able to spot that a sensor in the fuel tank made by a German supplier was doing terribly, producing a score of erroneous alarms for every valid one. The company could have handed that information to the supplier and requested the adjustment. In a more gentlemanly era of business it might have done just that. But the manufacturer had been spending a fortune on its analytics program. It wanted to use this information to recoup some of its investment.

The company pondered its options. Should it sell the data? How would the info be valued? What if the supplier balked, and the carmaker was stuck with a poorly functioning part? And it knew that if it handed over the information, similar parts that went into its competitors' vehicles would also be improved. Ensuring that the improvement would only benefit its own vehicles seemed a shrewder move. In the end, the auto manufacturer came up with a novel idea. It found a way to improve the part with modified software, received a patent on the technique, then sold the patent to the supplier — and earned a pretty penny in the process.

The new data intermediaries

Who holds the most value in the big-data value chain? Today the answer would appear to be those who have the mindset, the innovative ideas. As we saw from the dotcom era, those with a first-mover advantage can really prosper. But this advantage may not hold for very long. As the era of big data moves forward, others will adopt the mindset and the advantage of the early pioneers will diminish, relatively speaking.

Perhaps, then, the crux of the value is really in the skills? After all, a gold mine isn't worth anything if you can't extract the gold. Yet the history of computing suggests otherwise. Today expertise in database management, data science, analytics, machine-learning algorithms, and the like are in hot demand. But over time, as big data becomes more a part of everyday life, as the tools get better and easier to use, and as more people acquire the expertise, the value of the skills will also diminish in relative terms. Similarly, computer programming ability became more common between the 1960s and 1980s. Today, offshore outsourcing firms have reduced the value of programming even more; what was once the paragon of technical acumen is now an engine of development for the world's poor. This isn't to say that big-data expertise is unimportant. But it isn't the most crucial source of value, since one can bring it in from the outside.

Today, in big data's early stages, the ideas and the skills seem to hold the greatest worth. But eventually most value will be in the data itself. This is because we'll be able to do more with the information, and also because data holders will better appreciate the potential value of the asset they possess. As a result, they'll probably hold it more tightly than ever, and charge outsiders a high price for access. To continue with the metaphor of the gold mine: the gold itself will matter most.

However, there is an important dimension to data holders' long-term rise that deserves noting. In some cases, "data intermediaries" will emerge that are able to collect data from multiple sources, aggregate it, and do innovative things with it. The data holders will let these intermediaries perform this role because some of the data's value can only be reaped through them.

An example is Inrix, a traffic-analysis firm based outside Seattle. It compiles real-time geo-location data from 100 million vehicles in North America and Europe. The data comes from cars by BMW, Ford, and Toyota, among others, as well as from commercial fleets like taxis and delivery vans. It also obtains data from individual drivers' mobile phones (its free smartphone apps are important here: users get traffic info, Inrix gets their coordinates in return). Inrix combines this information with data on historical traffic patterns, weather, and other things like local events to predict how traffic will flow. The product from its data assembly line is relayed to cars' navigation systems, and is used by governments and commercial fleets.

Inrix is the quintessential independent data intermediary. It collects its information from numerous rival car companies and thereby generates a product more valuable than any of them could have achieved on its own. Each carmaker may have a few million data points from its vehicles on the road. Though it could use the data to predict traffic flows, those predictions wouldn't be very accurate or complete. The predictive quality improves as the amount of data increases. Also, the car companies may not have the skills: their competence is mostly bending metal, not pondering Poisson distributions. So they all have an incentive to turn to a third party to do the job. Besides, though traffic prediction is important to drivers, it hardly influences whether or not someone buys a particular car. So the competitors don't mind joining forces in this way.

Of course, firms in many industries have shared information before, notably insurance underwriters' laboratories and networked sectors like banking, energy, and telecoms, where exchanging information is critical to avoid problems and regulators at times require it.

Market research firms have aggregated industry data for decades, as have companies for specialized tasks like the auditing of newspaper circulation. For some trade associations, it is the core of what they do.

The difference today is that the data is now raw material entering the marketplace; an asset independent of what it had previously aimed to measure. For example, Inrix's information is more useful than it might seem on the surface. Its traffic analysis is used to measure the health of local economies because it can offer insights about unemployment, retail sales, and leisure activities. When the U.S. economic recovery started to sputter in 2011, signs of it were picked up by traffic analysis despite politicians' denials that it was happening: rush hours had become less crowded, suggesting more unemployment. Also, Inrix has sold its data to an investment fund that uses traffic patterns around a major retailer's stores as a proxy for its sales, which the fund uses to trade the company's shares before its quarterly earning announcements. More cars in the area correlate with better sales.

Other such intermediaries are cropping up within the big-data value chain. An early player was Hitwise, later bought by Experian, which struck deals with Internet service providers to collect their clickstream data in return for some extra income. The data was licensed for a small fixed fee rather than a percentage of the value it produced. Hitwise captured the majority of the value as the intermediary. Another example is Quantcast, which measures online traffic to websites to help them know more about their visitors' demographics and usage patterns. It gives away an online tool so sites can track visits; in return Quantcast gets to see the data, which enables it to improve its ad targeting.

These new intermediaries have identified lucrative niche positions without threatening the business models of the data holders from which they get their data. For the moment, Internet advertising is one of these niches, since that's where the most data is, and where there's a burning need to mine it to target ads. But as more of the world becomes datafied and more industries realize that their core business is learning from data, these independent information intermediaries will emerge elsewhere as well.

Some of the intermediaries may not be commercial enterprises, but nonprofits. For example, the Health Care Cost Institute was created in 2012 by a handful of America's biggest health insurers. Their combined data amounted to five billion (anonymized) claims involving 33 million people. Sharing the records let the firms spot trends that they might not have been able to see in their smaller individual datasets. Among the first findings was that U.S. medical costs had increased three times faster than inflation in 2009–10, but with pronounced differences at a granular level: emergency-room prices grew by 11 percent while nursing facilities' prices actually declined. Clearly health insurers would never have handed over their prized data to anything but a nonprofit intermediary. A nonprofit's motives are less suspect, and the organization can be designed with transparency and accountability in mind.

The variety of big-data firms shows how the value of information is shifting. In the case of Decide.com, the price data is provided by partner websites on a revenue-sharing basis. Decide.com earns commissions when people buy goods through the site, but the companies that supplied the data also get a piece of the action. This suggests a maturation in the way industry works with data: In the past, ITA didn't receive any commissions on the data it supplied Farecast, only a basic license fee. Now data providers are able to strike more appealing terms. For Etzioni's next startup, one can presume that he'll try to supply the data himself, since the value has migrated from the expertise to the idea and is now moving to the data.

Business models are being upended as the value shifts to those who control the data. The European carmaker that struck the intellectual property deal with its supplier had a strong in-house data-analysis team but needed to work with an outside technology vendor to uncover insights from the data. The tech firm was paid for its work, but the carmaker kept the bulk of the profits. Sniffing opportunity, however, the tech company has tweaked its business model to share some of the risk and reward with clients. It has experimented with working for a lower fee in return for sharing some of the wealth that its analysis unleashes. (As for auto-parts suppliers, it is probably safe to say that in the future they all will want to add measurement sensors to their products, or insist on access to performance data as a standard part of the sales contract, in order to continually improve their components.)

As for intermediaries, their lives are complicated because they need to convince companies of the value in sharing. For instance, Inrix has started to collect more than just geo-loco information. In 2012 it ran a trial of analyzing where and when cars' automatic braking systems (ABS) kicked in, for a carmaker that designed its telemetry system to collect the information in real time. The idea is that frequent triggering of the ABS on a particular stretch of road may imply that conditions there are dangerous, and that drivers should consider alternative routes. So with this data Inrix could recommend not only the shortest route but the safest one as well.

Yet the carmaker doesn't plan to share this data with others. Instead, it insists that Inrix deploy the system in its cars exclusively. The value of trumpeting the feature is seen to outweigh the gain from aggregating its data with others' data to improve the system's overall accuracy. That said, Inrix believes that, in time, all carmakers will see the utility of aggregating all their data. As a data intermediary, Inrix has a strong incentive to cling to such optimism: its business is built entirely on access to multiple data sources.

Companies are also experimenting with different organizational forms in the business of big data. Inrix didn't stumble upon its business model as many startups do — its role as an intermediary was established by design. Microsoft, which owned the essential patents to the technology, figured that a small, independent firm — rather than a big company — might be perceived as more neutral, and could bring together industry rivals and get the most from its intellectual property. Similarly, the MedStar Washington Hospital Center that used Microsoft's Amalga software to analyze patient readmissions knew exactly what it was doing with its data: the Amalga system was originally the hospital's own in-house emergency-room software, called Azyxxi, which it sold in 2006 to Microsoft so that it could be better developed.

In 2010 UPS sold an in-house data-analysis unit, called UPS Logistics Technologies, to the private equity firm Thoma Bravo. Now operating as Roadnet Technologies, the unit is freer to do route analysis for more than one company. Roadnet collects data from many clients to provide an industry-wide benchmarking service used by UPS and its competitors alike. As UPS Logistics, it never would have persuaded its parent firm's rivals to hand over their datasets, explains Roadnet chief executive Len Kennedy. But after it became independent, UPS's competitors felt more comfortable supplying their data, and ultimately everyone benefited from the improved accuracy that aggregation brings.

Evidence that data itself, rather than skills or mindset, will come to be most valued can be found in numerous acquisitions in the big-data business. For example, in 2006 Microsoft rewarded Etzioni's big-data mindset by buying Farecast for around $110 million. But two years later Google paid $700 million to acquire Farecast's data supplier, ITA Software.

The demise of the expert

In the movie *Moneyball,* about how the Oakland A's became a winning baseball team by applying analytics and new types of metrics to the game, there is a delightful scene in which grizzled old scouts are sitting around a table discussing players. The audience can't help cringing, not simply because the scene exposes the way decisions are made devoid of data, but because we've all been in situations where "certainty" was based on sentiment rather than science.

"He's got a baseball body . . . a good face," says one scout.

"He's got a beautiful swing. When it connects, he drives it, it pops off the bat," chimes in a frail, gray-haired fellow wearing a hearing aid. "A lot of pop off the bat," another scout concurs.

A third man cuts the conversation short, declaring, "He's got an ugly girlfriend."

"What does that mean?" asks the scout leading the meeting.

"An ugly girlfriend means no confidence," the naysayer explains matter-of-factly.

"OK," says the leader, satisfied and ready to move on.

After spirited banter, a scout speaks up who had been silent: "This guy's got an attitude. An attitude is good. I mean, he's the guy, walks into a room, and his dick's already been there two minutes." Adds another: "He passes the eye-candy test. He's got the looks, he's ready to play the part. He just needs some playing time."

"I'm just sayin'," reiterates the naysayer, "his girlfriend's a six — at best!"

The scene perfectly depicts the shortcomings of human judgment. What passes for reasoned debate is really based on nothing concrete. Decisions about millions of dollars' worth of player contracts are made on gut instinct, absent of objective measures. Yes, it is just a film, but real life isn't much different. Similar empty reasoning is employed from Manhattan boardrooms to the Oval Office to coffee shops and kitchen tables everywhere else.

Moneyball, based on the book by Michael Lewis, tells the true story of Billy Beane, the Oakland A's general manager who threw out the century-old rulebook on how to value players in favor of a math-infused method that looks at the game from a new set of metrics. Out went time-honored stats like "batting average" and in came seemingly odd ways of thinking about the game like "on-base percentage." The data-driven approach revealed a dimension to the sport that had always been present but hidden amid the peanuts and Cracker Jack. It didn't matter how a player got on base, via a bouncy grounder or an ignoble walk, so long as he got on. When the data showed that stealing bases was inefficient, out went one of the most exciting, but least "productive," elements of the game.

Amid considerable controversy, Beane enshrined in the team's front office the method known as sabermetrics, a term coined by the sportswriter Bill James in reference to the Society for American

Baseball Research, which had until then been the province of a geeky subculture. Beane was challenging the dogma of the dugout, just as Galileo's heliocentric views had affronted the authority of the Catholic Church. Ultimately he led the long-suffering team to a first-place finish in the American League West in the 2002 season, including a 20-game winning streak. From then on, statisticians supplanted the scouts as the sport's savants. And lots of other teams scrambled to adopt sabermetrics themselves.

In the same spirit, the biggest impact of big data will be that data-driven decisions are poised to augment or overrule human judgment. In his book *Super Crunchers,* the Yale economist and law professor Ian Ayers argued that statistical analyses force people to reconsider their instincts. Through big data, this becomes even more essential. The subject-area expert, the substantive specialist, will lose some of his or her luster compared with the statistician and data analyst, who are unfettered by the old ways of doing things and let the data speak. This new cadre will rely on correlations without prejudgments and prejudice, just as Maury didn't take at face value what wizened skippers had to say about a certain passage over a pint at the pub, but trusted the aggregated data to reveal practical truths.

We are seeing the waning of subject-matter experts' influence in many areas. In media, the content that gets created and publicized on websites like Huffington Post, Gawker, and Forbes is regularly determined by data, not just the judgment of human editors. The data can reveal what people want to read about better than the instincts of seasoned journalists. The online education company Coursera uses data on what sections of a video lecture students replay to learn what material may have been unclear, and feeds the information back to teachers so they can improve. As we noted earlier, Jeff Bezos got rid of in-house book reviewers at Amazon when the data showed that algorithmic recommendations drove more sales.

This means that the skills necessary to succeed in the workplace are changing. It alters what employees are expected to bring to their organizations. Dr. McGregor, caring for premature babies in Ontario, doesn't need to be the wisest doctor at the hospital, or the world's foremost authority on neonatal care, to produce the best results for her patients. In fact, she is not a medical physician at all — she holds a PhD in computer science. But she avails herself of data amounting to more than a decade of patient-years, which the computer crunches and she parlays into recommendations for treatment.

As we've seen, the pioneers in big data often come from fields outside the domain where they make their mark. They are specialists in data analysis, artificial intelligence, mathematics, or statistics, and they apply those skills to specific industries. The winners of Kaggle competitions, the online platform for big-data projects, are typically new to the sector in which they produce successful results, explains Kaggle's chief executive Anthony Goldbloom. A British physicist developed near-winning algorithms to predict insurance claims and identify defective used cars. A Singaporean actuary led a competition to predict biological responses to chemical compounds. Meanwhile, at Google's machine-translation group, the engineers celebrate their translations of languages that no one in the office speaks. Similarly, statisticians at Microsoft's machine-translation unit relish trotting out an old quip: that the quality of translations increases whenever a linguist leaves the team.

To be sure, subject-area experts won't die out. But their supremacy will ebb. From now on, they must share the podium with the big-data geeks, just as princely causation must share the limelight with humble correlation. This transforms the way we value knowledge, because we tend to think that people with deep specialization are worth more than generalists — that fortune favors depth. Yet expertise is like exactitude: appropriate for a small-data world where one never has enough information, or the right information, and thus has to rely on intuition and experience to guide one's way. In such a world, experience plays a critical role, since it is the long accumulation of latent knowledge — knowledge that one can't transmit easily or learn from a book, or perhaps even be consciously aware of — that enables one to make smarter decisions.

But when you are stuffed silly with data, you can tap that instead, and to greater effect. Thus those who can analyze big data may see past the superstitions and conventional thinking not because they're smarter, but because they have the data. (And being outsiders, they are impartial about squabbles within the field that may narrow an expert's vision to whichever side of a squabble she's on.) This suggests that what it takes for an employee to be valuable to a company changes. What you need to know changes, whom you need to know changes, and so does what you need to study to prepare for professional life.

Mathematics and statistics, perhaps with a sprinkle of programming and network science, will be as foundational to the modern workplace as numeracy was a century ago and literacy before that. In the past, to be an excellent biologist one needed to know lots of other biologists. That hasn't changed entirely. Yet today big-data breadth matters too, not just subject-expertise depth. Solving a puzzling biological problem may be as likely to happen through an association with an astrophysicist or a data-visualization designer.

Video gaming is one industry where the lieutenants of big data have already elbowed their way to stand beside the generals of expertise, transforming the industry in the process. The video-game sector is big business, reaping more than the Hollywood box office annually worldwide. In the past, companies would design a game, release it, and hope it became a hit. On the basis of sales data, firms would either prepare a sequel or start a new project. Decisions over the pace of play and elements of the games like characters, plot, objects, and events were based on the creativity of the designers, who took their jobs with the same seriousness as Michelangelo painting the Sistine Chapel. It was art, not science; a world of hunches and instincts, much like that of the baseball scouts in *Moneyball*.

But those days are over. Zynga's FarmVille, FrontierVille, FishVille, and other games are online and interactive. On the surface, online gaming allows Zynga to look at usage data and modify the games on the basis of how they're actually played. So if players are having difficulty advancing from one level to another, or tend to leave at a certain moment because the action loses its pace, Zynga can spot those problems in the data and remedy them. But what is less evident is that the company can tailor games to the traits of individual players. There is not one version of FarmVille — there are hundreds of them.

Zynga's big-data analysts study whether sales of virtual goods are affected by their color, or by players' seeing their friends using them. For example, after the data showed that FishVille players bought a translucent fish at six times the rate of other creatures, Zynga offered more translucent species and profited handsomely. In the game Mafia Wars, the data revealed that players bought more weapons with gold borders and purchased pet tigers that were all white.

These are not the sorts of things that a game designer toiling in a studio might have known, but the data spoke. "We are an analytics company masquerading as a gaming company. Everything is run by the numbers," explained Ken Rudin, then Zynga's analytics chief, before jumping ship to head analytics at Facebook. Of course harnessing data is no guarantee of business success, and Zynga's business has struggled, but it shows what is possible.

The shift to data-driven decisions is profound. Most people base their decisions on a combination of facts and reflection, plus a heavy dose of guesswork. "A riot of subjective visions — feelings in the solar plexus," in the poet W. H. Auden's memorable words. Thomas Davenport, a business professor at Babson College in Massachusetts and the author of numerous books on analytics, calls it "the golden gut." Executives are just sure of themselves from gut instinct, so they go with that. But this is starting to change as managerial decisions are made or at least confirmed by predictive modeling and big-data analysis.

For instance, The-Numbers.com uses lots of data and mathematics to tell independent Hollywood producers how much income a film is likely to earn long before the first scene is shot. The company's database crunches around 30 million records covering every commercial U.S. film going back decades. It includes each film's budget, genre, cast, crew, and awards, as well as revenue (from U.S. and international box office, overseas rights, video sales and rentals, and so on), and much more. The database also contains a ganglion of human connections, such as "this screenwriter worked with this director; this director worked with this actor," explains its founder and president, Bruce Nash.

The-Numbers.com is able to find intricate correlations that predict the income of film projects. Producers take that information to studios or investors to get financial backing. The firm can even tinker with variables to tell clients how to increase their haul (or minimize the risk of losses). In one instance, its analysis found that a project would have a far better chance of success if the male lead was an A-list actor: specifically, an Oscar-nominated one paid in the $5 million range. In another case, Nash informed the IMAX studio that a sailing documentary would probably be profitable only if its $12 million budget was reduced to $8 million. "It made the producer happy — the director less so," says Nash.

From whether to make a movie to what shortstop to sign, the shift in corporate decision-making is beginning to show up on bottom lines. Erik Brynjolfsson, a business professor at MIT's Sloan School of Management, and his colleagues studied the performance of companies that excel at data-driven decision-making and compared it with the performance of other firms. They found that productivity levels were as much as 6 percent higher at such firms than at companies that did not emphasize using data to make decisions. This gives the data-guided firms a significant leg up — though like the advantage of mindset and skills, it may be short-lived as more companies adopt big-data approaches to their business.

A question of utility

As big data becomes a source of competitive advantage for many companies, the structure of entire industries will be reshaped. The rewards, however, will accrue unequally. And the winners will be found among large and small firms, squeezing out the mass in the middle.

The largest players like Amazon and Google will continue to soar. Unlike the situation in the industrial age, however, their competitive advantage will not rest on physical scale. The vast technical infrastructure of data centers that they command is important but not their most essential quality. With abundant digital storage and processing available to lease inexpensively and add to within minutes, firms can adjust their amount of computing horsepower and storage to fit actual demand. By turning what had been a fixed cost into a variable one, this change erodes the advantages of scale based on technical infrastructure that large companies have long enjoyed.

Scale still matters, but it has shifted. What counts is scale in data. This means holding large pools of data and being able to capture ever more of it with ease. Thus large data holders will flourish as they gather and store more of the raw material of their business, which they can reuse to create additional value.

The challenge for the victors of a small-data world and for offline champions — companies like Walmart, Proctor & Gamble, GE, Nestlé, and Boeing — is to appreciate the power of big data and collect and use data more strategically. The aircraft engine-maker Rolls-Royce completely transformed its business over the past decade by analyzing the data from its products, not just building them. From its operations center in Britain, the company continuously monitors the performance of more than 3,700 jet engines worldwide to spot problems before breakdowns occur. It used data to help turn a manufacturing business into a razor-and-blades one: Rolls-Royce sells the engines but also offers to monitor them, charging customers based on usage time (and repairs or replaces them in case of problems). Services now account for around 70 percent of the civil-aircraft engine division's annual revenue.

Startups as well as old stalwarts in new business areas are positioning themselves to capture vast streams of data. Apple's foray into mobile phones is a case in point. Before the iPhone, mobile operators amassed potentially valuable usage data from subscribers but failed to capitalize on it. Apple, in contrast, demanded in its contracts with operators that it would receive much of the most useful information. By obtaining data from scores of operators around the world, Apple gets a far richer picture of cellphone use than any mobile carrier alone can see.

Big data offers exciting opportunities at the other end of the size spectrum as well. Smart and nimble small players can enjoy "scale without mass," in the celebrated phrase of Professor Brynjolfsson.

That is, they can have a large virtual presence without hefty physical resources, and can diffuse innovations broadly at little cost. Importantly, because some of the best big-data services are based primarily on innovative ideas, they may not require large initial investments. Small firms can license the data rather than own it, run their analysis on inexpensive cloud computing platforms, and pay the licensing fees with a percentage of income earned.

There's a good chance that these advantages at both ends of the spectrum will not be limited to data users but will accrue to data holders as well. Large data holders have strong incentives to add to their hoards of data, since doing so provides greater benefits at only marginal cost. First, they already have the infrastructure in place, in terms of storage and processing. Second, there is a special value in combining datasets. And third, a one-stop shop to obtain data simplifies life for data users.

Yet more intriguingly, a new breed of data holders may also emerge at the other extreme: individuals. As the value of data becomes increasingly apparent, people may want to flex their muscles as holders of information that pertains to them — for example, their shopping preferences, media-viewing habits, and perhaps health data too.

Personal-data ownership may empower individual consumers in ways that haven't been considered before. People may wish to decide for themselves whom to license their data to, and for how much. Of course, not everyone will want to flog his bits to the highest bidder; many will be content to see it reused for free in return for better service like accurate Amazon book recommendations and a better user experience on Pinterest, the digital pinboard and content sharing service. But for a significant number of digitally savvy consumers, the idea of marketing and selling their personal information may become as natural as blogging, tweeting, or editing a Wikipedia entry.

For this to work, however, more is needed than just a shift in consumer sophistication and preferences. Today it would be much too complicated and costly for people to license their personal data and for companies to transact with each individual to obtain it. More likely, we'll see the advent of new firms that pool data from many consumers, provide an easy way to license it, and automate the transactions. If their costs are low enough, and if enough people trust them, it is conceivable that a market for personal data could be established. Businesses such as Mydex in Britain and groups such as ID³, cofounded by Sandy Pentland, the personal-data analytics guru at MIT, are already working to make this vision a reality.

Until these intermediaries are up and running and data users have begun to use them, however, people desiring to become their own data holders have extremely limited options at their disposal. In the interim, to retain their options for a time when the infrastructure and intermediaries are in place, individuals may consider disclosing less rather than more.

For mid-sized companies, however, big data is less helpful. There are scale advantages to the very large, and cost and innovation advantages to the small, argues Philip Evans of the Boston Consulting Group, a prescient thinker on technology and business. In traditional sectors, medium-sized firms exist because they combine a certain minimum size to reap the benefits of scale with a certain flexibility that large players lack. But in a big-data world, there is no minimum scale that a company must reach to pay for its investments in production infrastructure. Big-data users wanting to remain flexible yet successful will find they no longer need to attain a threshold in size. Instead, they can remain small and still flourish (or be acquired by a big-data giant).

Big data squeezes the middle of an industry, pushing firms to be very large, or small and quick, or dead. Many traditional sectors will eventually be recast as big-data ones, from financial services to pharmaceuticals to manufacturing. Big data will not eliminate all mid-sized firms in all sectors, but it will certainly place pressure on companies in industries that are vulnerable to being shaken up by the power of big data.

Big data is poised to disrupt the competitive advantages of states as well. At a time when manufacturing has been largely lost to developing countries and innovation seems to be up for grabs, industrialized nations retain an advantage in that they hold the data and know how to use it. The bad news is that this advantage is not sustainable. As happened with computing and the Internet, the West's early lead in big data will diminish as other parts of the world adopt the technology. The good news for today's powerhouse firms from developed countries, however, is that big data will probably exacerbate corporate strengths and weaknesses. So if a company masters big data, it stands a chance of not only outperforming its peers but widening its lead.

The race is on. Just as Google's search algorithm needs users' data exhaust to work well, and just as the German car-parts supplier saw the importance of data to improve its components, so too all firms can gain by tapping data in clever ways.

Despite the rosy benefits, however, there are also reasons to worry. As big data makes increasingly accurate predictions about the world and our place in it, we may not be ready for its impact on our privacy and our sense of freedom. Our perceptions and institutions were constructed for a world of information scarcity, not surfeit. We explore the dark side of big data in the next chapter.

8

RISKS

FOR ALMOST FORTY YEARS, until the Berlin Wall came down in 1989, the East German state security agency known as the Stasi spied on millions of people. Employing around a hundred thousand full-time staff, the Stasi watched from cars and streets. It opened letters and peeked into bank accounts, bugged apartments and wiretapped phone lines. And it induced lovers and couples, parents and children, to spy on each other, betraying the most basic trust humans have in each other. The resulting files — including at least 39 million index cards and 70 miles of documents — recorded and detailed the most intimate aspects of the lives of ordinary people. East Germany was one of the most comprehensive surveillance states ever seen.

Twenty years after East Germany's demise, more data is being collected and stored about each one of us than ever before. We're under constant surveillance: when we use our credit cards to pay, our cellphones to communicate, or our Social Security numbers to identify ourselves. In 2007 the British media relished the irony that there were more than 30 surveillance cameras within 200 yards of the London apartment where George Orwell wrote *1984*. Well before the advent of the Internet, specialized companies like Equifax, Experian, and Acxiom collected, tabulated, and provided access to personal information for hundreds of millions of people worldwide. The Internet has made tracking easier, cheaper, and more useful. And clandestine three-letter government agencies are not the only ones spying on us. Amazon monitors our shopping preferences and Google our browsing habits, while Twitter knows what's on our minds. Facebook seems to catch all that information too, along with our social relationships. Mobile operators know not only whom we talk to, but who is nearby.

With big data promising valuable insights to those who analyze it, all signs seem to point to a further surge in others' gathering, storing, and reusing our personal data. The size and scale of data collections will increase by leaps and bounds as storage costs continue to plummet and analytic tools become ever more powerful. If the Internet age threatened privacy, does big data endanger it even more? Is that the dark side of big data?

Yes, and it is not the only one. Here, too, the essential point about big data is that a change of scale leads to a change of state. As we'll explain, this transformation not only makes protecting privacy much harder, but also presents an entirely new menace: penalties based on propensities. That is the possibility of using big-data predictions about people to judge and punish them even before they've acted. Doing this negates ideas of fairness, justice, and free will.

In addition to privacy and propensity, there is a third danger. We risk falling victim to a dictatorship of data, whereby we fetishize the information, the output of our analyses, and end up misusing it. Handled responsibly, big data is a useful tool of rational decision-making. Wielded unwisely, it can become an instrument of the powerful, who may turn it into a source of repression, either by simply frustrating customers and employees or, worse, by harming citizens.

The stakes are higher than is typically acknowledged. The dangers of failing to govern big data in respect to privacy and prediction, or of being deluded about the data's meaning, go far beyond trifles like targeted online ads. The history of the twentieth century is blood-soaked with situations in which data abetted ugly ends. In 1943 the U.S. Census Bureau handed over block addresses (but not street names and numbers, to maintain the fiction of protecting privacy) of Japanese-Americans to facilitate their internment. The Netherlands' famously comprehensive civil records were used by the invading Nazis to round up Jews. The five-digit numbers tattooed into the forearms of Nazi concentration-camp prisoners initially corresponded to IBM Hollerith punch-card numbers; data processing facilitated murder on an industrial scale.

Despite its informational prowess, there was much that the Stasi could not do. It could not know where everyone moved at all times or whom they talked to without great effort. Today, though, much of this information is collected by mobile phone carriers. The East German state could not predict which people would become dissidents, nor can we — but police forces are starting to use algorithmic models to decide where and when to patrol, which gives a hint of things to come. These trends make the risks inherent in big data as large as the datasets themselves.

Paralyzing privacy

It is tempting to extrapolate the danger to privacy from the growth in digital data and see parallels to Orwell's surveillance dystopia *1984*. And yet the situation is more complex. To start, not all big data contains personal information. Sensor data from refineries does not, nor does machine data from factory floors or data on manhole explosions or airport weather. BP and Con Edison do not need (or want) personal information in order to gain value from the analytics they perform. Big-data analyses of those types of information pose practically no risk to privacy.

Still, much of the data that's now being generated does include personal information. And companies have a welter of incentives to capture more, keep it longer, and reuse it often. The data may not even explicitly seem like personal information, but with big-data processes it can easily be traced back to the individual it refers to. Or intimate details about a person's life can be deduced.

For instance, utilities are rolling out "smart" electrical meters in the United States and Europe that collect data throughout the day, perhaps as frequently as every six seconds — far more than the trickle of information on overall energy use that traditional meters gathered.

Importantly, the way electrical devices draw power creates a "load signature" that is unique to the appliance. So a hot-water heater is different from a computer, which differs from marijuana grow-lights. Thus a household's energy use discloses private information, be it the residents' daily behavior, health conditions or illegal activities.

The important question, however, is not whether big data increases the risk to privacy (it does), but whether it changes the character of the risk. If the threat is simply larger, then the laws and rules that protect privacy may still work in the big-data age; all we need to do is redouble our existing efforts. On the other hand, if the problem changes, we may need new solutions.

Unfortunately, the problem has been transformed. With big data, the value of information no longer resides solely in its primary purpose. As we've argued, it is now in secondary uses.

This change undermines the central role assigned to individuals in current privacy laws. Today they are told at the time of collection which information is being gathered and for what purpose; then they have an opportunity to agree, so that collection can commence. While this concept of "notice and consent" is not the only lawful way to gather and process personal data, according to Fred Cate, a privacy expert at Indiana University, it has been transmogrified into a cornerstone of privacy principles around the world. (In practice, it has led to super-sized privacy notices that are rarely read, let alone understood — but that is another story.)

Strikingly, in a big-data age, most innovative secondary uses haven't been imagined when the data is first collected. How can companies provide notice for a purpose that has yet to exist? How can individuals give informed consent to an unknown? Yet in the absence of consent, any big-data analysis containing personal information might require going back to every person and asking permission for each reuse. Can you imagine Google trying to contact hundreds of millions of users for approval to use their old search queries to predict the flu? No company would shoulder the cost, even if the task were technically feasible.

The alternative, asking users to agree to any possible future use of their data at the time of collection, isn't helpful either. Such a whole-sale permission emasculates the very notion of informed consent. In the context of big data, the tried and trusted concept of notice and consent is often either too restrictive to unearth data's latent value or too empty to protect individuals' privacy.

Other ways of protecting privacy fail as well. If everyone's informa-tion is in a dataset, even choosing to "opt out" may leave a trace. Take Google's Street View. Its cars collected images of roads and houses in many countries. In Germany, Google faced widespread public and media protests. People feared that pictures of their homes and gar-dens could aid gangs of burglars in selecting lucrative targets. Un-der regulatory pressure, Google agreed to let homeowners opt out by blurring their houses in the image. But the opt-out is visible on Street View — you notice the obfuscated houses — and burglars may inter-pret this as a signal that they are especially good targets.

A technical approach to protecting privacy — anonymization — also doesn't work effectively in many cases. Anonymization refers to stripping out from datasets any personal identifiers, such as name, address, credit card number, date of birth, or Social Security number. The resulting data can then be analyzed and shared without compro-mising anyone's privacy. That works in a world of small data. But big data, with its increase in the quantity and variety of information, fa-cilitates re-identification. Consider the cases of seemingly unidentifi-able web searches and movie ratings.

In August 2006 AOL publically released a mountain of old search queries, under the well-meaning view that researchers could ana-lyze it for interesting insights. The dataset, of 20 million search que-ries from 657,000 users between March 1 and May 31 of that year, had been carefully anonymized. Personal information like user name and IP address were erased and replaced by unique numeric identifi-ers. The idea was that researchers could link together search queries from the same person, but had no identifying information.

Still, within days, the *New York Times* cobbled together searches like "60 single men" and "tea for good health" and "landscapers in Lilburn, Ga" to successfully identify user number 4417749 as Thelma

Arnold, a 62-year-old widow from Lilburn, Georgia. "My goodness, it's my whole personal life," she told the *Times* reporter when he came knocking. "I had no idea somebody was looking over my shoulder." The ensuing public outcry led to the ouster of AOL's chief technology officer and two other employees.

Yet a mere two months later, in October 2006, the movie rental service Netflix did something similar in launching its "Netflix Prize." The company released 100 million rental records from nearly half a million users — and offered a bounty of a million dollars to any team that could improve its film recommendation system by at least 10 percent. Again, personal identifiers had been carefully removed from the data. And yet again, a user was re-identified: a mother and a closeted lesbian in America's conservative Midwest, who because of this later sued Netflix under the pseudonym "Jane Doe."

Researchers at the University of Texas at Austin compared the Netflix data against other public information. They quickly found that ratings by one anonymized user matched those of a named contributor to the Internet Movie Database (IMDb) website. More generally, the research demonstrated that rating just six obscure movies (out of the top 500) could identify a Netflix customer 84 percent of the time. And if one knew the date on which a person rated movies as well, he or she could be uniquely identified among the nearly half a million customers in the dataset with 99 percent accuracy.

In the AOL case, users' identities were exposed by the content of their searches. In the Netflix case, the identity was revealed by a comparison of the data with other sources. In both instances, the companies failed to appreciate how big data aids de-anonymization. There are two reasons: we capture more data and we combine more data.

Paul Ohm, a law professor at the University of Colorado in Boulder and an expert on the harm done by de-anonymization, explains that no easy fix is available. Given enough data, perfect anonymization is impossible no matter how hard one tries. Worse, researchers have recently shown that not only conventional data but also the social graph — people's connections with one another — is vulnerable to de-anonymization.

In the era of big data, the three core strategies long used to ensure privacy — individual notice and consent, opting out, and anonymization — have lost much of their effectiveness. Already today many users feel their privacy is being violated. Just wait until big-data practices become more commonplace.

Compared with East Germany a quarter-century ago, surveillance has only gotten easier, cheaper, and more powerful. The ability to capture personal data is often built deep into the tools we use every day, from websites to smartphone apps. The data-recorders that are in most cars to capture all the actions of a vehicle a few seconds prior to an airbag activation have been known to "testify" against car owners in court in disputes over the events of accidents.

Of course, when businesses are collecting data to improve their bottom line, we need not fear that their surveillance will have the same consequences as being bugged by the Stasi. We won't go to prison if Amazon discovers we like to read Chairman Mao's "Little Red Book." Google will not exile us because we searched for "Bing." Companies may be powerful, but they don't have the state's powers to coerce.

So while they are not dragging us away in the middle of the night, firms of all stripes amass mountains of personal information concerning all aspects of our lives, share it with others without our knowledge, and use it in ways we could hardly imagine.

The private sector is not alone in flexing its muscles with big data. Governments are doing this too. For instance, the U.S. National Security Agency (NSA) is said to intercept and store 1.7 billion emails, phone calls, and other communications every day, according to a *Washington Post* investigation in 2010. William Binney, a former NSA official, estimates that the government has compiled "20 trillion transactions" among U.S. citizens and others — who calls whom, emails whom, wires money to whom, and so on.

To make sense of all the data, the United States is building giant data centers such as a $1.2 billion NSA facility in Fort Williams, Utah. And all parts of government are demanding more information than before, not just secretive agencies involved in counterterrorism. When the collection expands to information like financial transactions, health records, and Facebook status updates, the quantity being gleaned is unthinkably large. The government can't process so much data. So why collect it?

The answer points to the way surveillance has changed in the era of big data. In the past, investigators attached alligator clips to telephone wires to learn as much as they could about a suspect. What mattered was to drill down and get to know that individual. The modern approach is different. In the spirit of Google or Facebook, the new thinking is that people are the sum of their social relationships, online interactions, and connections with content. In order to fully investigate an individual, analysts need to look at the widest possible penumbra of data that surrounds the person — not just whom they know, but whom those people know too, and so on. This was technically very hard to do in the past. Today it's easier than ever. And because the government never knows whom it will want to scrutinize, it collects, stores, or ensures access to information not necessarily to monitor everyone at all times, but so that when someone falls under suspicion, the authorities can immediately investigate rather than having to start gathering the info from scratch.

The United States is not the only government amassing mountains of data on people, nor is it perhaps the most egregious in its practices. However, as troubling as the ability of business and government to know our personal information may be, a newer problem emerges with big data: the use of predictions to judge us.

Probability and punishment

John Anderton is the chief of a special police unit in Washington, D.C. This particular morning, he bursts into a suburban house moments before Howard Marks, in a state of frenzied rage, is about to plunge a pair of scissors into the torso of his wife, whom he found in bed with another man. For Anderton, it is just another day preventing capital crimes. "By mandate of the District of Columbia Precrime Division," he recites, "I'm placing you under arrest for the future murder of Sarah Marks, that was to take place today. . . ."

Other cops start restraining Marks, who screams, "I did not *do* anything!"

The opening scene of the film *Minority Report* depicts a society in which predictions seem so accurate that the police arrest individuals for crimes before they are committed. People are imprisoned not for what they did, but for what they are foreseen to do, even though they never actually commit the crime. The movie attributes this prescient and preemptive law enforcement to the visions of three clairvoyants, not to data analysis. But the unsettling future *Minority Report* portrays is one that unchecked big-data analysis threatens to bring about, in which judgments of culpability are based on individualized predictions of future behavior.

Already we see the seedlings of this. Parole boards in more than half of all U.S. states use predictions founded on data analysis as a factor in deciding whether to release somebody from prison or to keep him incarcerated. A growing number of places in the United States — from precincts in Los Angeles to cities like Richmond, Virginia — employ "predictive policing": using big-data analysis to select what streets, groups, and individuals to subject to extra scrutiny, simply because an algorithm pointed to them as more likely to commit crime.

In the city of Memphis, Tennessee, a program called Blue CRUSH (for Crime Reduction Utilizing Statistical History) provides police officers with relatively precise areas of interest in terms of locality (a few blocks) and time (a few hours during a particular day of the week). The system ostensibly helps law enforcement better target its scarce resources. Since its inception in 2006, major property crimes and violent offenses have fallen by a quarter, according to one measure (though of course, this says nothing about causality; there's nothing to indicate that the decrease is due to Blue CRUSH).

In Richmond, Virginia, police correlate crime data with additional datasets, such as information on when large companies in the city pay their employees or the dates of concerts or sports events. Doing so has confirmed and sometimes refined the cops' suspicions about crime trends. For example, Richmond police long sensed that there was a jump in violent crime following gun shows; the big-data analysis proved them right but with a wrinkle: the spike happened two weeks afterwards, not immediately following the event.

These systems seek to prevent crimes by predicting, eventually down to the level of individuals, who might commit them. This points toward using big data for a novel purpose: to prevent crime from happening.

A research project under the U.S. Department of Homeland Security called FAST (Future Attribute Screening Technology) tries to identify potential terrorists by monitoring individuals' vital signs, body language, and other physiological patterns. The idea is that surveilling people's behavior may detect their intent to do harm. In tests, the system was 70 percent accurate, according to the DHS. (What this means is unclear; were research subjects instructed to pretend to be terrorists to see if their "malintent" was spotted?) Though these systems seem embryonic, the point is that law enforcement takes them very seriously.

Stopping a crime from happening sounds like an enticing prospect. Isn't preventing infractions before they take place far better than penalizing the perpetrators afterwards? Wouldn't forestalling crimes benefit not just those who might have been victimized by them, but society as a whole?

But it's a perilous path to take. If through big data we predict who may commit a future crime, we may not be content with simply preventing the crime from happening; we are likely to want to punish the probable perpetrator as well. That is only logical. If we just step in and intervene to stop the illicit act from taking place, the putative perpetrator may try again with impunity. In contrast, by using big data to hold him responsible for his (future) acts, we may deter him and others.

Such prediction-based punishment seems an improvement over practices we have already come to accept. Preventing unhealthy, dangerous, or risky behavior is a cornerstone of modern society. We have made smoking harder to prevent lung cancer; we require wearing seatbelts to avert fatalities in car accidents; we don't let people board airplanes with guns to avoid hijackings. Such preventive measures constrain our freedom, but many see them as a small price to pay in return for avoiding much graver harm.

In many contexts, data analysis is already employed in the name of prevention. It is used to lump us into cohorts of people like us, and we are often characterized accordingly. Actuarial tables note that men over 50 are prone to prostate cancer, so members of that group may pay more for health insurance even if they never get prostate cancer. High-school students with good grades, as a group, are less likely to get into car accidents — so some of their less-learned peers have to pay higher insurance premiums. Individuals with certain characteristics are subjected to extra screening when they pass through airport security.

That's the idea behind "profiling" in today's small-data world. Find a common association in the data, define a group of people to whom it applies, and then place those people under additional scrutiny. It is a generalizable rule that applies to everyone in the group. "Profiling," of course, is a loaded word, and the method has serious downsides. If misused, it can lead not only to discrimination against certain groups but also to "guilt by association."

In contrast, big data predictions about people are different. Where today's forecasts of likely behavior — found in things like insurance premiums or credit scores — usually rely on a handful of factors that are based on a mental model of the issue at hand (that is, previous health problems or loan repayment history), with big data's non-causal analysis we often simply identify the most suitable predictors from the sea of information.

Most important, using big data we hope to identify specific individuals rather than groups; this liberates us from profiling's shortcoming of making every predicted suspect a case of guilt by association. In a big-data world, somebody with an Arabic name, who has paid in cash for a one-way ticket in first class, may no longer be subjected to secondary screening at an airport if other data specific to him make it very unlikely that he's a terrorist. With big data we can escape the straitjacket of group identities, and replace them with much more granular predictions for each individual.

The promise of big data is that we do what we've been doing all along — profiling — but make it better, less discriminatory, and more individualized. That sounds acceptable if the aim is simply to prevent unwanted actions. But it becomes very dangerous if we use big-data predictions to decide whether somebody is culpable and ought to be punished for behavior that has not yet happened.

The very idea of penalizing based on propensities is nauseating. To accuse a person of some possible future behavior is to negate the very foundation of justice: that one must have done something before we can hold him accountable for it. After all, thinking bad things is not illegal, doing them is. It is a fundamental tenet of our society that individual responsibility is tied to individual choice of action. If one is forced at gunpoint to open the company's safe, one has no choice and thus isn't held responsible.

If big-data predictions were perfect, if algorithms could foresee our future with flawless clarity, we would no longer have a choice to act in the future. We would behave exactly as predicted. Were perfect predictions possible, they would deny human volition, our ability to live our lives freely. Also, ironically, by depriving us of choice they would exculpate us from any responsibility.

Of course perfect prediction is impossible. Rather, big-data analysis will predict that for a specific individual, a particular future behavior has a certain probability. Consider, for example, research conducted by Richard Berk, a professor of statistics and criminology at the University of Pennsylvania. He claims his method can predict whether a person released on parole will be involved in a homicide (either kill or be killed). As inputs he uses numerous case-specific variables, including reason for incarceration and date of first offense, but also demographic data like age and gender. Berk suggests that he can forecast a future murder among those on parole with at least a 75 percent probability. That's not bad. However, it also means that should parole boards rely on Berk's analysis, they would be wrong as often as one out of four times.

But the core problem with relying on such predictions is not that they expose society to risk. The fundamental trouble is that with such a system we essentially punish people *before* they do something bad. And by intervening before they act (for instance by denying them parole if predictions show there is a high probability that they will murder), we never know whether or not they would have actually committed the predicted crime. We do not let fate play out, and yet we hold individuals responsible for what our prediction tells us they would have done. Such predictions can never be disproven.

This negates the very idea of the presumption of innocence, the principle upon which our legal system, as well as our sense of fairness, is based. And if we hold people responsible for predicted future acts, ones they may never commit, we also deny that humans have a capacity for moral choice.

The important point here is *not* simply one of policing. The danger is much broader than criminal justice; it covers all areas of society, all instances of human judgment in which big-data predictions are used to decide whether people are culpable for future acts or not. Those include everything from a company's decision to dismiss an employee, to a doctor denying a patient surgery, to a spouse filing for divorce.

Perhaps with such a system society would be safer or more efficient, but an essential part of what makes us human — our ability to choose the actions we take and be held accountable for them — would be destroyed. Big data would have become a tool to collectivize human choice and abandon free will in our society.

Of course, big data offers numerous benefits. What turns it into a weapon of dehumanization is a shortcoming, not of big data itself, but of the ways we use its predictions. The crux is that holding people culpable for predicted acts before they can commit them uses big-data predictions based on correlations to make causal decisions about individual responsibility.

Big data is useful to understand present and future risk, and to adjust our actions accordingly. Its predictions help patients and insurers, lenders and consumers. But big data does not tell us anything about causality. In contrast, assigning "guilt" — individual culpability — requires that people we judge have chosen a particular action. Their decision must have been causal for the action that followed. Precisely because big data is based on correlations, it is an utterly unsuitable tool to help us judge causality and thus assign individual culpability.

The trouble is that humans are primed to see the world through the lens of cause and effect. Thus big data is under constant threat of being abused for causal purposes, of being tied to rosy visions of how much more effective our judgment, our human decision-making of assigning culpability, could be if we only were armed with big-data predictions.

It is the quintessential slippery slope — leading straight to the society portrayed in *Minority Report,* a world in which individual choice and free will have been eliminated, in which our individual moral compass has been replaced by predictive algorithms and individuals are exposed to the unencumbered brunt of collective fiat. If so employed, big data threatens to imprison us — perhaps literally — in probabilities.

The dictatorship of data

Big data erodes privacy and threatens freedom. But big data also exacerbates a very old problem: relying on the numbers when they are far more fallible than we think. Nothing underscores the consequences of data analysis gone awry more than the story of Robert McNamara.

McNamara was a numbers guy. Appointed the U.S. secretary of defense when tensions in Vietnam started in the early 1960s, he insisted on getting data on everything he could. Only by applying statistical rigor, he believed, could decision-makers understand a complex situation and make the right choices. The world in his view was a mass of unruly information that if delineated, denoted, demarcated, and quantified could be tamed by human hand and would fall under human will. McNamara sought Truth, and that Truth could be found in data. Among the numbers that came back to him was the "body count."

McNamara developed his love of numbers as a student at Harvard Business School and then its youngest assistant professor at age 24. He applied this rigor during the Second World War as part of an elite Pentagon team called Statistical Control, which brought data-driven decision-making to one of the world's largest bureaucracies. Prior to this, the military was blind. It didn't know, for instance, the type, quantity, or location of spare airplane parts. Data came to the rescue. Just making armament procurement more efficient saved $3.6 billion in 1943. Modern war was about the efficient allocation of resources; the team's work was a stunning success.

At war's end, the group decided to stick together and offer their skills to corporate America. The Ford Motor Company was floundering, and a desperate Henry Ford II handed them the reins. Just as they knew nothing about the military when they helped win the war, so too were they clueless about car making. Still, the so-called "Whiz Kids" turned the company around.

McNamara rose swiftly up the ranks, trotting out a data point for every situation. Harried factory managers produced the figures he demanded — whether they were correct or not. When an edict came down that all inventory from one car model must be used before a new model could begin production, exasperated line managers simply dumped excess parts into a nearby river. The brass at headquarters nodded approvingly when the foremen sent back numbers confirming that the order had been obeyed. But the joke at the factory was that a fellow could walk on water — atop rusted pieces of 1950 and 1951 cars.

McNamara epitomized the mid-twentieth-century manager, the hyper-rational executive who relied on numbers rather than sentiments, and who could apply his quantitative skills to any industry he turned them to. In 1960 he was named president of Ford, a position he only held for a few weeks before President Kennedy appointed him secretary of defense.

As the Vietnam conflict escalated and the United States sent more troops, it became clear that this was a war of wills, not of territory. America's strategy was to pound the Viet Cong to the negotiation table. The way to measure progress, therefore, was by the number of enemy killed. The body count was published daily in the newspapers. To the war's supporters it was proof of progress; to critics, evidence of its immorality. The body count was the data point that defined an era.

In 1977, two years after the last helicopter lifted off the rooftop of the U.S. embassy in Saigon, a retired Army general, Douglas Kinnard, published a landmark survey of the generals' views. Called *The War Managers,* the book revealed the quagmire of quantification. A mere 2 percent of America's generals considered the body count a valid way to measure progress. Around two-thirds said it was often inflated. "A fake — totally worthless," wrote one general in his comments. "Often blatant lies," wrote another. "They were grossly exaggerated by many units primarily because of the incredible interest shown by people like McNamara," said a third.

Like the factory men at Ford who dumped engine parts into the river, junior officers sometimes gave their superiors impressive numbers to keep their commands or boost their careers — telling the higher-ups what they wanted to hear. McNamara and the men around him relied on the figures, fetishized them. With his perfectly combed-back hair and his flawlessly knotted tie, McNamara felt he could only comprehend what was happening on the ground by staring at a spreadsheet — at all those orderly rows and columns, calculations and charts, whose mastery seemed to bring him one standard deviation closer to God.

The use, abuse, and misuse of data by the U.S. military during the Vietnam War is a troubling lesson about the limitations of information in an age of small data, a lesson that must be heeded as the world hurls toward the big-data era. The quality of the underlying data can be poor. It can be biased. It can be mis-analyzed or used misleadingly. And even more damningly, data can fail to capture what it purports to quantify.

We are more susceptible than we may think to the "dictatorship of data" — that is, to letting the data govern us in ways that may do as much harm as good. The threat is that we will let ourselves be mindlessly bound by the output of our analyses even when we have reasonable grounds for suspecting something is amiss. Or that we will become obsessed with collecting facts and figures for data's sake. Or that we will attribute a degree of truth to the data which it does not deserve.

As more aspects of life become datafied, the solution that policymakers and businesspeople are starting to reach for first is to get more data. "In God we trust — all others bring data," is the mantra of the modern manager, heard echoing in Silicon Valley cubicles, on factory floors, and along the corridors of government agencies. The sentiment is sound, but one can easily be deluded by data.

Education seems on the skids? Push standardized tests to measure performance and penalize teachers or schools that by this measure aren't up to snuff. Whether the tests actually capture the abilities of schoolchildren, the quality of teaching, or the needs of a creative, adaptable modern workforce is an open question — but one that the data does not admit.

Want to prevent terrorism? Create layers of watch lists and no-fly lists in order to police the skies. But whether such datasets offer the protection they promise is in doubt. In one famous incident, the late Senator Ted Kennedy of Massachusetts was ensnared by the no-fly list, stopped, and questioned, simply for having the same name as a person in the database.

People who work with data have an expression for some of these problems: "garbage in, garbage out." In certain cases, the reason is the quality of the underlying information. Often, though, it is the misuse of the analysis that is produced. With big data, these problems may arise more frequently or have larger consequences.

Google, as we've shown in many examples, runs everything according to data. That strategy has obviously led to much of its success. But

it also trips up the company from time to time. Its co-founders, Larry
Page and Sergey Brin, long insisted on knowing all job candidates'
SAT scores and their grade point averages when they graduated from
college. In their thinking, the first number measured potential and
the second measured achievement. Accomplished managers in their
forties who were being recruited were hounded for the scores, to
their outright bafflement. The company even continued to demand
the numbers long after its internal studies showed no correlation between the scores and job performance.

Google ought to know better, to resist being seduced by data's false
charms. The measure leaves little room for change in a person's life. It
fails to count knowledge rather than book-smarts. And it may not reflect the qualifications of people from the humanities, where know-
how may be less quantifiable than in science and engineering. Google's
obsession with such data for HR purposes is especially queer considering that the company's founders are products of Montessori schools,
which emphasize learning, not grades. And it repeats the mistakes of
past technology powerhouses that vaunted people's résumés above
their actual abilities. Would Larry and Sergey, as PhD dropouts, have
stood a chance of becoming managers at the legendary Bell Labs? By
Google's standards, not Bill Gates, nor Mark Zuckerberg, nor Steve
Jobs would have been hired, since they lack college degrees.

The firm's reliance on data sometimes may seem overblown.
Marissa Mayer, when she was one of its top executives, once ordered
staff to test 41 gradations of blue to see which ones people used more,
to determine the color of a toolbar on the site. Google's deference to
data has been taken to extremes (even though choosing the right hue
earned Google millions, according to an engineer). In fact, Google's
obsession even sparked revolt.

In 2009 Google's top designer, Douglas Bowman, quit in a huff because he couldn't stand the constant quantification of everything. "I
had a recent debate over whether a border should be 3, 4 or 5 pix-
els wide, and was asked to prove my case. I can't operate in an environment like that," he wrote on a blog announcing his resignation.
"When a company is filled with engineers, it turns to engineering to

solve problems. Reduce each decision to a simple logic problem. That data eventually becomes a crutch for every decision, paralyzing the company."

Brilliance doesn't depend on data. Steve Jobs may have continually improved the Mac laptop over years on the basis of field reports, but he used his intuition, not data, to launch the iPod, iPhone, and iPad. He relied on his sixth sense. "It isn't the consumers' job to know what they want," he famously said, when telling a reporter that Apple did no market research before releasing the iPad.

In the book *Seeing Like a State,* the anthropologist James Scott of Yale University documents the ways in which governments, in their fetish for quantification and data, end up making people's lives miserable rather than better. They use maps to determine how to reorganize communities rather than learn anything about the people on the ground. They use long tables of data about harvests to decide to collectivize agriculture without knowing a whit about farming. They take all the imperfect, organic ways in which people have interacted over time and bend them to their needs, sometimes just to satisfy a desire for quantifiable order. The use of data, in Scott's view, often serves to empower the powerful.

This is the dictatorship of data writ large. And it was a similar hubris that led the United States to escalate the Vietnam War partly on the basis of body counts, rather than to base decisions on more meaningful metrics. "It is true enough that not every conceivable complex human situation can be fully reduced to the lines on a graph, or to percentage points on a chart, or to figures on a balance sheet," said McNamara in a speech in 1967, as domestic protests were growing. "But all reality can be reasoned about. And not to quantify what can be quantified is only to be content with something less than the full range of reason." If only the right data were used in the right way, not respected for data's sake.

Robert Strange McNamara went on to run the World Bank throughout the 1970s, then painted himself as a dove in the 1980s. He became an outspoken critic of nuclear weapons and a proponent of environmental protection. Later in life he underwent an intellectual conversion and produced a memoir, *In Retrospect,* that criticized the thinking behind the war and his own decisions as secretary of defense. "We were wrong, terribly wrong," he wrote. But he was referring to the war's broad strategy. On the question of data, and of body counts in particular, he remained unrepentant. He admitted many of the statistics were "misleading or erroneous." "But things you can count, you ought to count. Loss of life is one. . . ." McNamara died in 2009 at age 93, a man of intelligence but not of wisdom.

Big data may lure us to commit the sin of McNamara: to become so fixated on the data, and so obsessed with the power and promise it offers, that we fail to appreciate its limitations. To catch a glimpse of the big-data equivalent of the body count, we need only look back at Google Flu Trends. Consider a situation, not entirely implausible, in which a deadly strain of influenza rages across the country. Medical professionals would be grateful for the ability to forecast in real time the biggest hotspots by dint of search queries. They'd know where to intervene with help.

But suppose that in a moment of crisis political leaders argue that simply knowing where the disease is likely to get worse and trying to head it off is not enough. So they call for a general quarantine — not for all people in those regions, which would be unnecessary and overbroad. Big data allows us to be more particular. So the quarantine applies only to the individual Internet users whose searches were most highly correlated with having the flu. Here we have the data on whom to pick up. Federal agents, armed with lists of Internet Protocol addresses and mobile GPS information, herd the individual web searchers into quarantine centers.

But as reasonable as this scenario might sound to some, it is just plain wrong. Correlations do not imply causation. These people may or may not have the flu. They'd have to be tested. They'd be prisoners of a prediction, but more important, they'd be victims of a view of data that lacks an appreciation for what the information actually means. The point of the actual Google Flu Trends study is that certain search terms are *correlated* with the outbreak — but the correlation may exist because of circumstances like healthy co-workers hearing sneezes in the office and going online to learn how to protect themselves, not because the searchers are ill themselves.

The dark side of big data

As we have seen, big data allows for more surveillance of our lives while it makes some of the legal means for protecting privacy largely obsolete. It also renders ineffective the core technical method of preserving anonymity. Just as unsettling, big-data predictions about individuals may be used to, in effect, punish people for their propensities, not their actions. This denies free will and erodes human dignity.

At the same time, there is a real risk that the benefits of big data will lure people into applying the techniques where they don't perfectly fit, or into feeling overly confident in the results of the analyses. As big-data predictions improve, using them will only become more appealing, fueling an obsession over data since it can do so much. That was the curse of McNamara and is the lesson his story holds.

We must guard against overreliance on data rather than repeat the error of Icarus, who adored his technical power of flight but used it improperly and tumbled into the sea. In the next chapter, we'll consider ways that we can control big data, lest we be controlled by it.

9

CONTROL

CHANGES IN THE WAY WE produce and interact with information lead to changes in the rules we use to govern ourselves, and in the values society needs to protect. Consider an example from a previous data deluge, the one unleashed by the printing press.

Before Johannes Gutenberg invented moveable type around 1450, the spread of ideas in the West was largely limited to personal connections. Books were mostly confined to monastic libraries, tightly guarded by monks acting for the Catholic Church to protect and preserve its dominance. Outside the Church, books were extremely rare. A few universities had collected only dozens or perhaps a couple of hundred books. Cambridge University began the fifteenth century with a mere 122 tomes.

Within a few decades after Gutenberg's invention, his printing press had been replicated across Europe, making possible the mass production of books and pamphlets. When Martin Luther translated the Latin Bible into everyday German, people suddenly had a reason to become literate: reading the Bible themselves, they could bypass priests to learn the word of God. The Bible became a best seller. And once literate, people continued to read. Some even decided to write. In less than a person's life span, the flow of information had changed from a trickle to a torrent.

The dramatic change also fertilized the ground for new rules to govern the information explosion sparked by moveable type. As the secular state consolidated its power, it established censorship and licensing to contain and control the printed word. Copyright was established to give authors legal and economic incentives to create. Later, intellectuals pushed for rules to protect words from government suppression; by the nineteenth century, in a growing number of countries, freedom of speech was turned into a constitutional guarantee. But these rights came with responsibilities. As vitriolic newspapers trampled on privacy or slandered reputations, rules cropped up to shield people's private sphere and allow them to sue for libel.

Yet these changes in governance also reflect a deeper, more fundamental transformation of the underlying values. In Gutenberg's shadow, we first began to realize the power of the written word — and, eventually, the importance of information that spreads widely throughout society. As centuries passed, we opted for more information flows rather than less, and to guard against its excesses not primarily through censorship but through rules that limited the misuse of information.

As the world moves toward big data, society will undergo a similar tectonic shift. Big data is already transforming many aspects of our lives and ways of thinking, forcing us to reconsider basic principles on how to encourage its growth and mitigate its potential for harm. However, unlike our forebears during and after the printing revolution, we don't have centuries to adjust; perhaps just a few years.

Simple changes to existing rules will not be sufficient to govern in the big-data age and to temper big data's dark side. Rather than a parametric change, the situation calls for a paradigmatic one. Protecting privacy requires that big-data users become more accountable for their actions. At the same time, society will have to redefine the very notion of justice to guarantee human freedom to act (and thus to be held responsible for those actions). Lastly, new institutions and professionals will need to emerge to interpret the complex algorithms that underlie big-data findings, and to advocate for people who might be harmed by big data.

From privacy to accountability

For decades an essential principle of privacy laws around the world has been to put individuals in control by letting them decide whether, how, and by whom their personal information may be processed. In the Internet age, this laudable ideal has often morphed into a formulaic system of "notice and consent." In the era of big data, however, when much of data's value is in secondary uses that may have been unimagined when the data was collected, such a mechanism to ensure privacy is no longer suitable.

We envision a very different privacy framework for the big-data age, one focused less on individual consent at the time of collection and more on holding data users accountable for what they do. In such a world, firms will formally assess a particular reuse of data based on the impact it has on individuals whose personal information is being processed. This does not have to be onerously detailed in all cases, as future privacy laws will define broad categories of uses, including ones that are permissible without or with only limited, standardized safeguards. For riskier initiatives, regulators will establish ground rules for how data users should assess the dangers of a planned use and determine what best avoids or mitigates potential harm. This spurs creative reuses of the data, while at the same time it ensures that sufficient measures are taken to see that individuals are not hurt.

Running a formal big-data use assessment correctly and implementing its findings accurately offers tangible benefits to data users: they will be free to pursue secondary uses of personal data in many instances without having to go back to individuals to get their explicit consent. On the other hand, sloppy assessments or poor implementation of safeguards will expose data users to legal liability, and regulatory actions such as mandates, fines, and perhaps even criminal prosecution. Data-user accountability only works when it has teeth.

To see how this could happen in practice, take the example of the datafication of posteriors from Chapter Five. Imagine that a company sold a car antitheft service which used a driver's sitting posture as a unique identifier. Then, it later reanalyzed the information to predict drivers' "attention states," such as whether they were drowsy or tipsy or angry, in order to send alerts to other drivers nearby to prevent accidents. Under today's privacy rules, the firm might believe it needed a new round of notice and consent because it hadn't previously received permission to use the information in this way. But under a system of data-user accountability, the company would assess the dangers of the intended use, and if it found them minimal it could just go ahead with its plan — and improve road safety in the process.

Shifting the burden of responsibility from the public to the users of data makes sense for a number of reasons. They know much more than anybody else, and certainly more than consumers or regulators, about how they intend to use the data. By conducting the assessment themselves (or hiring experts to do it) they will avoid the problem of revealing confidential business strategies to outsiders. Perhaps most important, the data users reap most of the benefits of secondary use, so it's only fair to hold them accountable for their actions and place the burden for this review on them.

With such an alternative privacy framework, data users will no longer be legally required to delete personal information once it has served its primary purpose, as most privacy laws currently demand. This is an important change, since, as we've seen, only by tapping the latent value of data can latter-day Maurys flourish by wringing the most value out of it for their own — and society's — benefit. Instead, data users will be allowed to keep personal information longer, though not forever. Society needs to carefully weigh the rewards from reuse against the risks from too much disclosure.

To strike the appropriate balance, regulators may choose different time frames for reuse, depending on the data's inherent risk, as well as on different societies' values. Some nations may be more cautious than others, just as some sorts of data may be considered more sensitive than others. This approach also banishes the specter of "permanent memory" — the risk that one can never escape one's past because the digital records can always be dredged up. Otherwise our personal data hovers over us like the Sword of Damocles, threatening to impale us years hence with some private detail or regrettable purchase. Time limits also create an incentive for data holders to use it before they lose it. This strikes what we believe is a better balance for the big-data era: firms get the right to use personal data longer, but in return they have to take on responsibility for its uses as well as the obligation to erase personal data after a certain period of time.

In addition to a regulatory shift from "privacy by consent" to "privacy through accountability," we envision technical innovation to help protect privacy in certain instances. One nascent approach is the concept of "differential privacy": deliberately blurring the data so that a query of a large dataset doesn't reveal exact results but only approximate ones. This makes it difficult and costly to associate particular data points with particular people.

Fuzzing the information sounds as if it might destroy valuable insights. But it need not — or at least, the tradeoff can be favorable. For instance, experts in technology policy note that Facebook relies on a form of differential privacy when it reports information about its users to potential advertisers: the numbers it reports are approximate, so they can't help reveal individual identities. Looking up Asian women in Atlanta who are interested in Ashtanga yoga will produce a result such as "about 400" rather than an exact number, making it impossible to use the information to narrow down statistically on someone specific.

The shift in controls from individual consent to data-user accountability is a fundamental and essential change necessary for effective big-data governance. But it is not the only one.

People versus predictions

Courts of law hold people responsible for their actions. When judges render their impartial decisions after a fair trial, justice is done. Yet, in the era of big data, our notion of justice needs to be redefined to preserve the idea of human agency: the free will by which people choose their actions. It is the simple idea that individuals can and should be held responsible for their behavior, not their propensities.

Before big data, this fundamental freedom was obvious. So much so, in fact, that it hardly needed to be articulated. After all, this is the way our legal system works: we hold people responsible for their acts by assessing what they have done. In contrast, with big data we can predict human actions increasingly accurately. This tempts us to judge people not on what they did, but on what we predicted they would do.

In the big-data era we will have to expand our understanding of justice, and require that it include safeguards for human agency as much as we currently protect procedural fairness. Without such safeguards the very idea of justice may be utterly undermined.

By guaranteeing human agency, we ensure that government judgments of our behavior are based on real actions, not simply on big-data analysis. Thus government must only hold us responsible for our past actions, not for statistical predictions of future ones. And when the state judges previous actions, it should be prevented from relying solely on big data. For example, consider the case of nine companies suspected of price fixing. It is entirely acceptable to use big-data analyses to identify possible collusion so that regulators can investigate and build a case using traditional means. But these companies cannot be found guilty only because big data suggests that they probably committed a crime.

A similar principle should apply outside government, when businesses make highly significant decisions about us — to hire or fire, offer a mortgage, or deny a credit card. When they base these decisions mostly on big-data predictions, we recommend that certain safeguards must be in place. First is openness: making available the data and algorithm underlying the prediction that affects an individual. Second is certification: having the algorithm certified for certain sensitive uses by an expert third party as sound and valid. Third is disprovability: specifying concrete ways that people can disprove a prediction about themselves. (This is analogous to the tradition in science of disclosing any factors that might undermine the findings of a study.)

Most important, a guarantee on human agency guards against the threat of a dictatorship of data, in which we endow the data with more meaning and importance than it deserves.

It is equally crucial that we protect individual responsibility. Society will face a great temptation to stop holding individuals accountable and instead may shift to managing risks, that is, to basing decisions about people on assessments of possibilities and likelihoods of potential outcomes. With so much seemingly objective data available, it may seem appealing to de-emotionalize and de-individualize decision-making, to rely on algorithms rather than on subjective assessments by judges and evaluators, and to frame decisions not in the language of personal responsibility but in terms of more "objective" risks and their avoidance.

For example, big data presents a strong invitation to predict which people are likely to commit crimes and subject them to special treatment, scrutinizing them over and over in the name of risk reduction. People categorized in this way may feel, quite rightly, that they're being punished without ever being confronted and held responsible for actual behavior. Imagine that an algorithm identifies a particular teenager as highly likely to commit a felony in the next three years. As a result, the authorities assign a social worker to visit him once a month, to keep an eye on him and try to help him stay out of trouble.

If the teenager and his relatives, friends, teachers, or employers view the visits as a stigma, as they well may, then the intervention has the effect of a punishment, a penalty for an action that has not happened. And the situation isn't much better if the visits are seen not as a punishment but simply as an attempt to reduce the likelihood of future problems—as a way to minimize risk (in this case, the risk of a crime that would undermine public safety). The more we switch from holding people accountable for their acts to relying on data-driven interventions to reduce risk in society, the more we devalue the ideal of individual responsibility. The predictive state is the nanny state, and then some. Denying people's responsibility for their actions destroys their fundamental freedom to choose their behavior.

If the state bases many decisions on predictions and a desire to mitigate risk, our individual choices — and thus our individual freedom to act — no longer matter. Without guilt, there can be no innocence. Giving in to such an approach would not improve our society but impoverish it.

A fundamental pillar of big-data governance must be a guarantee that we will continue to judge people by considering their personal responsibility and their actual behavior, not by "objectively" crunching data to determine whether they're likely wrongdoers. Only that way will we treat them as human beings: as people who have the freedom to choose their actions and the right to be judged by them.

Breaking the black box

Computer systems currently base their decisions on rules they have been explicitly programmed to follow. Thus when a decision goes awry, as is inevitable from time to time, we can go back and figure out why the computer made it. For example, we can investigate questions like "Why did the autopilot system pitch the plane five degrees higher when an external sensor detected a sudden surge in humidity?" Today's computer code can be opened and inspected, and those who know how to interpret it can trace and comprehend the basis for its decisions, no matter how complex.

With big-data analysis, however, this traceability will become much harder. The basis of an algorithm's predictions may often be far too intricate for most people to understand.

When computers were explicitly programmed to follow sets of instructions, as with IBM's early translation program of Russian to English in 1954, a human could readily grasp why the software substituted one word for another. But Google Translate incorporates billions of pages of translations into its judgments about things like whether the English word "light" should be "lumière" or "léger" in French (that is, whether the word refers to brightness or to weight). It's impossible for a human to trace the precise reasons for the program's word choices because they are based on massive amounts of data and vast statistical computations.

Big data operates at a scale that transcends our ordinary understanding. For example, the correlation Google identified between a handful of search terms and the flu was the result of testing 450 million mathematical models. In contrast, Cynthia Rudin initially designed 106 predictors for whether a manhole might catch fire, and she could explain to Con Edison's managers why her program prioritized inspection sites as it did. "Explainability," as it is called in artificial intelligence circles, is important for us mortals, who tend to want to know why, not just what. But what if instead of 106 predictors, the system automatically generated a whopping 601 predictors, the vast majority of which had very low weightings but which, when taken together, improved the model's accuracy? The basis for any prediction might be staggeringly complex. What could she tell the managers then to convince them to reallocate their limited budget?

In these scenarios, we can see the risk that big-data predictions, and the algorithms and datasets behind them, will become black boxes that offer us no accountability, traceability, or confidence. To prevent this, big data will require monitoring and transparency, which in turn will require new types of expertise and institutions. These new players will provide support in areas where society needs to scrutinize big-data predictions and enable people who feel wronged by them to seek redress.

As a society, we've often seen such new entities emerge when a dramatic increase in the complexity and specialization of a particular field produced an urgent need for experts to manage the new techniques. Professions like law, medicine, accounting, and engineering underwent this very transformation more than a century ago. More recently, specialists in computer security and privacy have cropped up to certify that companies are complying with the best practices determined by bodies like the International Organization for Standards (which was itself formed to address a new need for guidelines in this field).

Big data will require a new group of people to take on this role. Perhaps they will be called "algorithmists." They could take two forms — independent entities to monitor firms from outside, and employees or departments to monitor them from within — just as companies have in-house accountants as well as outside auditors who review their finances.

THE RISE OF THE ALGORITHMIST

These new professionals would be experts in the areas of computer science, mathematics, and statistics; they would act as reviewers of big-data analyses and predictions. Algorithmists would take a vow of impartiality and confidentiality, much as accountants and certain other professionals do now. They would evaluate the selection of data sources, the choice of analytical and predictive tools, including algorithms and models, and the interpretation of results. In the event of a dispute, they would have access to the algorithms, statistical approaches, and datasets that produced a given decision.

Had there been an algorithmist on staff at the Department of Homeland Security in 2004, he might have prevented the agency from generating a no-fly list so flawed that it included Senator Kennedy. More recent instances where algorithmists could have played a role have happened in Japan, France, Germany, and Italy, where people have complained that Google's "autocomplete" feature, which produces a list of common search terms associated with a typed-in name, has defamed them. The list is largely based on the frequency of previous searches: terms are ranked by their mathematical probability. Still, which of us wouldn't be angry if the word "convict" or "prostitute" appeared next to our name when potential business or romantic partners turned to the Web to check us out?

We envision algorithmists as providing a market-oriented approach to problems like these that may head off more intrusive forms of regulation. They'd fill a need similar to the one accountants and auditors filled when they emerged in the early twentieth century to handle the new deluge of financial information. The numeric onslaught was hard for people to understand; it required specialists organized in an agile, self-regulatory way. The market responded by giving rise to a new sector of competitive firms specializing in financial surveillance. By offering this service, the new breed of professionals bolstered society's confidence in the economy. Big data could and should benefit from the similar confidence boost that algorithmists would provide.

EXTERNAL ALGORITHMISTS

We envision external algorithmists acting as impartial auditors to review the accuracy or validity of big-data predictions whenever the government requires it, such as under court order or regulation. They also can take on big-data companies as clients, performing audits for firms that want expert support. And they may certify the soundness of big-data applications like anti-fraud techniques or stock-trading systems. Finally, external algorithmists are prepared to consult with government agencies on how best to use big data in the public sector.

As in medicine, law, and other occupations, we envision that this new profession regulates itself with a code of conduct. The algorithmists' impartiality, confidentiality, competence, and professionalism are enforced by tough liability rules; if they fail to adhere to these standards, they'll be open to lawsuits. They can also be called on to serve as expert witnesses in trials, or to act as "court masters," experts appointed by judges to assist them in technical matters on particularly complex cases.

Moreover, people who believe they've been harmed by big-data predictions — a patient rejected for surgery, an inmate denied parole, a loan applicant denied a mortgage — can look to algorithmists much as they already look to lawyers for help in understanding and appealing those decisions.

INTERNAL ALGORITHMISTS

Internal algorithmists work inside an organization to monitor its big-data activities. They look out not just for the company's interests but also for the interests of people who are affected by its big-data analyses. They oversee big-data operations, and they're the first point of contact for anybody who feels harmed by their organization's big-data predictions. They also vet big-data analyses for integrity and accuracy before letting them go live. To perform the first of these two roles, algorithmists must have a certain level of freedom and impartiality within the organization they work for.

The notion of a person who works for a company remaining impartial about its operations may seem counterintuitive, but such situations are actually fairly common. The surveillance divisions at major financial institutions are one example; so are the boards of directors at many firms, whose responsibility is to shareholders, not management. And many media companies, including the *New York Times* and the *Washington Post,* employ ombudsmen whose primary responsibility is to defend the public trust. These employees handle readers' complaints and often chastise their employer publicly when they determine that it has done wrong.

And there's an even closer analogue to the internal algorithmist — a professional charged with ensuring that personal information isn't misused in the corporate setting. For instance, Germany requires companies above a certain size (generally ten or more people employed in processing personal information) to designate a data-protection representative. Since the 1970s, these in-house representatives have developed a professional ethic and an esprit de corps. They meet regularly to share best practices and training and have their own specialized media and conferences. Moreover, they've succeeded in maintaining dual allegiances to their employers *and* to their duties as impartial reviewers, managing to act as data-protection ombudsmen while also embedding information-privacy values throughout their companies' operations. We believe in-house algorithmists can do the same.

Governing the data barons

Data is to the information society what fuel was to the industrial economy: the critical resource powering the innovations that people rely on. Without a rich, vibrant supply of data and a robust market for services, the creativity and productivity that are possible may be stifled.

In this chapter we have laid out three fundamental new strategies for big-data governance, regarding privacy, propensity, and algorithm auditing. We're confident that with these in place the dark side of big data will be contained. Yet as the nascent big-data industry develops, an additional critical challenge will be to safeguard competitive big-data markets. We must prevent the rise of twenty-first-century data barons, the modern equivalent of the nineteenth-century robber barons who dominated America's railroads, steel manufacturing, and telegraph networks.

To control those earlier industrialists, the United States established antitrust rules that were extremely adaptable. Originally designed for the railroads in the 1800s, they were later applied to firms that were gatekeepers to the flow of information that businesses depend on, from National Cash Register in the 1910s, to IBM in the 1960s and later, Xerox in the 1970s, AT&T in the 1980s, Microsoft in the 1990s, and Google today. The technologies these firms pioneered became core components of the "information infrastructure" of the economy, and required the force of law to prevent unhealthy dominance.

To ensure the conditions for a bustling market for big data, we will need measures comparable to the ones that established competition and oversight in those earlier areas of technology. We should enable data transactions, such as through licensing and interoperability. This raises the issue of whether society might benefit from a carefully crafted and well-balanced "exclusion right" for data (similar to an intellectual property right, as provocative as this may sound!). Admittedly, achieving this would be a tall order for policymakers — and one fraught with risk for the rest of us.

It is obviously impossible to foretell how a technology will develop; even big data can't predict how big data will evolve. Regulators will need to strike a balance between acting cautiously and boldly — and the history of antitrust law points to one way this can be accomplished.

Antitrust regulation curbed abusive power. Yet strikingly, its principles translated beautifully from one sector to another, and across different types of network industries. It is just the sort of muscular regulation — which does not favor one sort of technology over another — that is useful, since it protects competition without presuming to do much more than that. Hence, antitrust may help big data steam ahead just as it did the railroads. Also, as some of the world's biggest data holders, governments ought to release their own data publicly. Encouragingly, some are already doing both these things — at least to an extent.

The lesson of antitrust regulation is that once overarching principles are identified, regulators can implement them to ensure the right degree of safeguards and support. Similarly, the three strategies we have put forward — shifting privacy protections from individual consent to data-users accountability; enshrining human agency amid predictions; and inventing a new caste of big-data auditors we call algorithmists — may serve as a foundation for effective and fair governance of information in the big-data era.

In many fields, from nuclear technology to bioengineering, we first build tools that we discover can harm us and only later set out to devise the safety mechanisms to protect us from those new tools. In this regard, big data takes its place alongside other areas of society that present challenges with no absolute solutions, just ongoing questions about how we order our world. Every generation must address these issues anew. Our task is to appreciate the hazards of this powerful technology, support its development — and seize its rewards.

Just as the printing press led to changes in the way society governs itself, so too does big data. It forces us to confront new challenges with new solutions. To ensure that people are protected at the same time as the technology is promoted, we must not let big data develop beyond the reach of human ability to shape the technology.

10

NEXT

MIKE FLOWERS WAS A LAWYER in the Manhattan district attorney's office in the early 2000s, prosecuting everything from homicides to Wall Street crimes, then made the shift to a plush corporate law firm. After a boring year behind a desk, he decided to leave that job too. Looking for something more meaningful, he thought of helping to rebuild Iraq. A friendly partner at the firm made a few calls to people in high places. The next thing Flowers knew, he was heading into the Green Zone, the secure area for American troops in the center of Baghdad, as part of the legal team for the trial of Saddam Hussein.

Most of his work turned out to be logistical, not legal. He needed to identify areas of suspected mass graves to know where to send investigators digging. He needed to ferry witnesses into the Green Zone without getting them blown up by the many IED (improvised explosive device) attacks that were a grim daily reality. He noticed that the military treated these tasks as information problems. And data came to the rescue. Intelligence analysts would combine field reports with details about the location, time, and casualties of past IED attacks to predict the safest route for that day.

On his return to New York City a few years later, Flowers realized that those methods marked a more powerful way to combat crime than he'd ever had at his disposal as a prosecutor. And he found a veritable soul mate in the city's mayor, Michael Bloomberg, who had made his fortune in data by supplying financial information to banks. Flowers was named to a special task force assigned to crunch the numbers that might unmask the villains of the subprime mortgage scandal in 2009. The unit was so successful that a year later Mayor Bloomberg asked it to expand its scope. Flowers became the city's first "director of analytics." His mission: to build a team of the best data scientists he could find and harness the city's untapped troves of information to reap efficiencies covering everything and anything.

Flowers cast his net wide to find the right people. "I had no interest in very experienced statisticians," he says. "I was a little concerned that they would be reluctant to take this novel approach to problem solving." Earlier, when he had interviewed traditional stats guys for the financial fraud project, they had tended to raise arcane concerns about mathematical methods. "I wasn't even thinking about what model I was going to use. I wanted actionable insight, and that was all I cared about," he says. In the end he picked a team of five people he calls "the kids." All but one were economics majors just a year or two out of school and without much experience living in a big city, and they all had something a bit creative about them.

Among the first challenges the team tackled was "illegal conversions" — the practice of cutting up a dwelling into many smaller units so that it can house as many as ten times the number of people it was designed for. They are major fire hazards, as well as cauldrons of crime, drugs, disease, and pest infestation. A tangle of extension cords may snake across the walls; hot plates sit perilously on top of bedspreads. People packed this tight regularly die in blazes. In 2005 two firefighters perished trying to rescue residents. New York City gets roughly 25,000 illegal-conversion complaints a year, but it has only 200 inspectors to handle them. There seemed to be no good way to distinguish cases that were simply nuisances from ones that were poised to burst into flames. To Flowers and his kids, though, this looked like a problem that could be solved with lots of data.

They started with a list of every property lot in the city — all 900,000 of them. Next they poured in datasets from 19 different agencies indicating, for example, if the building owner was delinquent in paying property taxes, if there had been foreclosure proceedings, and if anomalies in utilities usage or missed payments had led to any service cuts. They also fed in information about the type of building and when it was built, plus ambulance visits, crime rates, rodent complaints, and more. Then they compared all this information against five years of fire data ranked by severity and looked for correlations in order to generate a system that could predict which complaints should be investigated most urgently.

Initially, much of the data wasn't in usable form. For instance, the city's record keepers did not use a single, standard way to describe location; every agency and department seemed to have its own approach. The buildings department assigns every structure a unique building number. The housing preservation department has a different numbering system. The tax department gives each property an identifier based on borough, block, and lot. The police use Cartesian coordinates. The fire department relies on a system of proximity to "call boxes" related to the location of firehouses, even though call boxes are defunct. Flowers's kids embraced this messiness by devising a system that identifies buildings by using a small area in the front of the property based on Cartesian coordinates and then draws in geo-loco data from the other agencies' databases. Their method was inherently inexact, but the vast amount of data they were able to use more than compensated for the imperfections.

The team members weren't content just to crunch numbers, though. They went into the field with inspectors to watch them work. They took copious notes and quizzed the pros on everything. When one grizzled chief grunted that the building they were about to examine wouldn't be a problem, the geeks wanted to know why he felt so sure. He couldn't quite say, but the kids gradually determined that his intuition was based on the new brickwork on the building's exterior, which suggested to him that the owner cared about the place.

The kids went back to their cubicles and wondered how they could possibly feed "recent brickwork" into their model as a signal. After all, bricks aren't datafied — yet. But sure enough, a city permit is required for doing any external brickwork. Adding the permit information improved their system's predictive performance by indicating that some suspected properties were probably *not* major risks.

The analytics occasionally showed that some time-honored ways of doing things were not the best, just as the scouts in *Moneyball* had to accept the shortcomings of their intuition. For example, the number of calls to the city's "311" complaint hotline was considered to indicate which buildings were most in need of attention. More calls equaled more serious problems. But this turned out to be a misleading measure. A rat spotted on the posh Upper East Side might generate thirty calls within an hour, but it might take a battalion of rodents before residents in the Bronx felt moved to dial 311. Likewise, the majority of complaints about an illegal conversion might be about noise, not about hazardous conditions.

In June 2011 Flowers and his kids flipped the switch on their system. Every complaint that fell into the category of an illegal conversion was processed on a weekly basis. They gathered the ones that ranked in the top 5 percent for fire risk and passed them on to the inspectors for immediate follow-up. When the results came back, everyone was stunned.

Prior to the big-data analysis, inspectors followed up the complaints they deemed most dire, but only in 13 percent of cases did they find conditions severe enough to warrant a vacate order. Now they were issuing vacate orders on more than 70 percent of the buildings they inspected. By indicating which buildings most needed their attention, big data improved their efficiency fivefold. And their work became more satisfying: they were concentrating on the biggest problems. The inspectors' newfound effectiveness had spillover benefits, too. Fires in illegal conversions are 15 times more likely than other fires to result in injury or death for firefighters, so the fire department loved it. Flowers and his kids looked like wizards with a crystal ball that let them see into the future and predict which places were most risky. They took massive quantities of data that had been lying around for years, largely unused after it was collected, and harnessed it in a novel way to extract real value. Using a big corpus of information allowed them to spot connections that weren't detectable in smaller amounts — the essence of big data.

The experience of New York City's analytical alchemists highlights many of the themes of this book. They used a gargantuan quantity of data, not just some; their list of buildings in the city represented nothing less than N = all. The data was messy, such as location information or ambulance records, but that didn't deter them. In fact, the benefits of using more data outweighed the drawbacks of less pristine information. They were able to achieve their accomplishments because so many features of the city had been datafied (however inconsistently), allowing them to process the information.

The inklings of experts had to take a backseat to the data-driven approach. At the same time, Flowers and his kids continually tested their system with veteran inspectors, drawing on their experience to make the system perform better. Yet the most important reason for the program's success was that it dispensed with a reliance on causation in favor of correlation.

"I am not interested in causation except as it speaks to action," explains Flowers. "Causation is for other people, and frankly it is very dicey when you start talking about causation. I don't think there is any cause whatsoever between the day that someone files a foreclosure proceeding against a property and whether or not that place has a historic risk for a structural fire. I think it would be obtuse to think so. And nobody would actually come out and say that. They'd think, no, it's the underlying factors. But I don't want to even get into that. I need a specific data point that I have access to, and tell me its significance. If it's significant, then we'll act on it. If not, then we won't. You know, we have real problems to solve. I can't dick around, frankly, thinking about other things like causation right now."

When data speaks

The effects of big data are large on a practical level, as the technology is applied to find solutions for vexing everyday problems. But that is just the start. Big data is poised to reshape the way we live, work, and think. The change we face is in some ways even greater than those sparked by earlier epochal innovations that dramatically expanded the scope and scale of information in society. The ground beneath our feet is shifting. Old certainties are being questioned. Big data requires fresh discussion of the nature of decision-making, destiny, justice. A worldview we thought was made of causes is being challenged by a preponderance of correlations. The possession of knowledge, which once meant an understanding of the past, is coming to mean an ability to predict the future.

These issues are much more significant than the ones that presented themselves when we prepared to exploit e-commerce, live with the Internet, enter the computer age, or take up the abacus. The idea that our quest to understand causes may be overrated — that in many cases it may be more advantageous to eschew *why* in favor of *what* — suggests that the matters are fundamental to our society and our existence. The challenges posed by big data may not have set answers, either. Rather, they are part of the timeless debate over man's place in the universe and his search for meaning amid the hurly-burly of a chaotic, incomprehensible world.

Ultimately, big data marks the moment when the "information society" finally fulfills the promise implied by its name. The data takes center stage. All those digital bits that we have gathered can now be harnessed in novel ways to serve new purposes and unlock new forms of value. But this requires a new way of thinking and will challenge our institutions and even our sense of identity. The one certainty is that the amount of data will continue to grow, as will the power to process it all. But where most people have considered big data as a technological matter, focusing on the hardware or the software, we believe the emphasis needs to shift to what happens when the data speaks.

We can capture and analyze more information than ever before. The scarcity of data is no longer the characteristic that defines our efforts to interpret the world. We can harness vastly more data and in some instances, get close to all of it. But doing so forces us to operate in untraditional ways and, in particular, changes our idea of what constitutes useful information.

Instead of obsessing about the accuracy, exactitude, cleanliness, and rigor of the data, we can let some slack creep in. We shouldn't accept data that is outright wrong or false, but some messiness may become acceptable in return for capturing a far more comprehensive set of data. In fact, in some cases big and messy can even be beneficial, since when we tried to use just a small, exact portion of the data, we ended up failing to capture the breadth of detail where so much knowledge lies.

Because correlations can be found far faster and cheaper than causation, they're often preferable. We will still need causal studies and controlled experiments with carefully curated data in certain cases, such as designing a critical airplane part. But for many everyday needs, knowing *what* not *why* is good enough. And big-data correlations can point the way toward promising areas in which to explore causal relationships.

These quick correlations let us save money on plane tickets, predict flu outbreaks, and know which manholes or overcrowded buildings to inspect in a resource-constrained world. They may enable health insurance firms to provide coverage without a physical exam and lower the cost of reminding the sick to take their medication. Languages are translated and cars drive themselves on the basis of predictions made through big-data correlations. Walmart can learn which flavor Pop-Tarts to stock at the front of the store before a hurricane. (Answer: strawberry.) Of course, causality is nice when you can get it. The problem is that it's often hard to get, and when we think we've found it we're often deluding ourselves.

New tools, from faster processors and more memory to smarter software and algorithms, are only part of the reason we can do all this. While the tools are important, a more fundamental reason is that we have more data, since more aspects of the world are being datafied. To be sure, the human ambition to quantify the world long predated the computer revolution. But digital tools facilitate datafication greatly. Not only can mobile phones track whom we call and where we go, but the data they collect can be used to detect whether we're falling ill. Soon big data may be able to tell whether we're falling in love.

Our ability to do new, do more, do better, and do faster has the potential to unleash enormous value, creating new winners and losers. Much of the value of data will come from its secondary uses, its option value, not simply its primary use, as we're accustomed to think about it. As a result, for most types of data, it seems sensible to collect as much as one can and hold it as long as it adds value, and let others analyze it if they're better suited to extract its value (provided one can share in the lucre the analysis unleashes).

Companies that can situate themselves in the middle of information flows and can collect data will thrive. Harnessing big data effectively requires technical skills and a lot of imagination — a big-data mindset. But the crux of the value may go to those who hold the data. And sometimes an important asset will not be just the plainly visible information but the data exhaust created by people's interactions with information, which a clever company can use to improve an existing service or launch an entirely new one.

At the same time, big data presents us with huge risks. It renders ineffective the core technical and legal mechanisms through which we currently try to protect privacy. In the past what constituted personally identifiable information was well known — names, Social Security numbers, tax records, and so on — and hence relatively easy to protect. Today, even the most innocuous data can reveal someone's identity if a data collector has amassed enough of it. Anonymization or hiding in plain sight no longer works. Moreover, targeting an individual for surveillance now entails a more extensive invasion of privacy than ever before, since authorities not only want to see as much information about a person as possible, but also the widest range of relationships, connections, and interactions.

In addition to challenging privacy, these uses of big data raise another unique and troubling concern: the risk that we may judge people not just for their actual behavior but for propensities the data suggests they have. As big-data predictions become more accurate, society may use them to punish people for predicted behavior — acts they have not yet committed. Such predictions are axiomatically impossible to disprove; hence the people they accuse can never exculpate themselves. Punishment on this basis negates the concept of free will and denies the possibility, however small, that a person may choose a different path. As society assigns individual responsibility (and metes out punishment), human volition must be considered inviolable. The future must remain something that we can shape to our own design. If it does not, big data will have perverted the very essence of humanity: rational thought and free choice.

There are no foolproof ways to fully prepare for the world of big data; it will require that we establish new principles by which we govern ourselves. A series of important changes to our practices can help society as it becomes more familiar with big data's character and shortcomings. We must protect privacy by shifting responsibility away from individuals and toward the data users — that is, to accountable use. In a world of predictions, it's vital we ensure that human volition is held sacrosanct and we preserve not only people's capacity for moral choice but individual responsibility for individual acts. And society must design safeguards to allow a new professional class of "algorithmists" to assess big-data analytics — so that a world which has become less random by dint of big data does not turn into a black box, simply replacing one form of the unknowable with another.

Big data will become integral to understanding and addressing many of our pressing global problems. Tackling climate change requires analyzing pollution data to understand where best to focus our efforts and find ways to mitigate problems. The sensors being placed all over the world, including those embedded in smartphones, provide a cornucopia of data that will let us model global warming at a better level of detail. Meanwhile, improving and lowering the cost of healthcare, especially for the world's poor, will be in large part about automating tasks that currently seem to need human judgment but could be done by computer, such as examining biopsies for cancerous cells or detecting infections before symptoms fully emerge.

Big data has already been used for economic development and for conflict prevention. It has revealed areas of African slums that are vi-brant communities of economic activity by analyzing the movements of cellphone users. It has uncovered areas that are ripe for ethnic clashes and indicated how refugee crises might unfold. And its uses will only multiply as the technology is applied to more aspects of life.

Big data helps us do what we already do better, and it allows us to do new things altogether. Yet it is no magic wand. It won't bring about world peace, eradicate poverty, or produce the next Picasso. Big data can't make a baby — but it can save premature ones. In time, we will come to expect it to be used in almost every facet of life, and perhaps we'll be slightly alarmed when it's absent, in the same way that we expect a doctor to order an X-ray to uncover problems that couldn't possibly be gleaned from a physical exam.

As big data becomes commonplace, it may well affect how we think about the future. Around five hundred years ago, humanity went through a profound shift in its perception of time, as part of the move toward a more secular, science-based, and enlightened Europe. Before that, time was experienced as cyclical, and so was life. Every day (and year) was much like the one before, and even the end of life re-sembled its start, as adults again became childlike. Later, time came to be seen as linear — an unfolding sequence of days in which the world could be shaped and life's trajectory influenced. If earlier, the past, present, and future had all been fused together, now humanity had a past to look back upon, and a future to look forward to, as it shaped its present.

While the present could be molded, the future turned from some-thing perfectly predictable into something open, pristine — a vast, empty canvas that individuals could fill according to their own values and efforts. One of the defining features of modern times is our sense of ourselves as masters of our fate; this attitude sets us apart from our ancestors, for whom determinism of some form was the norm. Yet big-data predictions render the future less open and untouched. Rather than being a blank canvas, our future seems already sketched in faint traces that are discernible to those with the technology to make them apparent. This seems to diminish our capacity to shape our destiny. Potentiality is slaughtered on the altar of probability.

At the same time, big data may mean that we are forever prisoners of our previous actions, which can be used against us in systems that presume to predict our future behavior: we can never escape what has come before. "What's past is prologue," wrote Shakespeare. Big data enshrines this algorithmically, for ill as well as good. Will a world of predictions dampen our enthusiasm to greet the sunrise, our desire to put our own human imprint on the world?

The opposite is actually more likely. Knowing how actions may play out in the future will allow us to take remedial steps to prevent problems or improve outcomes. We will spot students who are starting to slip long before the final exam. We will detect tiny cancers and treat them before the full-blown disease has a chance to emerge. We will see the likelihood of unwanted teenage pregnancy or a life of crime and intervene to change, as much as we can, that predicted outcome. We will prevent deadly fires from consuming overcrowded New York tenements by knowing which buildings to inspect first.

Nothing is preordained, because we can always respond and react to the information we receive. Big data's predictions are not set in stone—they are only likely outcomes, and that means that if we want to change them we can do so. We may identify how to best greet the future and be its master, just as Maury found natural pathways within the vast, open space of wind and waves. And to accomplish this we won't need to comprehend the nature of the cosmos or prove the existence of the gods—big data will be good enough.

Even bigger data

As big data transforms our lives—optimizing, improving, making more efficient, and capturing benefits—what role is left for intuition, faith, uncertainty, and originality?

If big data teaches us anything, it is that just acting better, making improvements—without deeper understanding—is often good enough. Continually doing so is virtuous. Even if you don't know why your efforts work as they do, you're generating better outcomes than you would by not making such efforts. Flowers and his "kids" in New York may not embody the enlightenment of the sages, but they do save lives.

Big data is not an ice-cold world of algorithms and automatons. There is an essential role for people, with all our foibles, misperceptions and mistakes, since these traits walk hand in hand with human creativity, instinct, and genius. The same messy mental processes that lead to our occasional humiliation or wrongheadedness also give rise to successes and stumbling upon our greatness. This suggests that, just as we're learning to embrace messy data because it serves a larger purpose, we ought to welcome the inexactitude that is part of what it means to be human. After all, messiness is an essential property of both the world and our minds; in both cases, we only benefit by accepting it and applying it.

In a world in which data informs decisions, what purpose remains for people, or for intuition and going against the facts? If everyone appeals to the data and harnesses big-data tools, perhaps what becomes the central point of differentiation is unpredictability: the human element of instinct, risk-taking, accident, and error.

If so, then there will be a special need to carve out a place for the human: to reserve space for intuition, common sense, and serendipity to ensure that they are not crowded out by data and machine-made answers. What is greatest about human beings is precisely what the algorithms and silicon chips don't reveal, what they can't reveal because it can't be captured in data. It is not the "what is," but the "what is not": the empty space, the cracks in the sidewalk, the unspoken and the not-yet-thought.

This has important implications for the notion of progress in society. Big data enables us to experiment faster and explore more leads. These advantages should produce more innovation. But the spark of invention becomes what the data does not say. That is something that no amount of data can ever confirm or corroborate, since it has yet to exist. If Henry Ford had queried big-data algorithms for what his customers wanted, they would have replied "a faster horse" (to rephrase his famous saying). In a world of big data, it is our most human traits that will need to be fostered — our creativity, intuition, and intellectual ambition — since our ingenuity is the source of our progress.

Big data is a resource and a tool. It is meant to inform, rather than explain; it points us toward understanding, but it can still lead to misunderstanding, depending on how well or poorly it is wielded. And however dazzling we find the power of big data to be, we must never let its seductive glimmer blind us to its inherent imperfections.

The totality of information in the world — the ultimate N = all — can never be gathered, stored, or processed by our technologies. For example, the CERN particle-physics laboratory in Switzerland collects less than 0.1 percent of the information that is generated during its experiments — the rest, seemingly of no use, is left to dissipate into the ether. But this is hardly a new truth. Society has always been hobbled by the limitations of the tools we use to measure and know reality, from compass and sextant to telescope and radar to today's GPS. Our tools may be twice or ten times or a thousand times as powerful tomorrow as they are today, making what we know now seem minuscule then. Our current big-data world will, before long, look as quaint as the four kilobytes of writeable memory in Apollo 11's guidance control computer does now.

What we are able to collect and process will always be just a tiny fraction of the information that exists in the world. It can only be a simulacrum of reality, like the shadows on the wall of Plato's cave. Because we can never have perfect information, our predictions are inherently fallible. This doesn't mean they're wrong, only that they are always incomplete. It doesn't negate the insights that big data offers, but it puts big data in its place — as a tool that doesn't offer ultimate answers, just good-enough ones to help us now until better methods and hence better answers come along. It also suggests that we must use this tool with a generous degree of humility . . . and humanity.

NOTES

1. NOW

1   Google Flu Trends — Jeremy Ginsburg et al., "Detecting Influenza Epi-
    demics Using Search Engine Query Data," *Nature* 457 (2009), pp. 1012–14
    (http://www.nature.com/nature/journal/v457/n7232/full/nature07634
    .html).

2   Follow-on study of Google Flu Trends — A. F. Dugas et al., "Google Flu
    Trends: Correlation with Emergency Department Influenza Rates and
    Crowding Metrics," CID Advanced Access (January 8, 2012); DOI 10.1093
    /cid/cir883.

4   Buying airplane tickets, Farecast — The information comes from Kenneth
    Cukier, "Data, Data Everywhere," *The Economist* special report, February
    27, 2010, pp. 1–14, and from interviews with Etzioni between 2010 and 2012.
    Etzioni's Hamlet project — Oren Etzioni, C. A. Knoblock, R. Tuchinda, and
    A. Yates, "To Buy or Not to Buy: Mining Airfare Data to Minimize Ticket
    Purchase Price," SIGKDD '03, August 24–27, 2003 (http://knight.cis.tem
    ple.edu/~yates//papers/hamlet-kdd03.pdf).

5   Price Microsoft paid for Farecast — From media reports, notably "Secret
    Farecast Buyer Is Microsoft," Seattlepi.com, April 17, 2008 (http://blog
    .seattlepi.com/venture/2008/04/17/secret-farecast-buyer-is-microsoft
    /?source=mypi).

6   One way to think about big data — There is a loud and unproductive debate
    over the origin of the term "big data" and how to perfectly define it. The
    two words have occasionally appeared in unison for decades. A research
    report in 2001 by Doug Laney of Gartner set out the "three Vs" of big data
    (volume, velocity, and variety), which was useful for its time but imperfect.

7   Astronomy and DNA sequencing — Cukier, "Data, Data Everywhere."
    Billions of shares traded — Rita Nazareth and Julia Leite, "Stock Trading in

U.S. Falls to Lowest Level Since 2008," *Bloomberg,* August 13, 2012 (http://www.bloomberg.com/news/2012-08-13/stock-trading-in-u-s-hits-lowest-level-since-2008-as-vix-falls.html).

8   Google's 24 petabytes per day — Thomas H. Davenport, Paul Barth, and Randy Bean, "How 'Big Data' Is Different," *Sloan Review,* July 30, 2012, pp. 43–46 (http://sloanreview.mit.edu/the-magazine/2012-fall/54104/how-big-data-is-different/).

Facebook stats — Facebook IPO prospectus, "Form S-1 Registration Statement," U.S. Securities and Exchange Commission, February 1, 2012 (http://sec.gov/Archives/edgar/data/1326801/000119312512034517/d287954ds1.htm).

YouTube stats — Larry Page, "Update from the CEO," Google, April 2012 (http://investor.google.com/corporate/2012/ceo-letter.html).

Number of tweets — Tomio Geron, "Twitter's Dick Costolo: Twitter Mobile Ad Revenue Beats Desktop on Some Days," *Forbes,* June 6, 2012 (http://www.forbes.com/sites/tomiogeron/2012/06/06/twitters-dick-costolo-mobile-ad-revenue-beats-desktop-on-some-days/).

Information on the amount of data — Martin Hilbert and Priscilla López, "The World's Technological Capacity to Store, Communicate, and Compute Information" *Science,* April 1, 2011, pp. 60–65; Martin Hilbert and Priscilla López, "How to Measure the World's Technological Capacity to Communicate, Store and Compute Information?" *International Journal of Communication* 2012, pp. 1042–55 (http://www.ijoc.org/ojs/index.php/ijoc/article/viewFile/1562/742).

9   Estimate of the amount of stored information by 2013 — Cukier interview with Hilbert, 2012.

10   Printing press and eight million books; more produced since the founding of Constantinople — Elizabeth L. Eisenstein, *The Printing Revolution in Early Modern Europe* (Canto/Cambridge University Press, 1993), pp. 13–14.

Peter Norvig's analogy — From Norvig's talks based on the paper: A. Halevy, P. Norvig, and F. Pereira, "The Unreasonable Effectiveness of Data," *IEEE Intelligent Systems,* March/April 2009, pp. 8–12 (http://www.computer.org/portal/cms_docs_intelligent/intelligent/homepage/2009/x2exp.pdf). (Note that the title is a play on Eugene Wigner's article "The Unreasonable Effectiveness of Mathematics in the Natural Sciences" in which he considers why physics can be nicely expressed in basic math but the social sciences resist such tidy formulas. See E. Wigner, "The Unreasonable Effectiveness of Mathematics in the Natural Sciences," *Communications on Pure and Applied Mathematics* 13, no. 1 (1960), pp. 1–14.) Among Norvig's talks on the paper is "Peter Norvig — The Unreasonable Effectiveness of Data," lecture at University of British Columbia, YouTube, September 23, 2010 (http://www.youtube.com/watch?v=yvDCzhbjYWs).

On physical size affecting operative physical law (although not entirely correct), the often cited reference is to J. B. S. Haldane, "On Being the Right Size," *Harper's Magazine,* March 1926 (http://harpers.org /archive/1926/03/on-being-the-right-size/).

Picasso on the Lascaux images — David Whitehouse, "UK Science Shows Cave Art Developed Early," *BBC News Online,* October 3, 2001 (http:// news.bbc.co.uk/1/hi/sci/tech/1577421.stm).

2. MORE

19   Jeff Jonas quotation — Conversation with Jonas, December 2010, Paris.

21   History of the U.S. census — U.S. Census Bureau, "The Hollerith Machine" Online history. (http://www.census.gov/history/www/innovations/tech nology/the_hollerith_tabulator.html.

22   Neyman's contribution — William Kruskal and Frederick Mosteller, "Representative Sampling, IV: The History of the Concept in Statistics, 1895– 1939," *International Statistical Review* 48 (1980), pp. 169–195, pp. 187–188. Neyman's famous paper is Jerzy Neyman, "On the Two Different Aspects of the Representative Method: The Method of Stratified Sampling and the Method of Purposive Selection," *Journal of the Royal Statistical Society* 97, no. 4 (1934), pp. 558–625.
      A sample of 1,100 observations is sufficient — Earl Babbie, *Practice of Social Research* (12th ed. 2010), pp. 204–207.

24   The cellphone effect — "Estimating the Cellphone Effect," September 20, 2008   (http://www.fivethirtyeight.com/2008/09/estimating-cellphone -effect-22-points.html); for more on polling biases and other statistical insights see Nate Silver, *The Signal and the Noise: Why So Many Predictions Fail — But Some Don't* (Penguin, 2012).

25   Steve Jobs's gene sequencing — Walter Isaacson, *Steve Jobs* (Simon and Schuster, 2011), pp. 550–551.

27   Google Flu Trends predicting to city level — Dugas et al., "Google Flu Trends."
      Etzioni on temporal data — Interview by Cukier, October 2011.

28   John Kunze quotation — Jonathan Rosenthal, "Special Report: International Banking," *The Economist,* May 19, 2012, pp. 7–8.
      Sumo match fixing — Mark Duggan and Steven D. Levitt, "Winning Isn't Everything: Corruption in Sumo Wrestling," *American Economic Review* 92 (2002), pp. 1594–1605 (http://pricetheory.uchicago.edu/levitt/Papers /DugganLevitt2002.pdf).

29   Lytro's 11 million light rays — from Lytro's corporate website (http://www .lytro.com).

30   Replacing sampling in the social sciences — Mike Savage and Roger Burrows, "The Coming Crisis of Empirical Sociology," *Sociology* 41 (2007), pp. 885–899.

On analyzing comprehensive data from a mobile phone operator — J. P. On-nela et al., "Structure and Tie Strengths in Mobile Communication Net-works," *Proceedings of the National Academy of Sciences of the United States of America (PNAS)* 104 (May 2007), pp. 7332–36 (http://nd.edu/~dddas /Papers/PNAS0610245104v1.pdf).

3. MESSY

33   Crosby — Alfred W. Crosby, *The Measure of Reality: Quantification and Western Society, 1250–1600* (Cambridge University Press, 1997).

On Kelvin and Bacon quotations — These aphorisms are widely attributed to both men, though the actual expression in their written works is slightly different. In Kelvin, it's part of a longer quotation on measurement, from his lecture "Electrical Units of Measurement" (1883). For Bacon, it's con-sidered to be a loose translation from Latin, in *Meditationes Sacrae* (1597).

34   Many ways to refer to IBM — DJ Patil, "Data Jujitsu: The Art of Turning Data into Product," *O'Reilly Media,* July 2012 (http://oreillynet.com/oreilly /data/radarreports/data-jujitsu.csp?cmp=tw-strata-books-data-products).

35   30,000 trades per second on NYSE — Colin Clark, "Improving Speed and Transparency of Market Data," NYSE EURONEXT blog post, Jan-uary 9, 2011 (http://exchanges.nyx.com/cclark/improving-speed-and -transparency-market-data).

Idea that "2+2=3.9" — Brian Hopkins and Boris Evelson, "Expand Your Digital Horizon with Big Data," Forrester, September 30, 2011.

Improvements in algorithms — President's Council of Advisors on Science and Technology, "Report to the President and Congress, Designing a Dig-ital Future: Federally Funded Research and Development in Networking and Information Technology," December 2010, p. 71 (http://www.white house.gov/sites/default/files/microsites/ostp/pcast-nitrd-report-2010 .pdf).

36   Chess endgame tables — The most comprehensive endgame table publicly available, the Nalimov tableset (named after one of its creators), covers all games for six or fewer chess pieces. Its size exceeds seven terabytes, and compressing the information in it is a major challenge. See E. V. Nalimov, G. McC. Haworth, and E. A. Heinz, "Space-efficient Indexing of Chess Endgame Tables," *ICGA Journal* 23, no. 3 (2000), pp. 148–162.

Microsoft and algorithm performance — Michele Banko and Eric Brill, "Scaling to Very Very Large Corpora for Natural Language Disambigua-tion," Microsoft Research, 2001, p. 3 (http://acl.ldc.upenn.edu/P/P01/P01 -1005.pdf).

IBM demo, words, and quotation — IBM, "701 Translator," press release, IBM archives, January 8, 1954 (http://www-03.ibm.com/ibm/history /exhibits/701/701_translator.html). See also John Hutchins, "The First

Public Demonstration of Machine Translation: The Georgetown-IBM System, 7th January 1954," November 2005 (http://www.hutchinsweb.me.uk/GU-IBM-2005.pdf).

IBM Candide—Adam L. Berger et al., "The Candide System for Machine Translation," *Proceedings of the 1994 ARPA Workshop on Human Language Technology,* 1994 (http://aclweb.org/anthology-new/H/H94/H94-1100.pdf).

History of machine translation—Yorick Wilks, *Machine Translation: Its Scope and Limits* (Springer, 2008), p. 107.

38 Candide's millions of texts versus Google's billions of texts—Och interview with Cukier, December 2009.

Google's corpus of 95 billion sentences—Alex Franz and Thorsten Brants, "All Our N-gram are Belong to You," Google blog post, August 3, 2006 (http://googleresearch.blogspot.co.uk/2006/08/all-our-n-gram-are-belong-to-you.html).

39 Brown corpus and Google's 1 trillion words—Halevy, Norvig, and Pereira, "The Unreasonable Effectiveness of Data."

Quotation from paper Norvig co-authored—ibid.

40 BP pipe corrosion and hostile wireless environment—Jaclyn Clarabut, "Operations Making Sense of Corrosion," *BP Magazine,* issue 2 (2011) (http://www.bp.com/liveassets/bp_internet/globalbp/globalbp_uk_english/reports_and_publications/bp_magazine/STAGING/local_assets/pdf/BP_Magazine_2011_issue2_text.pdf). The difficulty of wireless data readings comes from Cukier, "Data, Data, Everywhere." The system is obviously not infallible: a fire at the BP Cherry Point refinery in February 2012 was blamed on a corroded pipe.

41 Billion Prices Project—From interview with co-founders with Cukier, October 2012. Also, James Surowiecki, "A Billion Prices Now," *The New Yorker,* May 30, 2011; data and details can be found on the project's website (http://bpp.mit.edu/); Annie Lowrey, "Economists' Programs Are Beating U.S. at Tracking Inflation," *Washington Post,* December 25, 2010 (http://www.washingtonpost.com/wp-dyn/content/article/2010/12/25/AR2010122502600.html).

42 On PriceStats as a check on national statistics—"Official Statistics: Don't Lie to Me, Argentina," *The Economist,* February 25, 2012 (http://www.economist.com/node/21548242).

Number of photos on Flickr—From Flickr website (http://www.flick.com). On the challenge to categorize information—See David Weinberger, *Everything Is Miscellaneous: The Power of the New Digital Disorder* (Times, 2007).

45 Pat Helland—Pat Helland, "If You Have Too Much Data Then 'Good Enough' Is Good Enough," *Communications of the ACM,* June 2011, pp. 40, 41. There is a vigorous debate within the database community about the models and concepts best able to meet the needs of big data. Helland rep-

resents the camp arguing for a radical break with tools used in the past. Microsoft's Michael Rys, in "Scalable SQL," *Communications of the ACM,* June 2011, p. 48, argues that much-adapted versions of existing tools will work fine.

46   Visa using Hadoop — Cukier, "Data, data everywhere."

47   Only 5 percent of information is structured-data — Abhishek Mehta, "Big Data: Powering the Next Industrial Revolution," Tableau Software White Paper, 2011 (http://www.tableausoftware.com/learn/whitepapers /big-data-revolution).

4. CORRELATION

50   Linden story as well as "Amazon voice" — Linden interview with Cukier, March 2012.
     WSJ on Amazon critics — As cited in James Marcus, *Amazonia: Five Years at the Epicenter of the Dot.Com Juggernaut* (New Press, 2004), p. 128.

51   Marcus quotation — Marcus, *Amazonia,* p. 199.

52   Recommendations one-third of Amazon's income — This figure has never been officially confirmed by the company but has been published in numerous analyst reports and articles in the media, including "Building with Big Data: The Data Revolution Is Changing the Landscape of Business," *The Economist,* May 26, 2011 (http://www.economist.com/node/18741392/). The figure was also referenced by two former Amazon executives in interviews with Cukier.
     Netflix price information — Xavier Amatriain and Justin Basilico, "Netflix Recommendations: Beyond the 5 stars (Part 1)," Netflix blog, April 6, 2012.

53   "Fooled by Randomness" — Nassim Nicholas Taleb, *Fooled by Randomness* (Random House, 2008); for more, see Nassim Nicholas Taleb, *The Black Swan: The Impact of the Highly Improbable* (2nd ed., Random House, 2010).

54   Walmart and Pop-Tarts — Constance L. Hays, "What Wal-Mart Knows About Customers' Habits," *New York Times,* November 14, 2004 (http:// www.nytimes.com/2004/11/14/business/yourmoney/14wal.html).

56   Examples of predictive models by FICO, Experian, and Equifax — Scott Thurm, "Next Frontier in Credit Scores: Predicting Personal Behavior," *Wall Street Journal,* October 27, 2011 (http://online.wsj.com/article/SB100 01424052970203687504576655182086300912.html).

57   Aviva's predictive models — Leslie Scism and Mark Maremont, "Insurers Test Data Profiles to Identify Risky Clients," *Wall Street Journal,* November 19, 2010 (http://online.wsj.com/article/SB10001424052748704648604575 620750998072986.html). See also Leslie Scism and Mark Maremont, "Inside Deloitte's Life-Insurance Assessment Technology," *Wall Street Journal,* November 19, 2010 (http://online.wsj.com/article/SB10001424052748 7041041044575622531084755588.html). See also Howard Mills, "Analytics:

Turning Data into Dollars," *Forward Focus,* December 2011 (http://www
.deloitte.com/assets/Dcom-UnitedStates/Local%20Assets/Documents
/FSI/US_FSI_Forward%20Focus_Analytics_Turning%20data%20
into%20dollars_120711.pdf).

Example of Target and pregnant teenager — Charles Duhigg, "How Companies Learn Your Secrets," *New York Times,* February 16, 2012 (http://www
.nytimes.com/2012/02/19/magazine/shopping-habits.html). The article is
adapted from Duhigg's book *The Power of Habit: Why We Do What We Do
in Life and Business* (Random House, 2012); Target has stated there are inaccuracies in media accounts of its activities but declines to say what those
inaccuracies are. Asked about the matter for this book, a Target spokesper-
son replied: "The goal is to use guest data to enhance the guest relationship
with Target. Our guests want to receive great value, relevant offers, and a
superior experience. Like many companies, we use research tools that help
us understand guest shopping trends and preferences so that we can give
our guests offers and promotions that are relevant to them. We take our responsibility to protect our guests' trust in us very seriously. One way we do
this is by having a comprehensive privacy policy that we share openly on
Target.com and by routinely educating our team members on how to secure our guests' information."

59 UPS analytics work — Cukier interviews with Jack Levis, 2012.

60 Preemies — Based on interviews with McGregor in 2010 and 2012. See also
Carolyn McGregor, Christina Catley, Andrew James, and James Padbury,
"Next Generation Neonatal Health Informatics with Artemis," in Euro-
pean Federation for Medical Informatics, *User Centred Networked Health
Care,* ed. A. Moen et al. (IOS Press, 2011), p. 117. Some material comes from
Cukier, "Data, Data, Everywhere."

61 On the correlation between happiness and income — R. Inglehart and H.-D.
Klingemann, *Genes, Culture and Happiness* (MIT Press, 2000).

62 On measles and health expenses, and on new non-linear tools for correlation analysis — David Reshef et al., "Detecting Novel Associations in Large
Data Sets," *Science* 334 (2011), pp. 1518–24.

64 Kahneman — Daniel Kahneman, *Thinking, Fast and Slow* (Farrar, Straus
and Giroux, 2011), pp. 74–75.

65 Pasteur — For readers interested in Pasteur's larger influence on how we
perceive things, we suggest Bruno Latour, *The Pasteurization of France*
(Harvard University Press, 1993).

Risk of catching rabies — Melanie Di Quinzio and Anne McCarthy, "Rabies
Risk Among Travellers," *CMAJ* 178, no. 5 (2008), p. 567.

66 Causality can rarely be proven — The Turing Award–winning computer
scientist Judea Pearl has developed a way to formally represent causal dynamics; while no formal proof, this offers a pragmatic approach to analyzing possible causal connections; see Judea Pearl, *Causality: Models, Reasoning and Inference* (Cambridge University Press, 2009).

67 Orange car example — Quentin Hardy. "Bizarre Insights from Big Data," nytimes.com, March 28, 2012 (http://bits.blogs.nytimes.com/2012/03/28 /bizarre-insights-from-big-data/); and Kaggle, "Momchil Georgiev Shares His Chromatic Insight from Don't Get Kicked," blog posting, February 2, 2012 (http://blog.kaggle.com/2012/02/02/momchil-georgiev-shares-his -chromatic-insight-from-dont-get-kicked/).

68 Weight of manhole covers, number of explosions, and height of the blast — Rachel Ehrenberg, "Predicting the Next Deadly Manhole Explosion," *Wired,* July 7, 2010 (http://www.wired.com/wiredscience/2010/07 /manhole-explosions).

Con Edison working with Columbia University statisticians — This case is described for the lay audience in Cynthia Rudin et al., "21st-Century Data Miners Meet 19th-Century Electrical Cables," *Computer,* June 2011, pp. 103–105. Technical descriptions of the work are available through Rudin's and her collaborators' academic articles on their websites, in particular Cynthia Rudin et al., "Machine Learning for the New York City Power Grid," *IEEE Transactions on Pattern Analysis and Machine Intelligence* 34, no. 2 (2012), pp. 328–345 (http://hdl.handle.net/1721.1/68634).

69 Messiness of the term "service box" — This list comes from Rudin et al., "21st-Century Data Miners Meet 19th-Century Electrical Cables."

Rudin quotation — From interview with Cukier, March 2012.

70 Anderson's views — Chris Anderson, "The End of Theory: The Data Deluge Makes the Scientific Method Obsolete," *Wired,* June 2008 (http://www .wired.com/science/discoveries/magazine/16-07/pb_theory/).

71 Anderson's backpedal — National Public Radio, "Search and Destroy," July 18, 2008 (http://www.onthemedia.org/2008/jul/18/search-and-destroy /transcript/).

72 On choices influencing our analysis — danah boyd and Kate Crawford. "Six Provocations for Big Data," paper presented at Oxford Internet Institute's "A Decade in Internet Time: Symposium on the Dynamics of the Internet and Society," September 21, 2011 (http://ssrn.com/abstract=1926431).

5. DATAFICATION

73 Details of Maury's life compiled from numerous works by and about him. They include Chester G. Hearn, *Tracks in the Sea: Matthew Fontaine Maury and the Mapping of the Oceans* (International Marine/McGraw-Hill, 2002); Janice Beaty, *Seeker of Seaways: A Life of Matthew Fontaine Maury, Pioneer Oceanographer* (Pantheon Books, 1966); Charles Lee Lewis, *Matthew Fontaine Maury: The Pathfinder of the Seas* (U.S. Naval Institute, 1927) (http:// archive.org/details/matthewfontainem00lewi); and Matthew Fontaine Maury, *The Physical Geography of the Sea* (Harper, 1855).

75   Maury quotations — From Maury, *Physical Geography of the Sea,* "Introduction," pp. xii, vi.

77   Car seat data — Nikkei, "Car Seat of Near Future IDs Driver's Backside," December 14, 2011.

78   Quantifying the world — Much of the authors' thinking on the history of datafication has been inspired by Crosby, *The Measure of Reality.*

80   Europeans were never exposed to abacuses — Ibid., 112.

      Calculating faster using Arabic numerals — Alexander Murray, *Reason and Society in the Middle Ages* (Oxford University Press, 1978), p. 166.

84   Total number of books published and Harvard study on Google book-scanning project — Jean-Baptiste Michel et al., "Quantitative Analysis of Culture Using Millions of Digitized Books," *Science* 331 (January 14, 2011), pp. 176–182 (http://www.sciencemag.org/content/331/6014/176.abstract). For a video lecture on the paper, see Erez Lieberman Aiden and Jean-Baptiste Michel, "What We Learned from 5 Million Books," TEDx, Cambridge, MA, 2011 (http://www.ted.com/talks/what_we_learned_from_5_million _books.html).

89   On wireless modules in cars and insurance — See Cukier, "Data, Data Everywhere."

      UPS's Jack Levis — Interview with Cukier, April 2012.

      Data on UPS's savings — Institute for Operations Research and the Management Sciences (INFORMS), "UPS Wins Gartner BI Excellence Award," 2011 (http://www.informs.org/Announcements/UPS-wins -Gartner-BI-Excellence-Award).

90   Pentland research — Robert Lee Hotz, "The Really Smart Phone," *Wall Street Journal,* April 22, 2011 (http://online.wsj.com/article/SB100014240 52748704547604576263261679848814.html).

91   Eagle's study of slums — Nathan Eagle, "Big Data, Global Development, and Complex Systems," Santa Fe Institute, May 5, 2010 (http://www.youtube .com/watch?v=yaivtqlu7iM). Also, interview with Cukier, October 2012.

92   Facebook data — From Facebook IPO Prospectus, 2012.

      Twitter data — Alexia Tsotsis, "Twitter Is at 250 Million Tweets per Day, iOS 5 Integration Made Signups Increase 3x," *TechCrunch,* October 17, 2011, http:// techcrunch.com/2011/10/17/twitter-is-at-250-million-tweets-per-day/.

      Hedge funds using twitter — Kenneth Cukier, "Tracking Social Media: The Mood of the Market," *Economist.com,* June 28, 2012 (http://www .economist.com/blogs/graphicdetail/2012/06/tracking-social-media).

93   Twitter and forecasting Hollywood box-office revenue — Sitaram Asur and Bernardo A. Huberman, "Predicting the Future with Social Media," *Proceedings of the 2010 IEEE/WIC/ACM International Conference on Web Intelligence and Intelligent Agent Technology,* pp. 492–499; online at http://www.hpl.hp.com/research/scl/papers/socialmedia/socialmedia .pdf.

Twitter and global moods — Scott A. Golder and Michael W. Macy, "Diurnal and Seasonal Mood Vary with Work, Sleep, and Daylength Across Diverse Cultures," *Science* 333 (September 30, 2011), pp. 1878–81.

Twitter and flu shots — Marcel Salathé and Shashank Khandelwal, "Assessing Vaccination Sentiments with Online Social Media: Implications for Infectious Disease Dynamics and Control," *PLoS Computational Biology,* October 2011.

94   IBM's "smart floor" patent — Lydia Mai Do, Travis M. Grigsby, Pamela Ann Nesbitt, and Lisa Anne Seacat. "Securing premises using surfaced-based computing technology," U.S. Patent number: 8138882. Issue date: March 20, 2012.

The quantified-self movement — "Counting Every Moment," *The Economist,* March 3, 2012.

Apple earbuds for bio-measurements — Jesse Lee Dorogusker, Anthony Fadell, Donald J. Novotney, and Nicholas R Kalayjian, "Integrated Sensors for Tracking Performance Metrics," U.S. Patent Application 20090287067. Assignee: Apple. Application Date: 2009-07-23. Publication Date: 2009-11-19.

Derawi Biometrics, "Your Walk Is Your PIN-Code," press release, February 21, 2011 (http://biometrics.derawi.com/?p=175).

iTrem information — See the iTrem project page of the Landmarc Research Center at Georgia Tech (http://eosl.gtri.gatech.edu/Capabilities /LandmarcResearchCenter/LandmarcProjects/iTrem/tabid/798/Default .aspx) and email exchange.

Kyoto researchers on tri-axial accelerometers — iMedicalApps Team, "Gait Analysis Accuracy: Android App Comparable to Standard Accelerometer Methodology," *mHealth,* March 23, 2012.

96   Newspapers gave rise to the nation state — Benedict Anderson, *Imagined Communities: Reflections on the Origin and Spread of Nationalism* (Verso, 2006).

Physicists suggest information is the basis of everything — Hans Christian von Baeyer, *Information: The New Language of Science* (Harvard University Press, 2005).

6. VALUE

98   Story of Luis von Ahn — Based on Cukier interviews with von Ahn from 2010. See also Clive Thompson, "For Certain Tasks, the Cortex Still Beats the CPU," *Wired,* June 25, 2007 (http://www.wired.com/techbiz/it/mag azine/15-07/ff_humancomp?currentPage=all); Jessie Scanlon, "Luis von Ahn: The Pioneer of 'Human Computation,'" *Businessweek,* November 3, 2008 (http://www.businessweek.com/stories/2008-11-03/luis-von-ahn

-the-pioneer-of-human-computation-businessweek-business-news
-stock-market-and-financial-advice). His technical description of reCaptchas is at Luis von Ahn et al., "reCAPTCHA: Human-Based Character Recognition via Web Security Measures," *Science* 321 (September 12, 2008), pp.
1465–68 (http://www.sciencemag.org/content/321/5895/1465.abstract).

100 Smith's pin factory — Adam Smith, *The Wealth of Nations* (reprint, Bantam
Classics, 2003), book I, chapter one. (A free electronic version is at http
://www2.hn.psu.edu/faculty/jmanis/adam-smith/Wealth-Nations.pdf).

101 Storage — Viktor Mayer-Schönberger, *Delete: The Virtue of Forgetting in the
Digital Age* (Princeton University Press, 2011), p. 63.

102 On electrical cars' power usage — IBM, "IBM, Honda, and PG&E Enable
Smarter Charging for Electric Vehicles," press release, April 12, 2012 (http://
www-03.ibm.com/press/us/en/pressrelease/37398.wss). Also see Clay Lu-
thy, "Guest Perspective: IBM Working with PG&E to Maximize the EV Potential" *PGE Currents* Magazine, April 13, 2012 (http://www.pgecurrents
.com/2012/04/13/ibm-working-with-pge-to-maximize-the-ev-potential).

105 Amazon and AOL's data — Cukier interview with Andreas Weigend, 2010
and 2012.
Nuance software and Google — Cukier, "Data, Data Everywhere."

106 Logistics company — Brad Brown, Michael Chui, and James Manyika, "Are
You Ready for the Era of 'Big Data'?" *McKinsey Quarterly*, October 2011, p.
10.

107 Telefonica monetizes mobile information — "Telefonica Hopes 'Big Data'
Arm Will Revive Fortunes," *BBC Online*, October 9, 2012. (http://www.bbc
.co.uk/news/technology-19882647).
Danish Cancer Society study — Patrizia Frei et al., "Use of Mobile Phones
and Risk of Brain Tumours: Update of Danish Cohort Study," *BMJ* 343
(2011) (http://www.bmj.com/content/343/bmj.d6387), and interview with
Cukier, October 2012.

109 Google's Street View's GPS records and self-driving car — Peter Kirwan,
"This Car Drives Itself," *Wired UK*, January 2012 (http://www.wired.co.uk
/magazine/archive/2012/01/features/this-car-drives-itself?page=all).

112 Google's spell check and quotation — Interview with Cukier at the Google-
plex in Mountain View, California, December 2009; some material also appeared in Cukier, "Data, Data Everywhere."

114 Hammerbacher's insight — Interview with Cukier, October 2012.
Barnes & Noble e-book data — Alexandra Alter, "Your E-Book Is Reading
You," *Wall Street Journal*, June 29, 2012 (http://online.wsj.com/article/SB1
0001424052702304870304577490950051438304.html).

115 Andrew Ng's Coursera class and data — Interview with Cukier, June 2012.

116 Obama's open government policy — Barack Obama, "Presidential memorandum," White House, January 21, 2009.

119 On Facebook's data's worth — For an excellent examination of the discrep-

ancy between market and book value for Facebook's IPO, see Doug Laney, "To Facebook You're Worth $80.95," *Wall Street Journal*, May 3, 2012 (http://blogs.wsj.com/cio/2012/05/03/to-facebook-youre-worth-80-95/). For valuing Facebook's discrete items, Laney extrapolated from Facebook's growth to estimate the 2.1 trillion pieces of content. In his *WSJ* article he valued the items at three cents each since he was using an earlier Facebook market valuation estimate of $75 billion. In the end, it was over $100 billion, or five cents, as we extrapolated ourselves based on his calculation.

Value gap of physical assets and intangible ones — Steve M. Samek, "Prepared Testimony: Hearing on Adapting a 1930's Financial Reporting Model to the 21st Century," U.S. Senate Committee on Banking, Housing and Urban Affairs, Subcommittee on Securities, July 19, 2000.

Value of intangibles — Robert S. Kaplan and David P. Norton, *Strategy Maps: Converting Intangible Assets into Tangible Outcomes* (Harvard Business Review Press, 2004), pp. 4–5.

122   Tim O'Reilly quotation — Interview with Cukier, February 2011.

7. IMPLICATIONS

123   Info on Decide.com — Cukier email exchange with Etzioni, May 2012.

125   McKinsey report — James Manyika et al., "Big Data: The Next Frontier for Innovation, Competition, and Productivity," McKinsey Global Institute, May 2011 (http://www.mckinsey.com/insights/mgi/research/technology _and_innovation/big_data_the_next_frontier_for_innovation), p. 10.
Hal Varian quotation — Interview with Cukier, December 2009.

126   Carl de Marcken quotation — Email exchange with Cukier, May 2012.

127   On MasterCard Advisors — Cukier interview with Gary Kearns, a MasterCard Advisors executive, at *The Economist*'s "The Ideas Economy: Information" conference, Santa Clara, California, June 8, 2011.

128   Accenture and city of St. Louis, Missouri — Cukier interview with municipal employees, February 2007.
Microsoft Amalga Unified Intelligence System — "Microsoft Expands Presence in Healthcare IT Industry with Acquisition of Health Intelligence Software Azyxxi," Microsoft press release, July 26, 2006 (http://www .microsoft.com/en-us/news/press/2006/jul06/07-26azyxxiacquisitionpr .aspx). The Amalga service is now a part of Microsoft's joint venture with General Electric called Caradigm.

129   Bradford Cross — Interviews with Cukier, March-October 2012.

132   Amazon and "collaborative filtering" — IPO Prospectus, May 1997 (http:// www.sec.gov/Archives/edgar/data/1018724/0000891020-97-000868 .txt).

133   Car's microprocessors — Nick Valery, "Tech.View: Cars and Software

Bugs," *Economist.com,* May 16, 2010 (http://www.economist.com/blogs
/babbage/2010/05/techview_cars_and_software_bugs).

Maury called ships "floating observatories" — Maury, *The Physical Geography of the Sea.*

135   Inrix — Cukier interview with executives, May and September, 2012.

137   On Health Care Cost Institute — Sarah Kliff, "A Database That Could Revolutionize Health Care," *Washington Post,* May 21, 2012.

Decide.com's data-usage agreement — Cukier email exchange with Etzioni, May 2012.

Google and ITA deal — Claire Cain Miller, "U.S. Clears Google Acquisition of Travel Software," *New York Times,* April 8, 2011 (http://www.nytimes.com/2011/04/09/technology/09google.html?_r=0).

138   Inrix and ABS — Cukier interview with Inrix executives, May 2012.

139   Roadnet story and Len Kennedy quotation — Interview with Cukier, May 2012.

Dialogue from film *Moneyball,* directed by Bennett Miller, Columbia Pictures, 2011.

142   McGregor's data amounting to more than a decade of patient-years — Interview with Cukier, May 2012.

Goldbloom quotation — Interview with Cukier, March 2012.

143   On Hollywood box office versus video game sales — For movies, see Brooks Barnes, "A Year of Disappointment at the Movie Box Office," *New York Times,* December 25, 2011 (http://www.nytimes.com/2011/12/26/business/media/a-year-of-disappointment-for-hollywood.html). For video games, see "Factbox: A Look at the $65 billion Video Games Industry," Reuters, June 6, 2011 (http://uk.reuters.com/article/2011/06/06/us-videogames-factbox-idUKTRE75552I20110606).

Zynga data analytics — Nick Wingfield, "Virtual Products, Real Profits: Players Spend on Zynga's Games, but Quality Turns Some Off," *Wall Street Journal,* September 9, 2011 (http://online.wsj.com/article/SB10001424053111904823804576502442835413446.html).

144   Ken Rudin quotation — From interview of Rudin by Niko Waesche, cited in Erik Schlie, Jörg Rheinboldt, and Niko Waesche, *Simply Seven: Seven Ways to Create a Sustainable Internet Business* (Palgrave Macmillan, 2011). p. 7.

Auden quotation — W. H. Auden, "For the Time Being," 1944.

Thomas Davenport quotation — Cukier interview with Davenport, December 2009.

The-Numbers.com — Cukier interviews with Bruce Nash, October 2011 and July 2012.

145   Brynjolfsson study — Erik Brynjolfsson, Lorin Hitt, and Heekyung Kim, "Strength in Numbers: How Does Data-Driven Decisionmaking Affect Firm Performance?" working paper, April 2011 (http://papers.ssrn.com/sol3/papers.cfm?abstract_id=1819486).

146   On Rolls-Royce — See "Rolls-Royce: Britain's Lonely High-Flier," *The Economist,* January 8, 2009 (http://www.economist.com/node/12887368). Figures updated from press office, November 2012.

Erik Brynjolfsson, Andrew McAfee, Michael Sorell, and Feng Zhu, "Scale Without Mass: Business Process Replication and Industry Dynamics," Harvard Business School working paper, September 2006 (http://www.hbs.edu/research/pdf/07-016.pdf also http://hbswk.hbs.edu/item/5532.html).

147   On the movement toward increasingly large data holders — See also Yannis Bakos and Erik Brynjolfsson, "Bundling Information Goods: Pricing, Profits, and Efficiency," *Management Science* 45 (December 1999), pp. 1613–30.

148   Philip Evans — Interviews with the authors, 2011 and 2012.

8. RISKS

150   On the Stasi — Much of the literature unfortunately is in German, but one well researched exception is Kristie Macrakis, *Seduced by Secrets: Inside the Stasi's Spy-Tech World* (Cambridge University Press, 2008); a very personal story is shared in Timothy Garton Ash, *The File* (Atlantic Books, 2008). We also recommend the Academy Award–winning movie *The Lives of Others,* directed by Florian Henckel von Donnersmark, Buena Vista/Sony Pictures, 2006.

Surveillance cameras near Orwell's home — "George Orwell, Big Brother Is Watching Your House," *The Evening Standard,* March 31, 2007 (http://www.thisislondon.co.uk/news/george-orwell-big-brother-is-watching-your-house-7086271.html).

On Equifax and Experian — Daniel J. Solove, *The Digital Person: Technology and Privacy in the Information Age* (NYU Press, 2004), pp. 20–21.

151   On block addresses of Japanese in Washington handed over to U.S. authorities — J. R. Minkel, "The U.S. Census Bureau Gave Up Names of Japanese-Americans in WW II," *Scientific American,* March 30, 2007 (http://www.scientificamerican.com/article.cfm?id=confirmed-the-us-census-b).

On data used by Nazis in the Netherlands — William Seltzer and Margo Anderson, "The Dark Side of Numbers: The Role of Population Data Systems in Human Rights Abuses," *Social Research* 68 (2001), pp. 481–513.

152   On IBM and the Holocaust — Edwin Black, *IBM and the Holocaust* (Crown, 2003).

On the amount of data smart meters collect — See Elias Leake Quinn, "Smart Metering and Privacy: Existing Law and Competing Policies; A Report for the Colorado Public Utility Commission," Spring 2009 (http://www.w4ar.com/Danger_of_Smart_Meters_Colorado_Report.pdf). See also Joel M. Margolis, "When Smart Grids Grow Smart Enough to Solve

Crimes," Neustar, March 18, 2010 (http://energy.gov/sites/prod/files/gc prod/documents/Neustar_Comments_DataExhibitA.pdf)

153   Fred Cate on notice and consent — Fred H. Cate, "The Failure of Fair Information Practice Principles," in Jane K. Winn, ed., *Consumer Protection in the Age of the "Information Economy"* (Ashgate, 2006), p. 341 et seq.

154   On the AOL data release — Michael Barbaro and Tom Zeller Jr., "A Face Is Exposed for AOL Searcher No. 4417749," *New York Times*, August 9, 2006. Also see Matthew Karnitschnig and Mylene Mangalindan, "AOL Fires Technology Chief After Web-Search Data Scandal," *Wall Street Journal*, August 21, 2006.

155   Netflix identified individual — Ryan Singel, "Netflix Spilled Your *Brokeback Mountain* Secret, Lawsuit Claims," *Wired*, December 17, 2009 (http://www .wired.com/threatlevel/2009/12/netflix-privacy-lawsuit/).

On the Netflix data release — Arvind Narayanan and Vitaly Shmatikov, "Robust De-Anonymization of Large Sparse Datasets," *Proceedings of the 2008 IEEE Symposium on Security and Privacy*, p. 111 et seq. (http://www .cs.utexas.edu/~shmat/shmat_oak08netflix.pdf); Arvind Narayanan and Vitaly Shmatikov, "How to Break the Anonymity of the Netflix Prize Dataset," October 18, 2006, arXiv:cs/0610105 [cs.CR] (http://arxiv.org/abs /cs/0610105).

On identifying people from three characteristics — Philippe Golle, "Revisiting the Uniqueness of Simple Demographics in the US Population," *Association for Computing Machinery Workshop on Privacy in Electronic Society* 5 (2006), p. 77.

On the structural weakness of anonymization — Paul Ohm, "Broken Promises of Privacy: Responding to the Surprising Failure of Anonymization," 57 *UCLA Law Review* 1701 (2010).

On anonymity of the social graph — Lars Backstrom, Cynthia Dwork, and Jon Kleinberg, "Wherefore Art Thou R3579X? Anonymized Social Networks, Hidden Patterns, and Structural Steganography," *Communications of the Association of Computing Machinery*, December 2011, p. 133.

156   Cars' "black boxes" — "Vehicle Data Recorders: Watching Your Driving," *The Economist*, June 23, 2012 (http://www.economist.com /node/21557309).

NSA data collection — Dana Priest and William Arkin, "A Hidden World, Growing Beyond Control," *Washington Post*, July 19, 2010 (http://projects .washingtonpost.com/top-secret-america/articles/a-hidden-world-growing-beyond-control/print/). Juan Gonzalez, "Whistleblower: The NSA Is Lying — U.S. Government Has Copies of Most of Your Emails," *Democracy Now*, April 20, 2012 (http://www.democracynow.org/2012/4/20/whistle blower_the_nsa_is_lying_us). William Binney, "Sworn Declaration in the Case of Jewel v. NSA," filed July 2, 2012 (http://publicintelligence.net /binney-nsa-declaration/).

How surveillance has changed with big data — Patrick Radden Keefe, "Can Network Theory Thwart Terrorists?" *New York Times,* March 12, 2006 (http://www.nytimes.com/2006/03/12/magazine/312wwln_essay.html).

158   Dialogue from *Minority Report,* directed by Steven Spielberg, Dream-Works/20th Century Fox, 2002. The dialogue we cite is very slightly abridged. The film is based on a 1958 short story by Philip K. Dick, but there are substantial differences between the two versions. Specifically, the opening scene of the cuckolded husband does not appear in the book, and the philosophical conundrum of pre-crime is presented more starkly in the Spielberg film than in the story. Hence we have chosen to draw our parallels with the film.

Examples of predictive policing — James Vlahos, "The Department Of Pre-Crime," *Scientific American* 306 (January 2012), pp. 62–67.

159   On the Future Attribute Screening Technology (FAST) — See Sharon Weinberger, "Terrorist 'Pre-crime' Detector Field Tested in United States," *Nature,* May 27, 2011 (http://www.nature.com/news /2011/110527/full/news.2011.323.html);   Sharon   Weinberger,   "Intent to Deceive," *Nature* 465 (May 2010), pp. 412–415. On the problem of false positives, see Alexander Furnas, "Homeland Security's 'Pre-Crime' Screening Will Never Work," *The Atlantic Online,* April 17, 2012 (http://www.theatlantic.com/technology/archive/2012/04/homeland -securitys-pre-crime-screening-will-never-work/255971/).

160   On students' grades and insurance premiums — Tim Query, "Grade Inflation and the Good-Student Discount," *Contingencies Magazine,* American Academy of Actuaries, May-June 2007 (http://www.contingencies.org /mayjun07/tradecraft.pdf).

On the perils of profiling — Bernard E. Harcourt, *Against Prediction: Profiling, Policing, and Punishing in an Actuarial Age* (University of Chicago Press, 2006).

161   On Richard Berk's work — Richard Berk, "The Role of Race in Forecasts of Violent Crime," *Race and Social Problems* 1 (2009), pp. 231–242, and email interview with Cukier, November 2012.

163   On McNamara's love of data — Phil Rosenzweig, "Robert S. McNamara and the Evolution of Modern Management," *Harvard Business Review,* December 2010 (http://hbr.org/2010/12/robert-s-mcnamara-and -the-evolution-of-modern-management/ar/pr).

164   On the Whiz Kids' success in World War II — John Byrne, *The Whiz Kids* (Doubleday, 1993).

On McNamara at Ford — David Halberstam, *The Reckoning* (William Morrow, 1986), pp. 222–245.

165   Kinnard book — Douglas Kinnard, *The War Managers* (University Press of New England, 1977), pp. 71–25. This section benefited from an email interview with Dr. Kinnard, via his assistant, for which the authors express their gratitude.

166 On quotation "In God we trust — all others bring data" — This is often attributed to W. Edwards Deming.

On Ted Kennedy and No-Fly List — Sara Kehaulani Goo, "Sen. Kennedy Flagged by No-Fly List," *Washington Post,* August 20, 2004, p. A01 (http://www.washingtonpost.com/wp-dyn/articles/A17073-2004Aug19.html).

167 Google's hiring practices — See Douglas Edwards, *I'm Feeling Lucky: The Confessions of Google Employee Number 59* (Houghton Mifflin Harcourt, 2011), p. 9. See also Steven Levy, *In the Plex* (Simon and Schuster, 2011), pp. 140–141. Ironically, Google's co-founders wanted to hire Steve Jobs as CEO (despite his lack of a college degree); Levy, p. 80.

Testing 41 gradations of blue — Laura M. Holson, "Putting a Bolder Face on Google," *New York Times,* March 1, 2009 (http://www.nytimes.com/2009/03/01/business/01marissa.html).

Google's chief designer's resignation — Quotation is excerpted (without ellipses for readability) from Doug Bowman, "Goodbye, Google," blog post, March 20, 2009 (http://stopdesign.com/archive/2009/03/20/goodbye-google.html).

168 Jobs quotation — Steve Lohr, "Can Apple Find More Hits Without Its Tastemaker?" *New York Times,* January 18, 2011, p. B1 (http://www.nytimes.com/2011/01/19/technology/companies/19innovate.html).

Scott book — James Scott, *Seeing Like a State: How Certain Schemes to Improve the Human Condition Have Failed* (Yale University Press, 1998).

McNamara quotation from 1967 — From address at Millsaps College in Jackson, Mississippi, quoted in *Harvard Business Review,* December 2010.

169 On McNamara's apologia — Robert S. McNamara with Brian VanDeMark, *In Retrospect: The Tragedy and Lessons of Vietnam* (Random House, 1995), pp. 48, 270.

9. CONTROL

171 On Cambridge University library book collection — Marc Drogin, *Anathema! Medieval Scribes and the History of Book Curses* (Allanheld and Schram, 1983), p. 37.

173 On accountability and privacy — The Center for Information Policy Leadership has been engaged in a multi-year project on the interface of accountability and privacy; see http://www.informationpolicycentre.com/accountability-based_privacy_governance/.

175 On expiration dates for data — Mayer-Schönberger, *Delete.*

"Differential privacy" — Cynthia Dwork, "A Firm Foundation for Private Data Analysis," *Communications of the ACM,* January 2011, pp. 86–95.

Facebook and differential privacy — A. Chin and A. Klinefelter, "Differential Privacy as a Response to the Reidentification Threat: The Facebook Advertiser Case Study," 90 *North Carolina Law Review* 1417 (2012); A.

Haeberlen et al., "Differential Privacy Under Fire," http://www.cis.upenn.edu/~ahae/papers/fuzz-sec2011.pdf.

176 Firms suspected of collusion — There is already work in this area; see Pim Heijnen, Marco A. Haan, and Adriaan R. Soetevent. "Screening for Collusion: A Spatial Statistics Approach," Discussion Paper TI 2012-058/1, Tinbergen Institute, The Netherlands, 2012 (http://www.tinbergen.nl/discussionpapers/12058.pdf).

182 On German corporate data-protection representatives — Viktor Mayer-Schönberger, "Beyond Privacy, Beyond Rights: Towards a 'Systems' Theory of Information Governance," 98 *California Law Review* 1853 (2010).

183 On interoperability — John Palfrey and Urs Gasser, *Interop: The Promise and Perils of Highly Interconnected Systems* (Basic Books, 2012).

10. NEXT

186 Mike Flowers and New York City's analytics — Based on interview with Cukier, July 2012. For a good description, see: Alex Howard, "Predictive data analytics is saving lives and taxpayer dollars in New York City," *O'Reilly Media*, June 26, 2012 (http://strata.oreilly.com/2012/06/predictive-data-analytics-big-data-nyc.html).

191 Walmart and Pop-Tarts — Hays, "What Wal-Mart Knows About Customers' Habits."

194 Big data's use in slums and in modeling refugee movements — Nathan Eagle, "Big Data, Global Development, and Complex Systems," http://www.youtube.com/watch?v=yaivtqlu7iM.

Perception of time — Benedict Anderson, *Imagined Communities* (Verso, 2006).

195 "What's past is prologue" — William Shakespeare, "The Tempest," Act 2, Scene I.

197 CERN experiment and data storage — Cukier email exchange with CERN researchers, November 2012.

Apollo 11's computer system — David A. Mindell, *Digital Apollo: Human and Machine in Spaceflight* (MIT Press, 2008).

BIBLIOGRAPHY

Alter, Alexandra. "Your E-Book Is Reading You." *Wall Street Journal,* June 29, 2012 (http://online.wsj.com/article/SB100014240527023048703045774909 50051438304.html).

Anderson, Benedict. *Imagined Communities,* New Edition. Verso, 2006.

Anderson, Chris. "The End of Theory." *Wired* 16, issue 7 (July 2008 (http://www .wired.com/science/discoveries/magazine/16-07/pb_theory).

Asur, Sitaram, and Bernardo A. Huberman. "Predicting the Future with Social Media." *Proceedings of the 2010 IEEE/WIC/ACM International Conference on Web Intelligence and Intelligent Agent Technology,* pp. 492–499. (An online version is available at http://www.hpl.hp.com/research/scl/papers/ socialmedia/socialmedia.pdf.)

Ayres, Ian. *Super Crunchers: Why Thinking-By-Numbers Is the New Way to Be Smart.* Bantam Dell, 2007.

Babbie, Earl. *Practice of Social Research,* 12th ed. 2010.

Backstrom, Lars, Cynthia Dwork, and Jon Kleinberg. "Wherefore Art Thou R3579X? Anonymized Social Networks, Hidden Patterns, and Structural Steganography." *Communications of the ACM,* December 2011, pp. 133–141.

Bakos, Yannis, and Erik Brynjolfsson. "Bundling Information Goods: Pricing, Profits, and Efficiency." *Management Science* 45 (December 1999), pp. 1613–30.

Banko, Michele, and Eric Brill. "Scaling to Very Very Large Corpora for Natural Language Disambiguation." Microsoft Research, 2001, p. 3 (http://acl.ldc .upenn.edu/P/P01/P01-1005.pdf).

Barbaro, Michael, and Tom Zeller Jr. "A Face Is Exposed for AOL Searcher No. 4417749." *New York Times,* August 9, 2006 (http://www.nytimes .com/2006/08/09/technology/09aol.html).

Barnes, Brooks. "A Year of Disappointment at the Movie Box Office," *New York Times,* December 25, 2011 (http://www.nytimes.com/2011/12/26/business/ media/a-year-of-disappointment-for-hollywood.html).

Beaty, Janice. *Seeker of Seaways: A Life of Matthew Fontaine Maury, Pioneer Oceanographer*. Pantheon Books, 1966.

Berger, Adam L., et al. "The Candide System for Machine Translation." *Proceedings of the 1994 ARPA Workshop on Human Language Technology* (1994) (http://aclweb.org/anthology-new/H/H94/H94-1100.pdf).

Berk, Richard. "The Role of Race in Forecasts of Violent Crime." *Race and Social Problems* 1 (2009), pp. 231–242.

Black, Edwin. *IBM and the Holocaust*. Crown, 2003.

boyd, danah, and Kate Crawford. "Six Provocations for Big Data." Research paper presented at Oxford Internet Institute's "A Decade in Internet Time: Symposium on the Dynamics of the Internet and Society," September 21, 2011 (http://ssrn.com/abstract=1926431).

Brown, Brad, Michael Chui, and James Manyika. "Are You Ready for the Era of 'Big Data'?" *McKinsey Quarterly*, October 2011, p. 10.

Brynjolfsson, Erik, Andrew McAfee, Michael Sorell, and Feng Zhu. "Scale Without Mass: Business Process Replication and Industry Dynamics." HBS working paper, September 2006 (http://www.hbs.edu/research/pdf/07-016.pdf; also http://hbswk.hbs.edu/item/5532.html).

Brynjolfsson, Erik, Lorin Hitt, and Heekyung Kim. "Strength in Numbers: How Does Data-Driven Decisionmaking Affect Firm Performance?" *ICIS 2011 Proceedings*, Paper 13 (http://aisel.aisnet.org/icis2011/proceedings/economicvalueIS/13; also available at http://papers.ssrn.com/sol3/papers.cfm?abstract_id=1819486).

Byrne, John. *The Whiz Kids*. Doubleday, 1993.

Cate, Fred H. "The Failure of Fair Information Practice Principles." In Jane K. Winn, ed., *Consumer Protection in the Age of the "Information Economy"* (Ashgate, 2006), p. 341 et seq.

Chin, A., and A. Klinefelter. "Differential Privacy as a Response to the Reidentification Threat: The Facebook Advertiser Case Study." 90 *North Carolina Law Review* 1417 (2012).

Crosby, Alfred. *The Measure of Reality: Quantification and Western Society, 1250–1600*. Cambridge University Press, 1997.

Cukier, Kenneth. "Data, Data Everywhere." *The Economist* Special Report, February 27, 2010, pp. 1–14.

——. "Tracking Social Media: The Mood of the Market." *Economist.com*, June 28, 2012 (http://www.economist.com/blogs/graphicdetail/2012/06/tracking-social-media).

Davenport, Thomas H., Paul Barth, and Randy Bean. "How 'Big Data' Is Different." *Sloan Review*, July 30, 2012 (http://sloanreview.mit.edu/the-magazine/2012-fall/54104/how-big-data-is-different/).

Di Quinzio, Melanie, and Anne McCarthy. "Rabies Risk Among Travellers." *CMAJ* 178, no. 5 (2008), p. 567.

Drogin, Marc. *Anathema! Medieval Scribes and the History of Book Curses.* Allanheld and Schram, 1983.

Dugas, A. F., et al. "Google Flu Trends: Correlation with Emergency Department Influenza Rates and Crowding Metrics." CID Advanced Access, January 8, 2012. DOI 10.1093/cid/cir883.

Duggan, Mark, and Steven D. Levitt. "Winning Isn't Everything: Corruption in Sumo Wrestling." *American Economic Review* 92 (2002), pp. 1594–1605 (http://pricetheory.uchicago.edu/levitt/Papers/DugganLevitt2002.pdf).

Duhigg, Charles. *The Power of Habit: Why We Do What We Do in Life and Business.* Random House, 2012.

Duhigg, Charles. "How Companies Learn Your Secrets." *New York Times,* February 16, 2012 (http://www.nytimes.com/2012/02/19/magazine/shopping-habits.html).

Dwork, Cynthia. "A Firm Foundation for Private Data Analysis." *Communications of the ACM,* January 2011, pp. 86–95 (http://dl.acm.org/citation.cfm?id=1866739.1866758).

Economist, The. "Rolls-Royce: Britain's Lonely High-Flier." *The Economist,* January 8, 2009 (http://www.economist.com/node/12887368).

——."Building with Big Data: The Data Revolution Is Changing the Landscape of Business." *The Economist,* May 26, 2011 (http://www.economist.com/node/18741392/).

——."Official Statistics: Don't Lie to Me, Argentina." *The Economist,* February 25, 2012 (http://www.economist.com/node/21548242).

——."Counting Every Moment." *The Economist,* March 3, 2012 (http://www.economist.com/node/21548493).

——."Vehicle Data Recorders: Watching Your Driving." *The Economist,* June 23, 2012 (http://www.economist.com/node/21557309).

Edwards, Douglas. *I'm Feeling Lucky: The Confessions of Google Employee Number 59.* Houghton Mifflin Harcourt, 2011.

Ehrenberg, Rachel. "Predicting the Next Deadly Manhole Explosion." *Wired,* July 7, 2010 (http://www.wired.com/wiredscience/2010/07/manhole-explosions).

Eisenstein, Elizabeth L. *The Printing Revolution in Early Modern Europe.* Cambridge University Press, 1993.

Etzioni, Oren, C. A. Knoblock, R. Tuchinda, and A. Yates. "To Buy or Not to Buy: Mining Airfare Data to Minimize Ticket Purchase Price." SIGKDD '03, August 24–27, 2003 (http://knight.cis.temple.edu/~yates//papers/hamlet-kdd03.pdf).

Frei, Patrizia, et al. "Use of Mobile Phones and Risk of Brain Tumours: Update of Danish Cohort Study." *BMJ* 2011, 343 (http://www.bmj.com/content/343/bmj.d6387).

Furnas, Alexander. "Homeland Security's 'Pre-Crime' Screening Will Never

Work." *The Atlantic Online,* April 17, 2012 (http://www.theatlantic.com/technology/archive/2012/04/homeland-securitys-pre-crime-screening-will-never-work/255971/).

Garton Ash, Timothy. *The File*. Atlantic Books, 2008.

Geron, Tomio. "Twitter's Dick Costolo: Twitter Mobile Ad Revenue Beats Desktop on Some Days." *Forbes,* June 6, 2012 (http://www.forbes.com/sites/tomiogeron/2012/06/06/twitters-dick-costolo-mobile-ad-revenue-beats-desktop-on-some-days/).

Ginsburg, Jeremy, et al. "Detecting Influenza Epidemics Using Search Engine Query Data." *Nature* 457 (2009), pp. 1012–14 (http://www.nature.com/nature/journal/v457/n7232/full/nature07634.html).

Golder, Scott A., and Michael W. Macy. "Diurnal and Seasonal Mood Vary with Work, Sleep, and Daylength Across Diverse Cultures." *Science* 333 (September 30, 2011), pp. 1878–81.

Golle, Philippe. "Revisiting the Uniqueness of Simple Demographics in the US Population." *Association for Computing Machinery Workshop on Privacy in Electronic Society* 5 (2006), pp. 77–80.

Goo, Sara Kehaulani. "Sen. Kennedy Flagged by No-Fly List." *Washington Post,* August 20, 2004, p. A01 (http://www.washingtonpost.com/wp-dyn/articles/A17073-2004Aug19.html).

Haeberlen, A., et al. "Differential Privacy Under Fire." In *SEC'11: Proceedings of the 20th USENIX conference on Security,* p. 33 (http://www.cis.upenn.edu/~ahae/papers/fuzz-sec2011.pdf).

Halberstam, David. *The Reckoning*. William Morrow, 1986.

Haldane, J. B. S. "On Being the Right Size." *Harper's Magazine,* March 1926 (http://harpers.org/archive/1926/03/on-being-the-right-size/).

Halevy, Alon, Peter Norvig, and Fernando Pereira. "The Unreasonable Effectiveness of Data." *IEEE Intelligent Systems,* March/April 2009, pp. 8–12.

Harcourt, Bernard E. *Against Prediction: Profiling, Policing, and Punishing in an Actuarial Age*. University of Chicago Press, 2006.

Hardy, Quentin. "Bizarre Insights from Big Data." *NYTimes.com,* March 28, 2012 (http://bits.blogs.nytimes.com/2012/03/28/bizarre-insights-from-big-data/).

Hays, Constance L. "What Wal-Mart Knows About Customers' Habits." *New York Times,* November 14, 2004 (http://www.nytimes.com/2004/11/14/business/yourmoney/14wal.html).

Hearn, Chester G. *Tracks in the Sea: Matthew Fontaine Maury and the Mapping of the Oceans*. International Marine/McGraw-Hill, 2002.

Helland, Pat. "If You Have Too Much Data then 'Good Enough' Is Good Enough." *Communications of the ACM,* June 2011, p. 40 et seq.

Hilbert, Martin, and Priscilla López. "The World's Technological Capacity to Store, Communicate, and Compute Information." *Science* 1 (April 2011), pp. 60–65.

——. "How to Measure the World's Technological Capacity to Communicate, Store and Compute Information?" *International Journal of Communication* (2012), pp. 1042–55 (ijoc.org/ojs/index.php/ijoc/article/viewFile/1562/742).

Holson, Laura M. "Putting a Bolder Face on Google." *New York Times*, March 1, 2009, p. BU 1 (http://www.nytimes.com/2009/03/01/business/01marissa.html).

Hopkins, Brian, and Boris Evelson. "Expand Your Digital Horizon with Big Data." Forrester, September 30, 2011.

Hotz, Robert Lee. "The Really Smart Phone." *Wall Street Journal*, April 22, 2011 (http://online.wsj.com/article/SB10001424052748704547604576263261679848814.html).

Hutchins, John. "The First Public Demonstration of Machine Translation: The Georgetown-IBM System, 7th January 1954." November 2005 (http://www.hutchinsweb.me.uk/GU-IBM-2005.pdf).

Inglehart, R., and H. D. Klingemann. *Genes, Culture and Happiness*. MIT Press, 2000.

Isaacson, Walter. *Steve Jobs*. Simon and Schuster, 2011.

Kahneman, Daniel. *Thinking, Fast and Slow*. Farrar, Straus and Giroux, 2011.

Kaplan, Robert S., and David P. Norton. *Strategy Maps: Converting Intangible Assets into Tangible Outcomes*. Harvard Business Review Press, 2004.

Karnitschnig, Matthew, and Mylene Mangalindan. "AOL Fires Technology Chief After Web-Search Data Scandal." *Wall Street Journal*, August 21, 2006.

Keefe, Patrick Radden. "Can Network Theory Thwart Terrorists?" *New York Times*, March 12, 2006 (http://www.nytimes.com/2006/03/12/magazine/312wwln_essay.html).

Kinnard, Douglas. *The War Managers*. University Press of New England, 1977.

Kirwan, Peter. "This Car Drives Itself." *Wired UK*, January 2012 (http://www.wired.co.uk/magazine/archive/2012/01/features/this-car-drives-itself).

Kliff, Sarah. "A Database That Could Revolutionize Health Care." *Washington Post*, May 21, 2012.

Kruskal, William, and Frederick Mosteller. "Representative Sampling, IV: The History of the Concept in Statistics, 1895–1939." *International Statistical Review* 48 (1980), pp. 169–195.

Laney, Doug. "To Facebook You're Worth $80.95." *Wall Street Journal*, May 3, 2012 (http://blogs.wsj.com/cio/2012/05/03/to-facebook-youre-worth-80-95/).

Latour, Bruno. *The Pasteurization of France*. Harvard University Press, 1993.

Levitt, Steven D., and Stephen J. Dubner. *Freakonomics: A Rogue Economist Explores the Hidden Side of Everything*. William Morrow, 2009.

Levy, Steven. *In the Plex*. Simon and Schuster, 2011.

Lewis, Charles Lee. *Matthew Fontaine Maury: The Pathfinder of the Seas*. U.S. Naval Institute, 1927.

Lohr, Steve. "Can Apple Find More Hits Without Its Tastemaker?" *New York Times*,

January 18, 2011, p. B1 (http://www.nytimes.com/2011/01/19/technology/companies/19innovate.html).

Lowrey, Annie. "Economists' Programs Are Beating U.S. at Tracking Inflation." *Washington Post*, December 25, 2010 (http://www.washingtonpost.com/wp-dyn/content/article/2010/12/25/AR2010122502600.html).

Macrakis, Kristie. *Seduced by Secrets: Inside the Stasi's Spy-Tech World*. Cambridge University Press, 2008.

Manyika, James, et al. "Big Data: The Next Frontier for Innovation, Competition, and Productivity." *McKinsey Global Institute*, May 2011 (http://www.mckinsey.com/insights/mgi/research/technology_and_innovation/big_data_the_next_frontier_for_innovation).

Marcus, James. *Amazonia: Five Years at the Epicenter of the Dot.Com Juggernaut*. The New Press, 2004.

Margolis, Joel M. "When Smart Grids Grow Smart Enough to Solve Crimes." Neustar, March 18, 2010 (http://energy.gov/sites/prod/files/gcprod/documents/Neustar_Comments_DataExhibitA.pdf).

Maury, Matthew Fontaine. *The Physical Geography of the Sea*. Harper, 1855.

Mayer-Schönberger, Viktor. "Beyond Privacy, Beyond Rights: Towards a 'Systems' Theory of Information Governance." 98 *California Law Review* 1853 (2010).

——. *Delete: The Virtue of Forgetting in the Digital Age*. Princeton University Press, 2nd ed., 2011.

McGregor, Carolyn, Christina Catley, Andrew James, and James Padbury. "Next Generation Neonatal Health Informatics with Artemis." In European Federation for Medical Informatics, *User Centred Networked Health Care*, ed. A. Moen et al. (IOS Press, 2011), p. 117 et seq.

McNamara, Robert S., with Brian VanDeMark. *In Retrospect: The Tragedy and Lessons of Vietnam*. Random House, 1995.

Mehta, Abhishek. "Big Data: Powering the Next Industrial Revolution." Tableau Software White Paper, 2011.

Michel, Jean-Baptiste, et al. "Quantitative Analysis of Culture Using Millions of Digitized Books." *Science* 331 (January 14, 2011), pp. 176–182 (http://www.sciencemag.org/content/331/6014/176.abstract).

Miller, Claire Cain. "U.S. Clears Google Acquisition of Travel Software." *New York Times*, April 8, 2011 (http://www.nytimes.com/2011/04/09/technology/09google.html?_r=0).

Mills, Howard. "Analytics: Turning Data into Dollars." *Forward Focus*, December 2011 (http://www.deloitte.com/assets/Dcom-UnitedStates/Local%20Assets/Documents/FSI/US_FSI_Forward%20Focus_Analytics_Turning%20data%20into%20dollars_120711.pdf).

Mindell, David A. *Digital Apollo: Human and Machine in Spaceflight*. MIT Press, 2008.

Minkel, J. R. "The U.S. Census Bureau Gave Up Names of Japanese-Amer-

icans in WW II." *Scientific American,* March 30, 2007 (http://www
.scientificamerican.com/article.cfm?id=confirmed-the-us-census-b).

Murray, Alexander. *Reason and Society in the Middle Ages.* Oxford University
Press, 1978.

Nalimov, E. V., G. McC. Haworth, and E. A. Heinz. "Space-Efficient Indexing of
Chess Endgame Tables." *ICGA Journal* 23, no. 3 (2000), pp. 148–162.

Narayanan, Arvind, and Vitaly Shmatikov. "How to Break the Anonymity of the
Netflix Prize Dataset." October 18, 2006, arXiv:cs/0610105 (http://arxiv.org
/abs/cs/0610105).

———. "Robust De-Anonymization of Large Sparse Datasets." *Proceedings of the
2008 IEEE Symposium on Security and Privacy,* p. 111 (http://www.cs.utexas
.edu/~shmat/shmat_oak08netflix.pdf).

Nazareth, Rita, and Julia Leite. "Stock Trading in U.S. Falls to Lowest Level Since
2008." *Bloomberg,* August 13, 2012 (http://www.bloomberg.com/news/2012
-08-13/stock-trading-in-u-s-hits-lowest-level-since-2008-as-vix-falls.html).

Negroponte, Nicholas. *Being Digital.* Alfred Knopf, 1995.

Neyman, Jerzy. "On the Two Different Aspects of the Representative Method:
The Method of Stratified Sampling and the Method of Purposive Selection."
Journal of the Royal Statistical Society 97, no. 4 (1934), pp. 558–625.

Ohm, Paul. "Broken Promises of Privacy: Responding to the Surprising Failure of
Anonymization." 57 *UCLA Law Review* 1701 (2010).

Onnela, J. P., et al. "Structure and Tie Strengths in Mobile Communication Networks." *Proceedings of the National Academy of Sciences of the United States
of America (PNAS)* 104 (May 2007), pp. 7332–36 (http://nd.edu/~dddas/
Papers/PNAS0610245104v1.pdf).

Palfrey, John, and Urs Gasser. *Interop: The Promise and Perils of Highly Interconnected Systems.* Basic Books, 2012.

Pearl, Judea. *Causality: Models, Reasoning and Inference,* 2nd ed. Cambridge University Press, 2009.

President's Council of Advisors on Science and Technology. "Report to the President and Congress, Designing a Digital Future: Federally Funded Research
and Development in Networking and Information Technology." December 2010 (http://www.whitehouse.gov/sites/default/files/microsites/ostp/
pcast-nitrd-report-2010.pdf).

Priest, Dana and William Arkin. "A Hidden World, Growing Beyond Control." *Washington Post,* July 19, 2010 (http://projects.washingtonpost.com/
top-secret-america/articles/a-hidden-world-growing-beyond-control/
print/).

Query, Tim. "Grade Inflation and the Good-Student Discount." *Contingencies
Magazine,* American Academy of Actuaries, May-June 2007 (http://www
.contingencies.org/mayjun07/tradecraft.pdf).

Quinn, Elias Leake. "Smart Metering and Privacy: Existing Law and Competing Policies; A Report for the Colorado Public Utility Commission." Spring

2009 (http://www.w4ar.com/Danger_of_Smart_Meters_Colorado_Report .pdf).

Reshef, David, et al. "Detecting Novel Associations in Large Data Sets." *Science* (2011), pp. 1518–24.

Rosenthal, Jonathan. "Banking Special Report." *The Economist,* May 19, 2012, pp. 7–8.

Rosenzweig, Phil. "Robert S. McNamara and the Evolution of Modern Management." *Harvard Business Review,* December 2010, pp. 87–93 (http://hbr .org/2010/12/robert-s-mcnamara-and-the-evolution-of-modern-manag ement/ar/pr).

Rudin, Cynthia, et al. "21st-Century Data Miners Meet 19th-Century Electrical Cables." *Computer,* June 2011, pp. 103–105.

———. "Machine Learning for the New York City Power Grid." *IEEE Transactions on Pattern Analysis and Machine Intelligence* 34.2 (2012), pp. 328–345 (http://hdl.handle.net/1721.1/68634).

Rys, Michael. "Scalable SQL." *Communications of the ACM,* June 2011, 48, pp. 48–53.

Salathé, Marcel, and Shashank Khandelwal. "Assessing Vaccination Sentiments with Online Social Media: Implications for Infectious Disease Dynamics and Control." *PlOS Computational Biology* 7, no. 10 (October 2011).

Savage, Mike, and Roger Burrows. "The Coming Crisis of Empirical Sociology." *Sociology* 41 (2007), pp. 885–899.

Schlie, Erik, Jörg Rheinboldt, and Niko Waesche. *Simply Seven: Seven Ways to Create a Sustainable Internet Business.* Palgrave Macmillan, 2011.

Scanlon, Jessie. "Luis von Ahn: The Pioneer of 'Human Computation.'" *Businessweek,* November 3, 2008 (http://www.businessweek.com/stories /2008-11-03/luis-von-ahn-the-pioneer-of-human-computation -businessweek-business-news-stock-market-and-financial-advice).

Scism, Leslie, and Mark Maremont. "Inside Deloitte's Life-Insurance Assessment Technology." *Wall Street Journal,* November 19, 2010 (http://on line.wsj.com/article/SB10001424052748704104104575622531084755588 .html).

———. "Insurers Test Data Profiles to Identify Risky Clients." *Wall Street Journal,* November 19, 2010 (http://online.wsj.com/article/SB100014240527487046 48604575620750998072986.html).

Scott, James. *Seeing Like a State: How Certain Schemes to Improve the Human Condition Have Failed.* Yale University Press, 1998.

Seltzer, William, and Margo Anderson. "The Dark Side of Numbers: The Role of Population Data Systems in Human Rights Abuses." *Social Research* 68 (2001) pp. 481–513.

Silver, Nate. *The Signal and the Noise: Why So Many Predictions Fail—But Some Don't.* Penguin, 2012.

Singel, Ryan. "Netflix Spilled Your *Brokeback Mountain* Secret, Lawsuit Claims." *Wired*, December 17, 2009 (http://www.wired.com/threatlevel/2009/12/netflix-privacy-lawsuit/).

Smith, Adam. *The Wealth of Nations* (1776). Reprinted Bantam Classics, 2003. A free electronic version is available (http://www2.hn.psu.edu/faculty/jmanis/adam-smith/Wealth-Nations.pdf).

Solove, Daniel J. *The Digital Person: Technology and Privacy in the Information Age*. NYU Press, 2004.

Surowiecki, James. "A Billion Prices Now." *New Yorker*, May 30, 2011 (http://www.newyorker.com/talk/financial/2011/05/30/110530ta_talk_surowiecki).

Taleb, Nassim Nicholas. *Fooled by Randomness: The Hidden Role of Chance in Life and in the Markets*. Random House, 2008.

——. *The Black Swan: The Impact of the Highly Improbable*. 2nd ed., Random House, 2010.

Thompson, Clive. "For Certain Tasks, the Cortex Still Beats the CPU." *Wired*, June 25, 2007 (http://www.wired.com/techbiz/it/magazine/15-07/ff_human comp?currentPage=all).

Thurm, Scott. "Next Frontier in Credit Scores: Predicting Personal Behavior." *Wall Street Journal*, October 27, 2011 (http://online.wsj.com/article/SB10001424052970203687504576655182086300912.html).

Tsotsis, Alexia. "Twitter Is at 250 Million Tweets per Day, iOS 5 Integration Made Signups Increase 3x." *TechCrunch*, October 17, 2011 (http://techcrunch.com/2011/10/17/twitter-is-at-250-million-tweets-per-day/).

Valery, Nick. "Tech.View: Cars and Software Bugs." *The Economist*, May 16, 2010 (http://www.economist.com/blogs/babbage/2010/05/techview_cars_and_software_bugs).

Vlahos, James. "The Department Of Pre-Crime." *Scientific American* 306 (January 2012), pp. 62–67.

Von Baeyer, Hans Christian. *Information: The New Language of Science*. Harvard University Press, 2005.

von Ahn, Luis, et al. "reCAPTCHA: Human-Based Character Recognition via Web Security Measures." *Science* 321 (September 12, 2008), pp. 1465–68 (http://www.sciencemag.org/content/321/5895/1465.abstract).

Watts, Duncan. *Everything Is Obvious Once You Know the Answer: How Common Sense Fails Us*. Atlantic, 2011.

Weinberger, David. *Everything Is Miscellaneous: The Power of the New Digital Disorder*. Times, 2007.

Weinberger, Sharon. "Intent to Deceive." *Nature* 465 (May 2010), pp. 412–415 (http://www.nature.com/news/2010/100526/full/465412a.html).

——. "Terrorist 'Pre-crime' Detector Field Tested in United States." *Nature*, May 27, 2011 (http://www.nature.com/news/2011/110527/full/news.2011.323.html).

Whitehouse, David. "UK Science Shows Cave Art Developed Early." *BBC News Online,* October 3, 2001 (http://news.bbc.co.uk/1/hi/sci/tech/1577421.stm).

Wigner, Eugene. "The Unreasonable Effectiveness of Mathematics in the Natural Sciences." *Communications on Pure and Applied Mathematics* 13, no. 1 (1960), pp. 1–14.

Wilks, Yorick. *Machine Translation: Its Scope and Limits.* Springer, 2008.

Wingfield, Nick. "Virtual Products, Real Profits: Players Spend on Zynga's Games, but Quality Turns Some Off." *Wall Street Journal,* September 9, 2011 (http://online.wsj.com/article/SB1000142405311904823804576502442842835413446.html).

ACKNOWLEDGMENTS

We both have been fortunate to work with and learn from an early giant in the field of information networks and innovation, Lewis M. Branscomb. His intellect, eloquence, energy, professionalism, wit, and never-ending curiosity continue to inspire us. And to his congenial and wise partner, Connie Mullin, we apologize for not heeding her suggestion to call the book "Superdata."

Momin Malik has been an excellent research assistant with his exceptional intellect and industriousness. We have the privilege of being represented by Lisa Adams and David Miller of Garamond Agency, who have simply been superb in every aspect. Eamon Dolan, our editor, has been phenomenal — a representative of the rare breed of editors who have an almost perfect sense of how to edit text and challenge our thinking, so that the result is much better than we ever could have hoped for. We thank everyone at Houghton Mifflin Harcourt, in particular Beth Burleigh Fuller and Ben Hyman. Also, Camille Smith for her expert copyediting. We are grateful to James Fransham of *The Economist* for his excellent fact-checking and shrewd criticisms of the manuscript.

We are especially thankful to all those big-data practitioners who spent time explaining their work, notably Oren Etzioni, Cynthia Rudin, Carolyn McGregor, and Mike Flowers.

. . .

For Viktor's individual acknowledgments: I thank Philip Evans, who is always thinking two steps ahead and expressing his ideas with precision and eloquence, for conversations spanning more than a decade.

I am also grateful to my former colleague David Lazer, who has been an early and strong big-data academic, and whose counsel I have sought many times.

I thank the participants of the 2011 Oxford Digital Data Dialogue (which focused on big data), and especially its co-chair Fred Cate, for most valuable discussions.

The Oxford Internet Institute, where I work, offered just the right environment for this book, with so many of my colleagues engaged in big-data research. I could not think of a better place to have written it. I also acknowledge with gratitude the support of Keble College, where I am a professorial fellow. Without that support, I would not have gotten access to some of the important primary sources used in the book.

The family always pays the biggest toll when one is writing a book. It is not only the many hours I have spent in front of the computer screen, away in the office, but also the many, many hours I have been physically present but lost in thought for which I need to ask forgiveness from my wife Birgit and from little Viktor. I promise I will try harder.

As for Kenn's individual acknowledgments: I am grateful to many great data scientists who helped, in particular Jeff Hammerbacher, Amr Awadallah, DJ Patil, Michael Driscoll, Michael Freed, and many folks at Google over the years (including Hal Varian, Jeremy Ginsberg, Peter Norvig, and Udi Manber, among others, while all-too-brief chats with Eric Schmidt and Larry Page were invaluable).

My thinking has been enriched by Tim O'Reilly, a savant of the Internet age. Also by Marc Benioff of Salesforce.com, who has been a teacher. Matthew Hindman's insights were immeasurable, as always. James Guszcza of Deloitte was incredibly helpful, as was Geoff Hyatt, an old friend and serial data entrepreneur. Special thanks go to Pete Warden, who is both a philosopher and a practitioner of big data.

Many friends offered ideas and advice, including John Turner, Angelika Wolf, Niko Waesche, Katia Verresen, David Wishart, Anna Petherick, Blaine Harden and Jessica Kowal. Others who inspired themes in the book include Blaise Aguera y Arcas, Eric Horvitz, David Auerbach, Gil Elbaz, Tyler Bell, Andrew Wyckoff and many others at the OECD, Stephen Brobst and the team at Teradata, Anthony Goldbloom and Jeremy Howard at Kaggle, Edd Dumbill, Roger Magoulas and the team at O'Reilly Media, and Edward Lazowska. James Cortada is pantheonic. Thanks also to Ping Li of Accel Partners and Roger Ehrenberg of IA Ventures.

At *The Economist,* my colleagues offered tremendous ideas and support. I particularly thank my editors Tom Standage, Daniel Franklin, and John Micklethwait, as well as Barbara Beck, who edited the special report "Data, Data Everywhere," which was the genesis of this book. Henry Tricks and Dominic Zeigler, my colleagues in Tokyo, were role models for always seeking out the novel and expressing it beautifully. Oliver Morton provided his customary wisdom when it was most needed.

The Salzburg Global Seminar in Austria offered the perfect combination of idyllic repose and intellectual inquisition that helped me write and think. An Aspen Institute roundtable in July 2011 sparked many ideas, for which I thank the participants and the organizer, Charlie Firestone. Also, my appreciation goes to Teri Elniski for her tremendous support.

Frances Cairncross, the Rector of Exeter College, Oxford, offered a tranquil place to stay and great encouragement. It is humbling to fix one's mind upon questions of technology and society that build on those she raised a decade and a half earlier in *The Death of Distance,* a work that inspired me as a young journalist. It was satisfying to cross the Exeter courtyard each morning knowing that I might pass along a torch she carried, though the flame burned so much more brightly in her hands.

My deepest appreciation goes to my family, who put up with me — or more commonly, with my absence. My parents, sister, and other relatives deserve thanks, but I reserve most of my gratitude for my wife Heather and our children Charlotte and Kaz, without whose support, encouragement, and ideas this book would not have been possible.

Both of us are grateful to so many people who have discussed the theme of big data with us, long before the term was even popularized. On that note, we reserve our particular thanks to the participants over the years at the Rueschlikon Conference on Information Policy, which Viktor co-organized and where Kenn was the rapporteur. We especially thank Joseph Alhadeff, Bernard Benhamou, John Seely Brown, Herbert Burkert (who introduced us to Commodore Maury), Peter Cullen, Ed Felten, Urs Gasser, Joi Ito, Jeff Jonas, Nicklas Lundblad, Douglas Merrill, Rick Murray, Cory Ondrejka, and Paul Schwartz.

VIKTOR MAYER-SCHÖNBERGER
KENNETH CUKIER
Oxford/London, August 2012

INDEX